Samuel Parsons

Landscape Gardening

Notes and suggestions on lawns and lawn planting--laying out and arrangement of country places, large and small parks, cemetery plots, and railway-station lawns--deciduous and evergreen trees and shrubs--the hardy border-bedding

Samuel Parsons

Landscape Gardening

Notes and suggestions on lawns and lawn planting--laying out and arrangement of country places, large and small parks, cemetery plots, and railway-station lawns--deciduous and evergreen trees and shrubs--the hardy border-bedding

ISBN/EAN: 9783337224349

Printed in Europe, USA, Canada, Australia, Japan

Cover: Foto ©Lupo / pixelio.de

More available books at **www.hansebooks.com**

THE POND EFFECT.—LOTUSES AND WATER-LILIES.

Frontispiece.

LANDSCAPE ✣
✣ GARDENING

NOTES AND SUGGESTIONS ON LAWNS AND LAWN PLANTING—LAYING OUT AND ARRANGEMENT OF COUNTRY PLACES, LARGE AND SMALL PARKS, CEMETERY PLOTS, AND RAILWAY-STATION LAWNS—DECIDUOUS AND EVERGREEN TREES AND SHRUBS—THE HARDY BORDER—BEDDING PLANTS—ROCKWORK, ETC.

BY

SAMUEL PARSONS, Jr.
SUPERINTENDENT OF PARKS, NEW YORK CITY

ILLUSTRATED

"I should prefer the delights of a garden to the dominion of a world."—JOHN ADAMS

G. P. PUTNAM'S SONS
NEW YORK   LONDON
27 WEST TWENTY-THIRD STREET   24 BEDFORD STREET, STRAND
The Knickerbocker Press
1900

COPYRIGHT, 1891
BY
SAMUEL PARSONS, JR.

The Knickerbocker Press, New York
Electrotyped, Printed, and Bound by
G. P. Putnam's Sons

CONTENTS.

	PAGE
INTRODUCTION	xi

CHAPTER I.
The Lawn 1

CHAPTER II.
The Treatment of Sloping Grounds 15

CHAPTER III.
Spring Effects on the Lawn 32

CHAPTER IV.
Trees and Shrubs for June Effects on the Lawn . 53

CHAPTER V.
The Flowers and Foliage of Summer 88

CHAPTER VI.
Green Autumnal Foliage . . . 106

CHAPTER VII.
Autumnal Color on the Lawn 114

CHAPTER VIII.
Lawn-Planting for Winter Effect . . 135

CHAPTER IX.
Garden Flowers 155

CHAPTER X.
Grandmother's Garden 201

CHAPTER XI.
Bedding Plants 216

CHAPTER XII.
The Ornamentation of Ponds and Lakes 238

CHAPTER XIII.
Lawn-Planting for Small Places 255

CHAPTER XIV.
City Parks 271

CHAPTER XV.
Railway, Churchyard, and Cemetery Lawn-Planting . 295

CHAPTER XVI.
Nookeries on the Home Grounds 307

CHAPTER XVII.
My Friend the Andromeda 312

ILLUSTRATIONS.

	PAGE
THE POND EFFECT—LOTUSES AND WATER-LILIES	*Frontispiece*
LAWN IN CENTRAL PARK, NEW YORK, NEAR THE NORTH END OF THE MALL	17
ROUGH UNGRADED BANK	18
CLOSELY MASSED ROCKS ON FINISHED STEEP BANK	19
PARTLY FINISHED ROCKY BANK READY FOR PLANTING	21
ENTRANCE TO CAVE IN THE RAMBLE, CENTRAL PARK, NEW YORK	23
STEPS LEADING TO CAVE IN THE RAMBLE, CENTRAL PARK, NEW YORK	25
STONE BRIDGE ADJOINING LARGE NATURAL ROCK, CENTRAL PARK, NEW YORK	27
YUCCA RECURVA	29
YELLOW JASMINE (*Jasminum nudiflorum*)	35
WEEPING GOLDEN BELL (*Forsythia suspensa*)	39
FLOWERING DOGWOOD (*Cornus Florida*)	40
DOUBLE-FLOWERING APPLE (*Pyrus spectabilis*)	41
THE DOUBLE-FLOWERING CHERRY (*Prunus cerasus, fl. pl.*)	42
SOULANGE'S MAGNOLIA (*Magnolia Soulangeana*)	43
* JAPAN WEEPING CHERRY	45
JAPANESE MAGNOLIA (*Magnolia stellata*)	46
ENGLISH HAWTHORN (*Cratægus oxyacantha*)	47
ENGLISH HAWTHORN (*Cratægus oxyacantha*)	48
DEUTZIA GRACILIS	49
AZALEA MOLLIS	49
TREE PEONY (*Paonia arborea*)	50
COMMON PURPLE LILAC (*Syringa vulgaris*)	51
JAPANESE MAPLE	58
HORSE-CHESTNUT TREES, CENTRAL PARK, NEW YORK	61
RED-FLOWERING HORSE-CHESTNUT (*Æsculus rubicunda*)	62
WHITE-FLOWERING HORSE-CHESTNUT (*Æsculus rubicunda*)	63
CHIONANTHUS VIRGINICA	64
RHODODENDRON	68
PINXTER FLOWER (*Azalea nudiflora*)	69
BROAD-LEAVED LAUREL (*Kalmia latifolia*)	69
GORDON'S MOCK ORANGE (*Philadelphus Gordonianus*)	72

* From a photograph taken by Mr. Paul Dana from a specimen on the lawn of Mr. Charles A. Dana, Dosoris, L. I.

ILLUSTRATIONS.

	PAGE
DEUTZIA CRENATA, *fl. pl.*	72
EXOCHORDA GRANDIFLORA	73
SWEET-SCENTED SHRUB (*Calycanthus Floridus*)	73
YELLOW JAPANESE KERRIA (*Kerria Japonica*)	73
RED-FLOWERING WEIGELIA (*Weigelia rosea*)	74
VIBURNUM OPULUS	75
FOUR GOOD CLEMATISES	76
WISTARIA SINENSIS	77
WISTARIA ARBOR, CENTRAL PARK, NEW YORK	79
JAPAN RAMANAS ROSE (*Rosa rugosa rubra*)	81
NOBLE SILVER FIR (*Abies nobilis*)	83
AMERICAN BEECHES (*Fagus ferruginea*)	93
DOUBLE-FLOWERING ALTHEA (*Hibiscus Syriacus, fl. pl.*)	99
SWEET PEPPER BUSH (*Clethra alnifolia*)	100
DWARF FLOWERING HORSE-CHESTNUT TREES (*Æsculus parviflora*)	101
CHINESE CYPRESS (*Glyptostrobus sinensis*)	102
JAPAN IVY (*Ampelopsis tricuspidata*)	103
DUTCHMAN'S PIPE (*Aristolochia sipho*)	104
SWEET-SCENTED CLEMATIS (*Clematis flammula*)	104
TRUMPET CREEPER (*Tecoma radicans*)	105
INDIAN BEAN (*Catalpa bignonioides*)	108
WEEPING BEECH (*Fagus sylvatica pendula*)	110
WEEPING BEECH IN WINTER	111
ELÆAGNUS LONGIPES	112
* KENTUCKY COFFEE-TREE	121
* LIQUID AMBAR	125
EUROPEAN OLEASTER (*Elæagnus hortensis*)	127
* ORIENTAL SPRUCE (*Picea Orientalis*)	141
WEEPING NORWAY SPRUCE AND DWARF PINE (*Picea excelsa inverta* and *Pinus strobus compacta*)	143
CEDAR OF LEBANON (*Cedrus Libani*)	144
BHOTAN PINE (*Pinus excelsa*)	145
* MUGHO PINE (*Pinus mughus*)	147
GINKGO TREE, IRISH YEWS, AND WEEPING SOPHORA	148
* JAPAN PARASOL PINE (*Sciadopitys verticillata*)	149
* OBTUSE-LEAVED JAPANESE CYPRESS (*Retinospora obtusa*)	151
PARSONS' SILVER FIR, WEEPING NORWAY SPRUCE, AND WEEPING LARCH	153
HEART-LEAVED SAXIFRAGE (*Saxifraga cordifolia*)	158
MOSS PINK (*Phlox subulata*)	159
EUROPEAN PASQUE-FLOWER (*Anemone pulsatilla*)	160
STEMLESS GENTIAN (*Gentiana acaulis*)	161
ALPINE BARRENWORT (*Epimedium Alpinum*)	162
ASTILBE JAPONICA	163
NOBLE FUMITORY (*Corydalis nobilis*)	163
BLEEDING HEART (*Dicentra spectabilis*)	164

* From a photograph taken by Mr. Paul Dana from a specimen on the lawn of Mr. Charles A. Dana, Dosoris, L. I.

ILLUSTRATIONS.

	PAGE
Spring Meadow Saffron (*Bulbocodium vernum*)	165
Poet's Narcissus (*Narcissus poeticus*)	166
Trumpet Major (*Narcissus major*)	166
Daffodil (*Narcissus pseudo-narcissus*)	167
Fragrant Jonquil (*Narcissus odorus*)	167
Crocus Vernus	168
Winter Aconites (*Eranthis hyemalis*)	168
Snowdrop (*Galanthus nivalis*)	169
Scarlet Turban Lily (*Lilium pomponium*)	169
Crucianella Stylosa	170
Lily of the Valley	171
Maiden's Pink (*Dianthus deltoides*), and the Nieremhergia Rivularis	172
Herbaceous Peony (*Pæonia officinalis*)	173
Slender-Leaved Peony (*Pæonia tenuifolia, fl. pl.*)	174
Sea Lavender (*Statice latifolia*)	174
Rock Tunica (*Tunica saxifraga*)	175
Achillea Ptarmica	176
Yellow Asphodel (*Asphodelus luteus*)	176
Yellow Chamomile (*Anthemis tinctoria*)	177
American Senna (*Cassia Marylandica*)	179
Gas Plant (*Dictamnus fraxinella*)	180
Gaillardia Grandiflora	181
Geranium Sanguineum	182
Bowman's Root (*Gillenia trifoliata*)	182
Plantain Lily (*Funkia ovata*)	183
German Iris (*Iris Germanica*)	184
Lilium Auratum	184
Lilium Speciosum	185
Turk's-Cap Lily (*Lilium superbum*)	185
Button Snakeroot (*Liatris spicata*)	186
Double Scarlet Lychnis (*Lychnis Chalcedonica, fl. pl.*)	186
Purple Loosestripe (*Lythrum salicaria*)	187
Purple Flowering Raspberry (*Rubus odoratus*)	188
Pentstemon Barbatus (var. *Torreyi*)	189
Large Bellflower (*Platycodon grandiflorum*)	189
Meadow Sweet (*Spiræa ulmaria*)	190
Gentian-Leaved Speedwell (*Veronica gentianoides*)	190
Red-Hot Poker (*Tritoma uvaria*)	192
Cardinal Flower (*Lobelia cardinalis*)	193
Leadwort (*Plumbago Larpenta*)	194
Stone Crop (*Sedum acre*)	195
Sedum Spectabile	195
Compass Plant (*Silphium laciniatum*)	196
Golden-Rod (*Solidago Canadensis*)	197
New York Iron-Weed (*Vernonia Novcboracensis*)	197
Christmas Rose (*Helleborus niger*)	198
Cobweb House-Leek (*Sempervivum arachnoideum*)	198

	PAGE
AUTUMN CROCUS (*Colchicum autumnale*)	199
SINGLE DAHLIAS	199
GARDEN PINK (*Dianthus plumarius*)	203
SWEET-WILLIAM (*Dianthus barbatus*)	203
FALL LARKSPUR (*Delphinium elatum*)	204
SINGLE HOLLYHOCKS	204
COREOPSIS LANCEOLATA	206
PRIVATE PLACE AT ORANGE, N. J., AS LAID OUT BY VAUX & CO.	207
CANADA COLUMBINE (*Aquilegia Canadensis*)	208
ERIANTHUS RAVENNÆ	209
FESTUCA GLAUCA	209
STIPA PENNATA	210
HAREBELL (*Campanula tenori*)	211
LIVER LEAF (*Hepatica triloba*)	212
JAPAN WIND-FLOWER (*Anemone Japonica—Honorine Joubert*)	213
BLUE VIOLET	214
WHITE VIOLET	214
PURPLE FOXGLOVE (*Digitalis purpurea*)	214
ORIENTAL POPPY (*Papaver bracteatum*)	215
JAPAN IRIS (*Iris Kæmpferi*)	215
DIAGRAM OF DECORATIVE BED	218
BED OF CANNAS, COLEUSES, AND ACALYPHAS	220
STUDY FOR BEDDING OF FOLIAGE PLANTS AGAINST A WALL	221
SWORD LILY (*Gladiolus*)	223
DIAGRAM OF BEDDING PLANTS	224
PLAN FOR ELLIPTICAL BEDS FOR MASSING COLORS	226
DOUBLE GERANIUM	231
SINGLE GERANIUM	231
SALVIA SPLENDENS	233
CANNA INDICA	233
BANANA PLANT (*Musa ensete*)	234
SOLANUM WARSCEWICZIOIDES	235
ELEPHANT EAR (*Caladium esculentum*)	235
NEW SINGLE TULIPS	236
GREEN-LEAVED BAMBOO (*Arundo donax*)	242
PAMPAS GRASS (*Gynerium argenteum*)	243
EULALIA (*Japonica zebrina*)	244
BORDER OF THE FOUNTAIN, UNION SQUARE, NEW YORK,—LOTUSES AND WATER-LILIES	245
ARRANGEMENT OF LOTUSES AND LILY-PADS	247
GROUP OF JAPANESE LOTUSES (*Nelumbium speciosum*)	248
ARRANGEMENT OF WATER-LILIES AND PAPYRUS	250
CENTRE OF THE FOUNTAIN, UNION SQUARE, NEW YORK	252
BETHESDA FOUNTAIN BASIN, CENTRAL PARK, NEW YORK	253
SMALL HOME LAWN	259
SUGGESTIONS FOR LAWN-PLANTING	263
A STUDY FOR LAWN-PLANTING	267

ILLUSTRATIONS.

	PAGE
THE MALL, CENTRAL PARK, NEW YORK	275
* THE ISLAND, NEAR BRIDGE, CENTRAL PARK, NEW YORK	279
THE CAVE LANDING ON THE LAKE, CENTRAL PARK, NEW YORK	281
NORTH MEADOW, CENTRAL PARK, NEW YORK	283
OVERHANGING ROCK NEAR 110TH STREET AND SEVENTH AVENUE, CENTRAL PARK, NEW YORK	285
A GORGE IN CENTRAL PARK	287
A CHURCH LAWN	299
A BURIAL PLOT	305

* From a photograph taken by Mr. E. P. Fowler.

INTRODUCTION.

IN presenting to the reader the following brief and unpretending chapters, I am fully aware that the subject of landscape gardening is receiving at my hands unsystematic and insufficient treatment. At the very outset, therefore, I wish to say that the principal feeling that has inspired the present undertaking has been a desire to arouse, by simple desultory talks, increased enthusiasm for lawn-making among men of moderate means.

Most people have some land, or can in this country readily get it. As a rule, however, they accomplish little towards the proper development of the landscape-gardening capabilities of such land as they have. The hired man generally advises them to a considerable degree, and then carries out the plans agreed upon, without much let or hindrance from the employer, or comprehension of the comparative value of the completed work.

There is no doubt that nurserymen's catalogues furnish much valuable advice concerning the best methods of growing certain plants, as well as extensive lists of their various species and varieties; but this cannot be considered an adequate or even an attractive way of treating the subject of landscape gardening. The discussions of plants are sufficiently alluring, I will acknowledge, and the colored pictures and woodcuts are unquestionably effective in arresting the eye and securing interest of a certain kind. In a word, nurserymen's catalogues are intended for one definite purpose—namely, that of tempting the reader to purchase plants, and to that end they are admirably adapted. To the development of a sound taste for the practice of genuine landscape gardening these catalogues can of course contribute comparatively little. And yet the material, the trees and shrubs, they discuss, must always form an important and very essential part of any satisfactory treatise on landscape gardening.

On the other hand, to write such works as those of Price, Gilpin, Repton, and Downing, while requiring ability and experience of a high order, does not satisfy what seems to me a particular need of the present time. Wealth and taste are being rapidly diffused among all classes. The book, therefore, that is needed for this purpose is, it seems to me, one that will stimulate interest in an inexpensive style of landscape gardening by enunciating a few practical fundamental principles, and giving an account of some examples of well laid out grounds. With this, should naturally be included a description of some of the best lawn-plants.

My chief confidence in the value of such a work lies, I confess, chiefly in the superior effect the illustrations may have in inspiring interest in the subject, and leading the reader to pursue his investigations farther a-field. I have also myself lived among choice ornamental trees all my life, and had the opportunity of studying many examples of landscape gardening in numerous more or less professional visits to country-places in America. My position of Superintendent of Parks in New York for nearly ten years, moreover, gives some additional reasons for undertaking to make a few suggestions and notes by the way that may be helpful to others.

The first chapter that I propose to undertake in the series of what should be termed talks, rather than serious discussions, will be on the subject of the actual lawn considered by itself. Having duly considered the best methods of making a lawn, and arrived at the final conviction that lawn-making requires considerable practical knowledge and skill, we will be likely to meet the question, "But how do you make your roads?" To this I shall be obliged to reply: "That, although I have arrived at certain conclusions about road-making, I do not deem the subject as clearly within the proper scope of landscape gardening."

Roadmaking is distinctly within the province of the engineer, and all over the civilized world the subject has been exhaustively treated by learned experts, who have set forth their views in prize essays and more extended treatises. But I must say this much, earnestly and from an experience that has been checkered by good and bad results, that you had better give your roads only enough curve or crown to shed water properly. It will be also found in many places, even within the home grounds, that gutters by the side of the road are essential; and invariably well-assorted broken stones should underlie the driveway for the purpose of drainage. With the additional oft-quoted remark on the maintenance of roads, that "a stitch in time saves nine," I shall forego all further talk in these pages about the construction of paths and roads.

The question of the curves or course of paths and roads, in relation to adjacent lands and buildings, is, however, a legitimate query for the reader to make, and of that I shall have something definite to say. Roads and paths are, it must be confessed, necessary evils that add no landscape beauty to the place, and must be simply tolerated because they are needed to get about the grounds. In devising the location and course of roads and paths, it becomes, therefore, our duty to seek to minimize their essential ugliness, and to contrive how to manage with as few of them as possible.

Constructing lawns and laying out lines of paths and roads having been discussed, the plan of my chapters next induces me to ask the reader to imagine a rough, undulating country-place with, perhaps, a ravine or two on one side of it. As one looks at the natural arrangement of rocks on the hillside it should be readily apparent that the treatment of steep and sloping grounds needs consideration as well as that of the more level lawns. Trees, shrubs, flower gardens, and level lawns,—every one knows something of them. There are few, however, who have ever given serious thought to artificial sloping grounds and rockwork studied from natural models found in the hills about us. Some of us have without question studied such work in Central Park, New York City, and in Prospect Park, Brooklyn, L. I. There are, of course, a few other examples in the country of this genuine American landscape architecture, but to not many, I fancy, has it occurred to treat sloping grounds in any definite and specialized way.

I used the term American landscape architecture advisedly, for my words in these chapters are chiefly addressed to inhabitants of America, living in a region between North Carolina on the one side and Maine on the other, and bounded on the west by the Rocky Mountains. The principles and general theory of arranging grounds will doubtless be much the same the world over, but the selection and treatment of plants must vary constantly. The plants that do well in this part of North America will not necessarily succeed in England and on the Continent, while in the same latitude in California the same trees will perhaps fail lamentably.

Trees and shrubs therefore must be studied carefully with due regard to their environment, and in these chapters I have moreover undertaken to classify them in a somewhat general way in accordance with their suitability to the different seasons. I contend that this grouping of trees and shrubs is not sufficiently looked after when lawns are planted. On Morningside Park, New York, for instance, a whole hillside is systematically planted, on account of their rich color in autumn, with white dogwood *(Cornus florida)*, Andromeda arborea *(or Oxydendrum arboreum)*, liquidambar, scarlet maple, sumach, *Rhus Osbecki*, etc. At another point many spring-blooming plants are massed, and throughout all the tree and shrub groupings come more or less spring-, summer-, or fall-blooming kinds scattered about at frequent intervals. In regard to the employment of bright-colored trees and shrubs, such as Japanese maples, purple beeches, and golden oaks, it is important to say that self-restraint is advisable. Coloring of the brightest kind is valuable duly and properly related to the general mass of the foliage of trees and shrubs. The color scheme of tree and shrub plantation should be, as a rule, in tones of green. Subsidiary masses may, however, have yellowish or reddish tones, and even a main mass might be, in some cases, attractively designed with only purple beech or golden oak.

It seems fitting to explain here what I consider the proper way to treat shrubs viewed in mass and viewed individually. I approach this question with some hesitation, because it is easy, in talking of such matters, to find one's self landed in a tangle of unprecise phrases, such as mystery, blending, gardenesque, picturesque, etc., etc. There is doubtless a particular composition that should be devised for every landscape-gardening picture, and a broad comprehensive scheme of a high order of art may be thus unquestionably established. Foreground, middle-distance, and background need due consideration, and proper relations of this kind may be unquestionably established. Trees may be massed on the higher levels, and may straggle down hillsides, and may be grouped and emphasized at certain points in a thoroughly artistic manner. The stretches of lawn and vistas of trees may extend, seemingly, to great distances on comparatively small places, and many charming effects and surprises in variation of sky-line and mystery of far-reaching background may undoubtedly be contrived with success.

Do not let me give the impression that I question the possibility of creating, as it were, all these delightful features of the lawn. Only, and here I will speak frankly and from considerable experience, do not undertake too much of this kind of thing yourself; you may fail. Trees will die when they have grown to considerable size at artistically critical points, or they will fail to grow to just the height and diameter required, and a weak realization of the desired effect will be attained.

But to return to the question of treating trees and shrubs considered in mass and considered individually. The tendency of those who think of the trees in mass and in their mass relations, is to crowd them too much with their companions, to fail to comprehend their appearance at maturity, and thus develop their proper effect imperfectly. Such a tendency is apt to "crib and confine" the trees, and to undertake to make them do duty after a fashion that is not altogether adapted to their nature; that is, if it is not altogether a case of round pegs for square holes, to force them just a little. On the other hand, the person who dwells specially on the development of the individual character of a plant is liable to err in another way, and to sacrifice the broad effects and harmoniously combined relations of trees to the exhibition of characteristic and highly perfected individual excellences.

For most lawns a middle way of arrangement may

be pursued with reasonable satisfaction which will secure good mass effects and a fair consideration for the characteristics of individual specimens. There will be the open centre of lawn grass and the border plantation of mixed trees and shrubs and herbaceous plants with a moderately diversified sky-line. Outlying specimens of choice trees and shrubs will vary the outline of the masses here and there, and perhaps stand alone at a few points without shrubs. Excessive cribbing and confining will be prevented by planting the trees forty to fifty feet apart, and the shrubs eight to ten feet apart, with small ones two to four feet apart. A simple negative rule for the arrangement of trees, shrubs, and herbaceous plants is to never plant them in a continuous straight line, but in groups with curving boundaries and placed on the specially prepared crests of swelling spots or portions of the lawn. Trees and shrubs thus placed are favorably exhibited and enabled to show their peculiar beauties better than on a flat surface.

There are a few simple things pertaining to landscape gardening, such as irregular sky-lines and border lines of shrub and tree groups, open lawn centres, and boundary plantations, attention to which will be likely to secure a pleasing effect, even though one foregoes any attempt to realize the higher and more subtle features of the art. Another way to simplify and, to my mind, greatly improve the arrangement of trees and shrubs is to group a lot of one kind of plants together, a hundred *Spiræa opulifolia* here, fifty *Spiræa Thunbergii* there, and so on. It is a large and specially effective method of treatment, and really easy of accomplishment.

Where a junction of two paths or roads is made, this method of arrangement looks well, for a considerable plantation should be here so contrived as to cover all points of connection and give the impression of an unseen way through a large grove or group. The question of shade and shade trees is one that must never be ignored. No landscape art can afford to slight the practical necessity for shade. All along, and about twenty feet from the drives and walks, and not less than fifty feet from the house, shade trees, elms, maples, etc., should stand at distances of from fifty to seventy-five feet from each other. But beware of, in this way, encroaching on the open centre lawns. Nothing can be a worse practice in landscape gardening.

I shall have occasion to speak of pruning hereafter specifically, but I desire to say in a general way here that self-restraint in pruning is a good habit to acquire. To cut and chop trees and shrubs every year may be a more pernicious practice than to leave them entirely alone. It is safe to say that what we want in a tree or shrub is to see its special and most characteristic beauty. If it naturally weeps or spreads, or is pyramidal, we want to see that special peculiarity naturally developed and not pruned into some monotonous semi-artificial shape. Rather if it be symmetrically inclined, lop off a branch here and there to emphasize its symmetrical habit; if it be weeping, increase its weeping habit by cutting away shoots that may show an upright tendency. If it be an early-blooming shrub, do not cut off the already formed flower buds in winter simply because that season happens to be the natural season for pruning wood, whether bud-bearing or not. Let the spent flowering wood be removed as in the case of *Forsythia*, as soon as the plant has done blooming, thus relieving the interior of the plant from being clogged, and paving the way for increased abundance and beauty of flowers the following spring. Generally speaking, it might be said that trees and shrubs do not really require pruning at all, except the removal of dead and deformed portions of the growth.

As regards the selection of trees and shrubs given in these chapters I have to say that, although it comprises a comparatively small list, it yet includes a number of the best kinds as well as such as in most cases can be readily obtained from leading tree and plant growers. I have endeavored to point out in every case the peculiar attractions that render the plants suited to the lawn, and have avoided as much as practicable all technical botanical terms that might be puzzling to the reader. Every one should know these plants intimately, know them as friends that he ought to see every day on his lawn. And it is in the office of such house friends, as the Germans would say, that I have endeavored to consider them.

My statements concerning the hardiness and time of blooming of plants must not be taken as absolutely precise. I can only offer the general conclusions of my individual experience. Nature performs strange freaks. A plant may bloom three weeks later next year than it did this, or two shrubs may have bloomed at the same time last year and this year one may flower a week earlier than the other.

The same varying rule applies to the hardiness of plants. For years we will find a certain variety, say of rhododendrons, hardy, and then will come a peculiar season, when a number of what we have previously considered tender kinds will survive, and the heretofore entirely hardy one will go. In judging and determining the value and peculiarities of a variety in any given locality we must be governed by the conclusions of a very considerable experience and then be prepared for occasional and startling surprises.

In the discussion of foliage bedding and the use of hardy herbaceous perennials, I have endeavored to give a distinctly formulated system based on the fundamental and general principles of landscape gardening; and to simplify their treatment and make it as definite and precise as possible. The illustration of the herbaceous bedding treatment is to be found in the chapter on "Grandmother's Garden." I should like very much to recommend more highly the use of hardy herbaceous plants in rockwork, on edges of lawns, in the long grass, and especially in shady woods. They are very charming in such places, but it is not easy to manage them, and they will require much renewing. And that reminds me to say that the reason why many plantations of hardy herbaceous perennials grow beautifully less in flower and foliage year by year is that they need renewing. Once in three or four years many of the plants of herbaceous borders should be taken up, divided and set out again, and in spots where any of them have died, new ones planted.

After discussing trees, shrubs, herbaceous perennial plants, and bedding plants, which constitute the material of landscape gardening, I have undertaken to set forth in a few sketches drawn from the resources of personal experience, the best way to use this material. There are doubtless many other landscape-gardening problems to be solved and other kinds of grounds to be laid out than those indicated in these chapters, but I think, however, that a number of the most constantly recurring ones have been fairly considered.

Before concluding this introduction I desire to express my obligation for assistance in preparing these chapters to Mr. Calvert Vaux, Landscape Architect of the Department of Public Parks, New York, to Mr. George C. Woolson, Superintending Gardener of the Park Department, and to Mr. J. François Huss, General Foreman of Construction Work in the Park Department.

In the preparation of the illustrations I am greatly indebted to Mr. Paul Dana, Commissioner of the Department of Public Parks, New York, for the loan and reproduction of seven excellent photographs, taken by himself, from the unsurpassed tree specimens growing on his father's, Mr. Charles A. Dana's, great country-place at Dosoris, L. I. An excellent photograph of an island in the lake, Central Park, New York, is also reproduced with the permission of Dr. E. P. Fowler.

CHAPTER I.

THE LAWN.

TO the minds of most readers the lawn suggests simply grass. We say we will walk on the lawn, and the thought of soft, velvety, newly cut grass immediately arises. In an ordinary sense, the lawn includes trees, shrubs, flowers, rocks, etc., but in actual fact, I believe, the idea of mown grass is first and foremost in the mind when the word *lawn* is used. I am therefore going to limit my remarks to the more or less level grass spaces that are open and agreeable to those who care to wander over their close-cut surface.

Among shrubs, rocks, and flowers, one should not, and would not be likely to care to wander. Here the grass would be naturally allowed to grow longer, and the interlacing branches and irregular grass surface would impede progress. The open close-cut grass space is, moreover, the lawn proper for all purposes of occupation.

During hot weather, when it is not actually raining, we confine ourselves to the foot-paths or carriage-roads of the place where gravel, stone, boards, or asphalt afford safe and convenient promenade almost immediately after a downfall of rain. Later on, however, when the sun comes out and dries up the moisture, we may enjoy perhaps for days, in the American climate, the great open spaces of greensward, which we propose to call the lawn. Here, in a sense, the family may be said, during certain seasons, to live for a large portion of the time. As soon as the dew is off, should there be any, some elder member of the family will be found wandering about, looking for flowers, or simply breathing the fresh morning air. Soon little children dash out, chasing butterflies or tumbling over each other in simple glee of existence, revelling in the feeling of the rich, soft, thick turf. Later, perhaps, comes a game of ball or tag among the older boys, which can only be played satisfactorily on the lawn. Finally, in the evening, at sunset, and later, the family may again linger on the lawn to enjoy the soft turf and long shadows on the greensward.

The pleasures of sight, and varied movement, it is acknowledged, are increased a hundred-fold by the studied comfort and adornment of the house itself in the special features of carpets, and walls, and chairs, and tables. Why should we not then seek to extend the sphere of our artistic endeavor to perfecting and ornamenting our lawns? It should, after all, be considered as much a part of the house domain as the verandah.

Feeling the importance, therefore, of making the lawn a place for the family to occupy, as though it were a part of the actual house, I am going to try to tell the reader just how to go to work to make his lawn so that it can be actually used as well as looked at. In this country especially, we see a great many poor lawns and very few good ones, and a poor lawn should be considered as inexcusable a home-feature as a ragged or soiled carpet. We often fail to make good roads and walks, and tree and shrub plantations, but we more often fail to make good lawns.

The reason for this may be found in the fact that when we make a road or walk of gravel, or asphalt, or other artificial material, we generally have a clear idea of the result we shall attain; when we plant trees we can foresee, with some degree of certainty, what their future comparatively unhampered growth will be, but, least of all, does this apply to lawns, as lawns are usually made in this country to-day.

I do not propose in my present remarks to allow myself to be drawn, however, into the fascinating discussion, introduced by Mr. James B. Olcott, of the Connecticut Agricultural Experiment Station, concerning the use of selected pieces of pure grass sod for making lawns. Experiments in this direction may, and doubtless will, finally enable us to make lawns possessing a beauty and durability under the stress of daily occupation, of which we have little conception at present.

But I will say now and here, that sad experience has proved long ago that want of pure grass seed, and the right variety of grass seed, is one of the chief causes of the failure and uncertainty of lawns. Seedsmen cannot furnish pure grass seed, because no one grows pure grass seed, and certainly not the best sorts of seed for making good greensward.

But in order to make the best greensward that we can reasonably expect to obtain, in view of the practice of the present day, let us take an ordinary piece of ground in the rough, covered with stones, wild turf, and weeds. It must not be an extreme case of sand or clay. Special ways of treatment would have to be devised for these, and we might imagine fifty cases, each of which would require a different mode of treatment. We had better, therefore, confine ourselves to an average or ordinary example of the way to make a lawn. This supposition would include a moderately heavy loam, some stone, and many weeds.

The first thing to be considered in such cases is the drainage; I mean the drainage of the lawn, and not of the roads. People are apt to stop when they have drained their roads and walks, and forget that the lawn requires such a thing as drainage.

I am not, however, going to linger much on this question, supremely important though it be to many lawns. The fact is, our average lawn does not need any drainage, except where in some limited spot water is apt to lie a part of the year. In such cases, drains of horse-shoe, or four-inch round tile, should be laid to some main drain, or open gutter along a road or street. No doubt there are cases of only moderately heavy loam, where the moisture sticks and lingers, in an undue degree, and here under-drainage is needed. Under-drainage on ordinary lawns will be only required in limited areas, that is in valleys or hollows made by the lay of the land.

This question of under-drainage once settled and relegated to the realm of scientific treatises, to which this book does not purport to belong, we should also point out that it is necessary to so grade the lawn as to properly distribute the surface water.

What, then, is the first thing to be done to our lawn in the rough after the problems of under-drainage and surface distribution of water have been disposed of? Why, simply to cart off the stones and cut down the weeds with a scythe. The ground thus roughly cleaned, the next thing is to plow it up or spade it at least a foot deep. If the subsoil is not actually sandy, it will be well to go farther down. Deep culture is of great value to a lawn. It ensures better resistance to droughts and a more even and luxuriant growth of grass.

I am coming now to a point that is of the utmost importance to the development of a good lawn, and that is the removal of all weeds, stones, and roots from the soil to a foot or more in depth. On the proper removal and burning of these weeds and roots the ultimate success of the lawn largely depends. Once plowing, raking, forking, and burning may not suffice; twice may not, and even three times may not, but no matter how many may be needed, they must be given. Deep and thorough culture is a necessity to a lawn, absolute and fundamental. There is no cause, perhaps, more prolific of bad lawns than poor culture. I care not what tools you use, plow or spade (ordinarily the plow should suffice), tilth and cleanness of soil you must have. By cleanness, of course, I mean, at the best, approximate cleanness, for millions of embryo seeds must lurk in most soils, clean them as often as you will. But if you will clean them again and again, by plowing and raking, you will find that the young grass will get a better chance to occupy the ground with their root feeders before the roots of the weeds enter in and take possession.

Having accomplished the plowing and cleaning, the next thing is to do the grading. Now the grading is a nice operation, which requires not only a good knowledge of landscape gardening but an intuitive, artistic conception of the best effect that can be produced under existing circumstances. It is not easy to convey any broad and generally reliable suggestions on this subject, so much depends on individual surroundings and peculiarities of position. However, I will endeavor to convey some idea of what I mean.

In the first place, the reader may, for instance, fancy himself at his front door-step as the most important point from which he should view his lawn. From this point he must look on the view as a picture with an open centre and boundary enclosure, the lawn being, for convenience of illustration, the open centre, and the trees, shrubs, and flowers the boundary enclosure. I insist upon this illustration because I want it understood that the lawn is to be open; there may be allowed a few outlying trees and shrubs and flowers, but the lawn is to be practically open, closely cut greensward, suitable for people to walk about on and children to play on without obstruction. If this end is not accomplished, I consider the lawn a failure.

Looking from the front door-steps, we must first consider our lawn as a comparatively flat surface—in a word, as level. Of course nature does nothing stiffly or on abrupt or rigid lines. Her work is one of infinite gradations or shadings. What appears to us as level at a little distance, when we approach it may prove to be a gentle swell.

As we walk over a natural vale, or lawn—if I may be allowed the term,—we find a continual change in the grade of the surface. If we should attempt to make level an artificial lawn we could not do it. We would only succeed in making stiff lines and awkward transitions of grade. At the outset, therefore, long, swelling, easy lines of grade should be sought. For the better effect of the boundary enclosure of trees and shrubs and flowers, the lawn should be made hollowing, and for the better enjoyment of those walking over its surface, this hollowing should be easy and closely approaching the level.

It is evident that this theory of grading will apply equally well to ground sloping down or up from the front of the house, only the general slope should be not too steep or the pleasure of walking on it will be diminished. I shall speak of this further when I consider the treatment of sloping grounds that cannot be properly termed lawns. I desire to say that so important do I consider it that all lawns should be in part at least more or less level that I would be willing in grading to remove a large amount of earth entirely, or mound it up at the front along the road or at the sides, in order to secure this level lawn effect. The sense of the repose, comfort, and beauty associated with the idea of a lawn disappears when it grows steep.

Let me say, however, that I do not wish to indicate that the lawn should be made only in front of the house. It may be even better arranged at the back of the house. All considerable lawns are improved by isolating from them the carriage drives and even the foot-paths. The most agreeable way of arranging a house and grounds, if convenience will permit it, is to have the drives and walks come in from the highway, merely turning about a small grass plot. With the hall and kitchen and other business parts of the house on this side, it is desirable then to have the library and living rooms open out on the main lawn, and if possible the finest view. You have thus the best part of the home grounds to yourself undisturbed by carriages or undesirable foot passengers.

Seclusion and the shutting in of the lawn as part of the actual home has always a peculiar charm of its own. I would not, as a rule, emulate the strict exclusiveness of our English brethren who, in so many cases, shut themselves in with great stone walls, but I would fence myself round about in some way. I would surround the home lawns with masses of trees and shrubs, and so dispose the main lawn in connection with the house as to make it my own special and peculiar domain.

Having plowed, cleaned, and roughly graded the lawn into a comparatively level, gently swelling surface, the next thing is to cover it over with a heavy coat of rich manure, twenty-five, thirty, forty, fifty loads to the acre. Spread it on liberally, all you can get under, provided it is well decomposed. Use thoroughly decayed composted stable manure if you can get it; if not, bone-dust, wood-ashes, superphosphate of lime, nitrate of ammonia, etc.

What is required in the manure is plenty of ammonia, then phosphoric acid, lime, soda, potash, and magnesia, etc., but when you use these salts of soda, potash, etc., as concentrated fertilizers, you may happen not to apply them in proper quantities. Bone-dust acts slowly on grass lands, though well, and so does wood-ashes with its phosphates and potash salts, but stable manure, with the one drawback of sometimes bringing in foul weeds, seems to act more quickly and at the same time as permanently as any other fertilizer. People try everything else, but come back to the properly composted heap of barnyard manure, with the feeling that therein lies their true source of strength for creating permanently rich grass lands. There is doubtless a large percentage of a load of stable manure that is of little use to the land, but the application of fifty loads of manure to an acre seems to present the nutriment in a form and combination that will do the land the most good. There is not much scientific theory in these suggestions about manuring lawns, I know, but you will find it is plain common-sense. Experiment with artificial manures all you can, but let it be at first on a small scale, and it will repay your trouble by the information gained as to what your special soil actually needs. Do the bulk of your fertilizing with barnyard manure and your average results will be satisfactory ; then if your other experiments develop some peculiar need of your soil, you can give up the barnyard manure, and use for a while some concentrated special fertilizer.

Now that your land is graded, and the surface covered with fertilizing material, the next thing is to dig or plow lightly the entire surface of the ground and then harrow and hand-rake it thoroughly, and remove again entirely all stones, roots, and foul weeds that come to the surface. It is wonderful how these stones, roots, and weeds, crop out with repeated plowing, harrowing, and raking. The supply seems in many soils unlimited. As I have said, however, already, thoroughness in such work is of vital importance to the success of the lawn. The raking is of importance, moreover, to secure fine pulverizing of the top soil intended to receive the grass seed.

But the question that now arises is, what kind of grass seed shall be used? The seedsman will give you a mixture of lawn grass seed, and if the business firm be reputable, it will doubtless produce fair results. Let us, however, look a little closer into the matter. I have said that very little conception generally exists of the actual appearance of any lawn that is in process of construction, that is, that has been recently sown. And in considering this question of the best kind of grass seed, we begin to realize the truth of this assertion.

In the first place, grass seed of any kind can be seldom secured reasonably pure. Any seedsman, if he be candid, will tell you that. He will, doubtless, say in addition, what is true, that grass seed is a great deal cleaner now than it was a few years ago. Better methods of cleaning grass seed have been devised, and more pains are taken to secure this desirable result. But the question still remains, what kind of grass seed shall we use? There are, as all persons at all acquainted with grasses know, hundreds of varieties, many, very many that are not named in the catalogues of seedsmen.

Of these, one perhaps is best suited to this particular soil, and on the next field another is required. This one does well here, that kind dies out there. What are we to do? It is verily a puzzle. And then after all, we cannot hope to get really pure seed of the kind we select at last. We sow it, and with it will spring up some unknown grass or weed that will destroy entirely the effect we have expected.

Grass sods of some pure, rich-looking, and permanent variety might be used with success, but where are they to be obtained in quantities? To make a lawn with grass sod would be more expensive than with grass seed, but if selected grass sod could be obtained, it would doubtless produce far better, more enduring and attractive results. In view, however, of the entire lack at present of nurseries or plots of the right kind of sod, we are obliged to fall back on the ordinary grass seeds that can be purchased of reputable seedsmen at the present time.

In the first place, when you go to the seedsman do not buy a lawn grass mixture. Do the mixing yourself if there is to be any. It will be cheaper and better. Secondly and lastly, limit yourself to two or three kinds that are likely to grow well in the particular kind of soil you expect to sow. There is a prevailing desire to sow white clover on the lawn. Now I contend that white clover is out of place on the lawn. To me a greensward of red top or Kentucky blue grass is always more attractive than one mottled with white clover.

Then as to the mixture of grasses, there is, to my mind, a great deal of current error. Why not select a strong, vigorous variety that grows tolerably thick-set, and sow that only. If you sow twenty other kinds, they will all probably be run out in a few years by this and some other strong-growing variety that may come in by accident. The important thing is to secure a variety that will spring up vigorously and take possession of the soil before other less attractive grasses and weeds occupy the ground.

In order to accomplish this, we may be even obliged to select a somewhat coarse variety. On the lawns of Central Park, for instance, a great deal of Kentucky blue grass has been used, not because it is, by any means, the most attractive of grasses, but because it is vigorous and holds its own even on sandy ground, and makes a fairly good-looking sod. This kind and herds' grass, or red top, form the staple of most lawn-grass mixtures used in the United States. Rhode Island bent grass is highly valued by many, and makes an excellent sod, particularly in a moist climate. Red top in a sandy soil is apt to die off in droughts occurring just after germination. Its first growth is not, in such cases, quite vigorous enough, although the quality of the sod it produces is much finer than that of Kentucky blue grass. Another objection to red top seed is its general impurity as found in the market.

Having secured our seed, such as it is, the next question is, in what quantities and how shall we sow it? Again comes in the question of the quality of soil, its comparative moisture, and its cleanness. Under the most favorable circumstances a large proportion of the seed sown will fail to germinate. It is therefore wise to sow grass seed liberally. The price of grass seed is comparatively low. I have consequently not hesitated to use, in some cases, six bushels of Kentucky blue grass or red top to the acre, although seedsmen only advise two or three. The art of sowing grass seed properly requires some experience to acquire. The great difficulty is to sow it evenly. Like mowing and other farming operations, it takes trouble to learn how to sow grass seed properly. You must get up early in the morning before the wind has risen. You must consider the direction from which the wind blows and do a good many things that can hardly be set down intelligently on paper.

When the seed is sown the next thing is to rake with a fine-toothed iron rake the entire lawn over thoroughly. Some people content themselves with a harrow for such work, but it does imperfect work at best. After the raking a heavy iron roller should be used at once over every part where the seed is sown. This sets the seed in the ground firmly and helps wonderfully to secure an even mat of grass, especially if a drought sets in soon after the sowing. It is a good plan also to continue this rolling once or twice after the grass has started and before it is fit to mow.

The first cutting with the mowing machine should come as soon as the grass is high enough for the knives of the machine to fairly take hold. Frequent mowing during the early development of the lawn tends to thicken and strengthen the growth of lawn grass and thus keep down objectionable wild grasses and weeds.

Having reached this point, however, in the construction of a lawn, most people are liable to consider that nothing more than an occasional mowing is needed. And just here a great mistake is made, and the establishment of a reasonably perfect lawn retarded, or, in most cases, absolutely prevented. Perhaps I may startle some one when I state that to keep up a good lawn, in many places, requires as much careful and continual culture, with our present quality of seed, as to keep a flower-bed in order; but it is a fact. And why should we not consider the well-being of each spear of grass as important as that of each coleus or geranium in the flower-bed. The spear of grass is actually the most important factor in the enjoyment of the home grounds.

Viewing the matter in this light, we should not hesitate to weed the lawn all summer if necessary, to water it daily in dry weather, and yearly renew bare spots with better soil, to cover it with seed again, and fertilize the entire surface with frequent applications of manure, and in addition to roll it from time to time when the ground is soft. In the course of years, however, the good results of such work must tell, and the necessity for it become much diminished; but vigilance and intelligent culture will be always and continually required under the most favorable circumstances.

CHAPTER II.

THE TREATMENT OF SLOPING GROUNDS.

 AM convinced that the reader will find this subject a novel one. The principles governing it are not, so far as I am aware, laid down in the books, and yet some of the most charming effects of our best park lawns come from an accidental or intentional arrangement of the kind I am about to describe.

There are certain primary conditions or divisions that make up all parks or home-grounds. Walks, drives, greensward or lawns, plantations, whether trees, shrubs, or flowers, and the intermediate spaces that may be called "sloping grounds," make up characteristic landscape-gardening effects. These sloping grounds may come down to the drives or walks or they may slope upward, in steps as it were, to higher lawns or plateaus. They may be made of turf, rocks, vines or trees, shrubs or perennial plants, of each alone, or of all, or of only part mingled together. The lawn itself we have decided to consider for the purpose of comfortable and pleasant occupation as level or slightly hollowing.

The accompanying illustration will convey some idea of what I mean by a slightly hollowing lawn. This surface is to my mind quite as irregular as one would desire for pleasant walking, and anything more irregular I should call sloping grounds, and not properly a lawn. We may find attractive sloping grounds all ready-made for us by nature or we may be obliged to humbly follow her lead and treat more or less artificially our sloping grounds after the fashion practised by the natural forces about us.

The hardest part of such work is to keep from exaggerating nature or repeating over and over again some one of her ways of doing things. It should be always remembered, in landscape gardening, that nature never repeats herself. A torrent of rain rushes down a hillside and ploughs furrows or heaps piles of stones in its path and partially covers them with earth from above, but it never ploughs the same kind of furrow twice or heaps up the earth and stones again in the same way. There will be, indeed a certain similarity in the trend of the furrows and the course of the rolling stones. This may be largely established by the character and pitch of the slope, or it may come from the general direction of the storms.

Keeping this in mind, we will proceed to consider the best way to treat sloping grounds of obvious steepness. There are two kinds of steep sloping ground in connection with lawns which require special modes of handling. One we may describe as artificially irregular, and the other as only in part artificially irregular. A portion of it may be

LAWN IN CENTRAL PARK, NEW YORK, NEAR THE NORTH END OF THE MALL

already found in place, and to attain the desired effect it may be simply necessary to supplement it with work of a similar character. The wholly artificial sloping ground will be required where it is necessary to support a steep bank connected with a terrace or upper lawn plateau. It may be also required in the immediate vicinity of a house, or, as in the illustration, along a skirting boundary wall. The second kind consists in great part of a mass of natural rock, which, cropping out of a hillside, separates a lower from a higher lawn, or borders a path or roadway, or body of water, or a plantation and lawn.

In order to explain more satisfactorily the proper method of treating sloping grounds, I have employed three illustrations of the work of actually constructing such features. In the first illustration, a rough ungraded bank in Central Park is shown; then another, where the workmen

ROUGH UNGRADED BANK.

have finished grading a piece of ground and a steep bank at one end.

It will be noticed that the bank is very steep and needs to be kept up to its abrupt angle. If such a place were subjected to the action of the elements for years, with the soil as full of boulders as it is in the immediate neighborhood, you would find that, in time, a state of things would be established like the one seen in the illustration below.

CLOSELY-MASSED ROCKS ON FINISHED STEEP BANK.

Gullies of different depths and like general direction would course down between half-uncovered rocks that may have been long embedded there or may have rolled down to this point. Above, just over the rocks, will appear mounded up earth as though soil had washed down and collected above the stone obstruction.

Sometimes there will be several of these rocks clustered together and holding up a steep portion of the banks, and again, considerable spaces will occur without rocks, but they may still be slightly gullied or lightly scooped out, as it were, by the elements over a considerable area. The entire bank, finished on these natural lines, is sodded, as it is too steep to retain and properly germinate grass seed. Rains would be sure to wash the seed away.

It will be seen by this brief explanation that rockwork must be constructed on nature's lines after a careful study and analysis of nature's methods of doing such work.

The illustration of the next bank shows the way to treat sloping grounds where the steepness is not so great. Here larger areas are open and longer gullies appear where the sweep of the water has apparently had more opportunity to leave broad marks.

The placing of these rocks requires much art. It will be seen that they are not set parallel with each other, but that they have a likeness of setting, as if a gully had been opened behind them, and that its course had determined the dip and set of the rocks. The gullies naturally have also the same general similarity, although throughout the whole arrangement extends the greatest diversity of formation.

Thus far I have spoken of and illustrated entirely artificial rockwork, and of course artificial rockwork may take special forms. It may be a bank to be treated with rocks, as we have seen, or it may be a group of stones to protect a tree, around which earth is to be filled. The curves of drives may need rocks to fend off carriage-wheels, or there may be an extended terrace, in front or on the side of the house, that must be held in with rocks. In each and every case the simple object to be sought is to make the effect look entirely natural, as if it had been brought about in long course of time under the stress of wind and rain.

There is also the second or semi-artificial rockwork to be considered, the kind that is a supplementary rockwork to that already standing naturally in place. Instances of

PARTLY FINISHED ROCKY BANK READY FOR PLANTING.

this kind are to be found everywhere in countries where stone abounds, along paths and roads, between upper and lower lawns, near the house, and along boundary lines. In fact, they may be found everywhere as problems distinctly in sight and requiring treatment. I except of course rocks that stand up in the middle of roads or paths. From such places the rock must be simply removed at least two feet below the surface of the ground. Many lawns turn brown in summer on account of the proximity of rock to the surface.

If you will note the illustration of a charming lawn of Central Park near the Webster Statue and the head of the Mall, you will see how the rocks crop out of the outskirts of the territory. It is in the neighborhood of these rocks, where they have not been blasted away sufficiently, that the first effects of drought are felt. The lawn of the illustration is like a shallow bowl, beautifully modelled, and, as already noted, it represents the extreme of irregularity that should be given a lawn.

Many of the rocks around it are natural, but in order to supplement and complete their attractions others have been set contiguous to them in such a manner as to make the whole seem to be an entirely natural effect.

Let us now turn to the illustration of the Cave in the Ramble, Central Park. It is an excellent example of this semi-artificial rockwork. In the first place, it should be explained that the entire Cave and the hollow space around it were found originally to be filled up to a high level with rich mould. For the sake of the mould, all the soil was carted out, leaving a great excavation not very unlike

ENTRANCE TO CAVE IN THE RAMBLE, CENTRAL PARK, NEW YORK.

what we see in the picture. Just here, however, came in the art.

In carrying out the work of park construction, all the desirable effects were simply emphasized and completed. On top of the solid wall of rock adjoining, more rocks were set, while on the other side where little but earth probably appeared in the original excavation, many large rocks were set on edge as if they had accidentally slid down to their present position. The planting of trees and vines and the laying of a convenient walk to the Cave complete the entirely natural effect presented by the picture.

The illustration of the steps to the Cave is introduced principally to show the proper method of treating such places. The most perfect rustic steps are of course rough-hewn slabs of stone, but as these are often hardly agreeable to the feet, good practice has accepted the cut granite step, roughly edged. This somewhat artificial-looking stone does not look well directly alongside the greensward, and the turf at that point is liable to be kicked to pieces by the feet of those passing up and down the steps. It will be seen in the picture how this difficulty is overcome by bordering all the steps with large stones set so as to look as natural as possible. No rustic steps should indeed be set without this border or natural coping of rockwork.

In another illustration taken from Central Park will be seen the way in which a shore should be treated where a great mass of rock extends sheer down into the depths of the pool. By looking closely you will see two large rocks lying in the water. Although they seem to have only happened there, it should be understood that they were care-

STEPS LEADING TO CAVE IN THE RAMBLE, CENTRAL PARK, NEW YORK.

fully placed at the very point they occupy to increase the desired natural effect. Where the shore is less occupied by a huge mass of rock, and yet is steep, a good-sized stone, set here and there in the water, is very effective. The shore line should be diversified by pushing out a cluster of stones at one point, and at another flanking a bay with a broad long rock with its base in the water. At the lowest part of the bank there may be arranged with good effect a sandy beach.

The rocks, I should explain, must not be clustered too thickly on a bank. There should be plenty of plant space between the rocks, otherwise they will appear to be simply an artificial heap of stones. Some rocks will of course be contiguous, but many of the others should in that case be kept farther apart. I doubt if, in most cases, such a bank should have more than half its surface covered with rocks. The rest should be turf, vines, or trees and shrubs, and the manner of using grass and plants in rockwork is a distinguishing mark of the best landscape-gardening art.

This reference to trees and shrubs leads me to the consideration of the remaining and specially important part of the treatment of sloping grounds, namely, the use of turf and plants of all kinds in connection with rockwork. The illustrations show many large trees and shrubs mingled with the rocks, and numerous Virginia creepers and other vines trailing over their surface in such a manner and thickness as to relieve the solid character of the stony masses.

It is important to observe the practice of so pruning and training vines in such places as to always leave exposed something of the general effect and contour of the rock.

STONE BRIDGE ADJOINING LARGE NATURAL ROCK, CENTRAL PARK, NEW YORK.

As a rule, the vines should be planted in the deepest soil near the top of the rock, and not at the base. The exception to this rule is the *Ampelopsis tricuspidata* or Japan ivy. Wherever this excellent vine is planted in rockwork, it should stand at the base of a rock, and thus climb up by means of its rootlets, rather than fall over and lose its most characteristic effect. It is a thick-growing vine, and completely covers any moderate-sized space it seizes on. Thinning out this vine is not easy. It does not look natural for some time after being thinned out, no matter how much care is taken. For this reason, the Japan ivy is not to be generally commended for covering rocks. Such vines as Virginia creeper, honeysuckles, Virginia silk, *Akebia quinata*, trumpet creeper *(Tecoma radicans)*, clematis, Dutchman's pipe, bitter-sweet *(Celastrus scandens)*, and above all Wistaria, are always found picturesque-looking on rocks.

Trees and shrubs should be planted on the higher portions of the banks or sloping grounds, and not usually in the valleys or hollows. This arrangement tends to increase the effect of the irregularity of the grounds and emphasizes the higher points that manifestly require emphasis.

Some of the best trees and shrubs for planting among rocks are those that weep or droop, or are irregular and picturesque-looking. Among trees I may name as specially suitable for this purpose, the varieties of Japanese maple *(Acer polymorphum)*, the alders, *Andromeda arborea*, *Aralia spinosa* (Hercules' club), *Aralia Japonica*, white birch, European and American hornbeam, white-flowering dogwood, *Cratægus Crus-galli* (the cock-spur thorn), *C. coccinea*, weeping beech, honey-locust, Kentucky coffee tree, weeping larch, pyramidal oak, Lombardy poplar, *Rhus aromatica* and *Rhus glabra laciniata* or cut-leaved sumach, the ginkgo tree *(Salisburia adiantifolia)*, *Salix rosmarinifolia* (rosemary-leaved willow), and the Japan weeping *(Sophora)*. Some of the shrubs suitable for rocky regions are the Ghent or hardy azalea, *Clethra alnifolia, Cornus sanguinea alba* (the red-twigged dogwood), *Daphne Genkwa, Deutzia gracilis, Elæagnus hortensis, Elæagnus longipes, Euonymus alatus, Forsythia suspensa, Fothergilla alnifolia, Genista scoparia* (Scotch broom), *Genista tinctoria, Itea Virginica, Kerria Japonica, Jasminum nudiflorum, Lonicera fragrantissima, Lycium barbarum, Myrica cerifera, Prinos verticillata, Prunus maritima, Rhodotypus kerrioides, Rubus odoratus, Sambucus nigra aurea, Spiræa Reevesiana, S. callosa, S. callosa alba, S. opulifolia, Symphoricarpus vulgaris, S. racemosa, Tamarix Africana, T. Indica, Viburnum opulus, Yucca filamentosa,* and *Y. recurva.*

YUCCA RECURVA.

The best evergreens for rockwork are the weeping hemlock, the weeping Norway spruce or *Picea excelsa inverta, Picea excelsa elata, Cedrus Atlantica, Juniperus Virginiana* (the red cedar), *J. prostrata, J. squamata, J.*

tamariscifolia (all three known as the creeping juniper), *J. Sabina* or savin juniper, *Abies pectinata pendula* (weeping silver fir), *Pinus Cembra, Pinus Mugho, Retinospora obtusa, R. filifera pendula, Sciadopitys verticillata,* the Japan parasol pine, rhododendrons, *Azalea amœna, Cotoneaster buxifolia, Cratægus* or *Cotoneaster pyracantha, Kalmia latifolia* (broad-leaved laurel), *Berberis* or *Mahonia Aquifolium,* and *M. Japonicum.*

There are also a large number of hardy herbaceous perennials that are peculiarly well suited to rockwork.

A word, before closing this chapter, on the kind of rock-treatment that generally passes for good work among gardeners. It generally consists of an irregular pile of stones, with a little soil tucked in pockets here and there for the reception of vines and flowers. The stones chosen are frequently brought from a considerable distance in order to secure the very quality they should not have, viz., that of strangeness and unlikeness to the common rock seen at home. Flowers and vines may, of course, be attractive in themselves, growing out of a pile of stones, but unrelated stones heaped up in a mass, that is in no sense in key or harmony with the rest of the landscape, have no excuse for their special arrangement in a landscape-gardener's picture.

It is to be regretted that landscape gardeners so often fail to grasp the combined possibilities and proper relations of the different features of the places they undertake to treat. If they could only look upon their work in a large and artistic manner, they would see that rocks planted in the ground at the points where they would appear most natural and most needed contribute to secure some of the

TREATMENT OF SLOPING GROUNDS. 31

best effects of the entire lawn. Heaps of stones, on the other hand, set on end with their points sticking up, even with the nested vines and flowers, always serve to mar the repose of the place.

CHAPTER III.

SPRING EFFECTS ON THE LAWN.

PRINGTIME is the season of buds. Now everything is swelling with revived life and ecstasy. The new year is growing, and nature is bursting with all possible haste into the full perfection of June. Some specially endowed plants actually reach their goal of bloom before summer sets her seal-warrant on their perfection, but they do it in many cases only by presenting their flowers on twigs and branches, which scarcely as yet show their leaves.

So many plants have this habit of flowering before their leaves appear that I propose to dwell chiefly on their intrinsic peculiarities as dominating the most characteristic portions of spring effects on the lawn. I always fancy April and early May as the true springtide of the year. Late May is generally June in appearance as far as the effects of grass, foliage, and flowers go. The hurry and activity of the bright early spring days have passed by the middle of May, and we find ourselves fast settling down into the slumberous rich fulness of content inspired by the gracious conditions of early summer. The activities of spring have culminated into the restfulness of summer.

It is the activities of spring, however, that I wish to consider at present, fully believing that no more charming subject can enchain our attention than the simultaneous unfolding, as it were, of the leaf and flower bud of all nature. It is a new birth, and inspires all the glad feelings associated with an actual resurrection. The very sight of nature at this season is a positive delight, and the lawn, so planted as to exhibit properly the glories of this season, will surely gain a charm unspeakable. Nor is the charm less for people generally, but rather more, because in a full community of interest in this particular season every one feels, recognizes, and takes possession of the evident charm as common property. There is none of the elusiveness of some of the shy beauties of other parts of the year.

As we walk upon the tender, emerald greensward we luxuriate and glory in the very bounteousness with which nature is renewing her mysterious powers about us. We are insatiable; we demand the evident presence of spring everywhere on the lawn. The object is not yet the rich composition of color in fall effects, not yet the quiet subdued masses of late summer foliage, nor even the broad glow and gleam of June.

In contemplating once more the wonderful mystery of renewed creation, exemplified by freshly budding leaf and flower, we simply seek with avidity something of special spring foliage and bloom everywhere. It is not enough to see this foliage and bloom freshly put forth at our doorstep, but their beauty must appear on all sides, under the trees, down by the stream, in a part of every shrub group, on the vines of the porch or boundary wall—in short, on every spot where their presence will not unduly usurp the province of the flowers and foliage of other seasons of the year.

Unlike the fall effects, moreover, which are specially effective on a large lawn, the beauties of spring ornamental plants may be restricted to very small dimensions, and actually in such cases furnish lovely lawn-planting effects from the very charm alone of their detail.

You will perceive, therefore, that my endeavor in treating of spring on the lawn resolves itself into comparatively simple descriptions of lovely bits of color and form in actual process of being wrought into the most charming lawn-planting combinations. I would not imply that these processes are not going on during the entire summer, only that now we feel them to be a dominant feature of the time. They are in full action all around us, and we are in sympathy with them more than at any other time of the year.

There are several plants that sometimes bloom even in winter, if the season is mild. These plants must of course be considered the earliest of flowering shrubs, and bearing, as they must at this early season, their flowers before their leaves, our attention is naturally given chiefly to their flowers.

The first I call to mind is an old shrub common in many unpretending gardens, *Jasminum nudiflorum*, the yellow jasmine which a mild February has often seen in bloom. The flowers are yellow, small, and bright, and studded on smooth, slender, green stems. It is vigorous and easily transplanted, and should have a place on every lawn, old-fashioned though it be. The yellow jasmine may occupy very suitably a position in a group, but it also makes a lovely sweet-scented plant for early spring bloom, or may be even trained on a trellis as a climber.

At some point near a path or near the house, or, best of all, on the outskirts of *Rhododendron Catawbiense* groups, may be used an allied and equally aristocratic plant, *Rhododendron dauricum*. Why aristocratic it may not be easy to explain in set terms, for the application of such an adjective is doubtless fanciful; yet I always feel a certain respect that is more than mere admiration for the dignified beauty of the rhododendron family. Its members are so excellent for their grand forms and exquisite color that they quite cast into the shade the homely though undoubted charms of the yellow jasmine. In this case I wish to pay my respects to the *Rhododendron Dauricum*, a species that in England often blooms in midwinter. Even in New England a few mild February days may coax and surprise

YELLOW JASMINE.
(JASMINUM NUDIFLORUM.)

the dark glowing red of its flower into sudden full-blown beauty. This rhododendron is quite dwarf in its nature and not at all spreading. It is not indeed specially conspicuous among its relatives, except for the extreme earliness of its flowers. The leaves are small, and not always as lustrous as the broad foliage of *Rhododendron Catawbiense* and *R. maximum*.

But there are other trees and shrubs not far behind this *Rhododendron Dauricum* and yellow jasmine. The scarlet maple, which we saw a few months since dyed during the yearly process of decay with lovely crimson, is now scarcely less attractive. Almost before we fairly begin to feel that spring is upon us we note with sudden pleasure the bare branches of the scarlet maple studded with minute red buds over the entire tree, literally jewelled with the first bursting luxuriance of spring. These leaf-buds are accompanied, if not entirely outstripped, by the flowers, a common peculiarity of the inflorescence of all early spring-blooming plants. The flowers of the scarlet maple are of course most noteworthy, and are the special cause of the bejewelled appearance of the branches.

Thus far we have dwelt particularly on the flowers of spring, but we must be careful not to forget the equally attractive charms of the unfolding leaf. The mysterious processes of the early development of the leaf reveal exquisite shadings and tints and a marvellous delicacy of form seldom to be found in such bright, rich beauty as in the budding of this maple.

Who has not likewise enjoyed the pushing forth of the pussies or catkins of willow and alder? Delightful in their rich, cool green last fall, we find ourselves again in early spring dwelling on the same pleasant leaf colors gradually developed, but preceded by the lovely silvery flower-buds known as pussies or catkins.

There are European alders and several well-known American alders that it would be well to employ for their charming appearance at this season. *Alnus imperialis laciniata*, the cut-leaved alder, and *Alnus firma*, the Japan alder, are also fine in early spring.

All willows are effective in early spring, but the goat willow, *Salix caprea*, parent of the weeping Kilmarnock willow, is particularly noteworthy for attractive early spring development. In similar fashion the royal willow *(Salix regalis)*, the common weeping willow, and the rosemary willow distinguish themselves, furnishing us the delightful bits of cool silvery-gray or olive-green color so characteristic of much of the foliage of the early days of spring.

It would seem as if the birch was lovely during every hour of the year, for even winter landscapes are greatly beautified by the birch's picturesque white stems and delicate branching. In spring, however, the soft delicate satin sheen of its unfolding leaf-buds are dainty and surpassingly beautiful to those who will take the trouble to examine their refined charms. For early spring purposes the ordinary American birches, the canoe birch, and black and yellow birches and the common European birch are sufficient. The cut-leaved and purple-leaved birches of course stand eminent among rare trees for their distinctive beauty.

While on the subject of attractive early spring foliage, we should dwell especially on the larches. The tender soft shining green of their young foliage is not surpassed in color by their leaf clothing of any other season of the year. It matters little which larch we take—the vigorous Japan leptolepsis, or glauca, or the grotesque weeping form, or Dahurica, or even the common European and American species or type—their charming spring tints are alike lovely. Larches look well and do well in outlying low portions of the lawn, and are especially valuable for this soft and tender springtime beauty. If planted too near the house, the rusty hue of midsummer they present, obtrudes itself unpleasantly on the eye.

The aspen poplar *(Populus tremuloides)* also develops beautiful early unfoldings of the leaf. It is, moreover, almost as attractive in form and tint as the alders and birches. All this we must remember is embryonic foliage, for early spring is properly the season of leaf, buds, and early flowers. Indeed, flowers are the crown and charm of spring, just as leaves almost exclusively adorn the noteworthy plants of midsummer and fall. As a rule, we have properly no developed foliage with early spring effects; so although during our discussion we have been led, almost unconsciously, into dwelling on certain lovely leaf-buds of spring, we will henceforth devote ourselves conscientiously and exclusively to the flowers that constitute spring's special wreath of glory.

We have considered one charming yellow flower, *Jasminum nudiflorum*, but a better and more effective bloom appears almost as early on the long sweeping branches of the well-known *Forsythia viridissima* or golden bell. This shrub graces the dooryard of nearly every home that attempts to grow any ornamental plants whatever. Yet its fresh bright charms never weary the eye, especially when we come to realize its hardy vigor and fitness for ready transplanting and its abundant display of flowers.

There are two or three kinds, but *viridissima* is the favorite, with little show of justice, for *suspensa* presents more regular and attractive curves, and is particularly effective on rockwork, and *Fortunii*, an erect form, is fine in every way.

One of the commonest and best shrubs that bloom in these early spring days is the *Cydonia Japonica*, the Japan quince. It has grown to be a favorite deciduous shrub, alike in the office of hedge, group, or single specimen, and proves itself worthy of all its popularity by its rich bloom, great hardiness, and bright green foliage. *Pyrus Japonica* we used to call it, before botanists taught us better, and few who enjoy hardy trees

WEEPING GOLDEN BELL.
(FORSYTHIA SUSPENSA.)

and shrubs at all have failed to note time and again its many excellent and lovely qualities. But the blossom, its chief and peculiar spring attraction, is not always of the glowing brilliant red so familiar to all who have known the *Pyrus Japonica* at all. Red is indeed the color of the best-known kinds; but there are varieties bearing pinkish-white flowers, and others, like *alba simplex*, pure white in their loveliness. Others are distinctly striped red and white, and still others glow with rich salmon color. There is a large-flowered kind recently introduced from Japan called *Cydonia Japonica grandiflora*, bearing flowers nearly double the size of our common form, with richly blended colors of salmon red and white. Do not forget, therefore, to use the different varieties of these Japan quinces.

The white flowering dogwood *(Cornus florida)* should stand on every lawn. It is hardy, picturesque in growth, and charming in spring with its masses of pure white flowers, and is, moreover, an American shrub or tree, and therefore deserves employment for American planting.

There are two or three dainty little flowers that come very early in spring, before the leaves appear. I dwell on them with special pleasure because their beauty is shy and modest, more like that of the violet, and because they afford a strong contrast to the glowing brilliance of the Japan quince. *Rhodora Canadensis*, the choicest of these, is little known except to botanists and true plant lovers, not certainly because it is rare, for it grows in the woods of New England in considerable quantities, and could be transplanted while young with little difficulty. Indeed, I cannot account satisfactorily for the neglect of such a beautiful and abundant native flower. Perhaps like a good many other

FLOWERING DOGWOOD.
(CORNUS FLORIDA.)

beautiful things that do not flaunt their charms before the eye of the passer-by, it has been simply overlooked. Exquisite as all its tints are, they are yet quiet, Quaker-like, and almost neutral in effect. The slender stems or branches are a delicate drab, and the flowers have that tender violet or mauve tint so difficult to describe and yet so charming to dwell on minutely. These flowers are numerous and appear early. When we light, therefore, unexpectedly on a cluster of rhodoras in some retired nook, they impress us as one of the most exquisite indications of settled spring.

DOUBLE-FLOWERING APPLE.
(PYRUS SPECTABILIS.)

Only less dainty than the rhodora is the *Daphne Mezereum*, bearing many early small flowers on brown erect stems. The color of these flowers is also neutral, a violet purple, very different and less exquisite than the rhodora. Very different, too, are the leaves. Indeed, the entire plant is less choice in every way, but, bearing flowers very early, before the leaves appear, it forms on the outskirts of deciduous groups, or better still, standing alone, a noteworthy feature on the lawn.

Smaller and more exquisite is the Japan *Daphne Genkwa*, another, but more dwarf, slender-growing shrub, with numerous long downy twigs, which in early spring, before the leaves appear, are thickly garnished with violet-colored tubular flowers rather less than an inch long. This daphne seldom attains a height of more than three feet, and has fine delicate foliage. It is one of the more recent valuable introductions from Japan, and should be planted in angles of the house or in similar retired spots where numbers of it can be set out together without being overwhelmed by the more striking effect of other plants.

Almost as early as the plants already mentioned are the blossoms of the various fruits, apples, cherries, plums, and peaches. In this case, however, I do not refer to the simple blossoms familiar to all in dooryard or orchard, but to special varieties that have changed—developed—their fruit-producing blossoms into larger and more beautiful, though sterile flowers. These flowers are variously colored, and double the size of the ordinary forms.

THE DOUBLE-FLOWERING CHERRY. (PRUNUS CERASUS, FL. PL.)

There are several varieties of double-flowering apples, some with blooms more or less shaded with pink, some red, and others with leaves variegated. *Acubæfolia* is an instance of the last form, and among the others are

SOULANGE'S MAGNOLIA. (MAGNOLIA SOULANGEANA.)

coronaria odorata, double pink, double crimson, and, above all, *Malus Halleana* and *spectabilis* from Japan, with flowers of a deep lively rose at the base, and a lighter shade at the edges. This last is unquestionably the most ornamental of the double-flowering apples. The old white double-flowering cherry is another early and most charming tree, only surpassed in form by the highly-prized weeping cherry of Japan, the flowers of which, however, are smaller and more pink than those of our flowering cherry. Double-flowering cherries, peaches, and plums are all attractive at this season.

The Japan Judas tree must receive a distinguished position among the early spring flowers of any lawn, for its long shrubby stems look rich and peculiar at that season, wreathed and studded with reddish-purple clinging flowers.

Of like peculiar habit are the Asiatic magnolias, chief among which for early blooming is the Japanese *Magnolia stellata*, with its delicate white star-like blossoms resting on firm compact stems. The better-known Chinese magnolias, *conspicua*, *Soulangeana*, *Norbetiana*, and *Lennei*, are each grand in their way, but come later than *stellata*, although still before the leaves appear. *Soulangeana* is the most vigorous and hardy, and best fitted for general popularity, but *conspicua* is, after all, the magnolia chief and peculiar among its race for choice beauty. It has not as sweet an odor or so dainty a development as *M. stellata*, but it is grander and more generally effective in appearance. A large tree of *M. conspicua* is a beautiful sight when arrayed in full bloom, especially if there has been, as often occurs in April, a light fall of snow. The great white regular cups of the flowers cover the entire contour of the tree, until as we gaze on it we could fancy, in the absence of foliage, we were looking on a white cloud. Snow adds greatly to the effect by harmoniously blending with the mass of these myriads of flowers. Like many plants, however, it is in this peculiar attractiveness of the early flower that we find its weakness. Late frosts sometimes catch and destroy the blooms of *conspicua*, which fact, notwithstanding the superior excellence of *conspicua* above *Soulangeana*, gives a decided advantage to the latter on account of its somewhat later bloom.

Norbetiana is but a slenderer, smaller form of *Soulangeana*, with flowers of similar tint and time of blooming.

JAPAN WEEPING CHERRY.

M. Lennei, however, is later in flowering, the latest of the Chinese magnolias, if we except perhaps the bloom of *M. purpurea* and its variety *gracilis*, which come about the same time. *Lennei* has the inner surface of its petal slightly tinted with red, but the outer side is solid, rich, royal purple. The flower itself is large, larger than those of any of the hardy magnolias, if we except possibly *tripetala*, and, of course, the enormous petals of *M. macrophylla*.

The lawn planter must not neglect the attractions of *M. gracilis*. It is, indeed, a variety of *M. purpurea*, an Asiatic magnolia, by no means hardy in America, but its seedling, *gracilis*, is hardier. *M. gracilis* displays on its petals the deepest purple of the family. It is, moreover, a low shrub like *M. Halleana (stellata)* with a comparatively slender and more elegant growth.

JAPANESE MAGNOLIA.
(MAGNOLIA STELLATA.)

Few hardy plants possess more noble ornamental qualities than Asiatic magnolias, but it must be conceded that while young they are somewhat more liable to injury from sudden changes in winter and early spring than some other plants. This is a weakness truly, but such excellence is surely worthy of a little protection for a few years and frequent transplanting in the nursery before permanent setting out, in order to secure the fibrous roots necessary to successful removal.

The consideration of the weakness of magnolias reminds us of the difficulties in growing the early flowering European thorns in many sections of this country. Notwithstanding the blight that attacks the thorn, it is easy to find

ENGLISH HAWTHORN. (CRATÆGUS OXYACANTHA.)

enough healthy specimens here and there to warrant our employing it in well drained, rich, loamy soil. The early and rich-hued blossoms of the thorn give it a charm that must always make it welcome as one of our choicest spring flowers. Bright bark and fresh young budding foliage add to the beauty of the flowers, but the flowers are quite sufficient of themselves to justify the renown for beauty belonging of old to the hawthorn of England.

This hawthorn has been improved and improved until there are double white varieties, double pink, double scarlet, double crimson, or single flowering scarlet, pink, etc., of less striking color and form. Paul's double red stands very high among red hawthorns, and some of the white flowering varieties are equally excellent. Hawthorns should be planted either singly or in groups by themselves. Their peculiar habit does not allow them to form entirely harmonious relations with other shrubs in the same group.

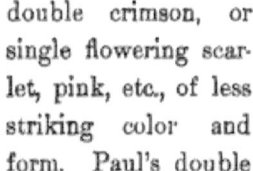

ENGLISH HAWTHORN.
(CRATÆGUS OXYACANTHA.)

I must not forget to mention among early-blooming plants the low-growing form of *Deutzia gracilis*, piled in May with masses of the most lovely small white flowers. Florists prize the flowers of the *Deutzia gracilis* highly for forcing, and no more attractive snow-white dainty clusters can be found on any of the hardy plants of the lawn.

Nor must I neglect the rich purple crimson and bronze-green foliage of *Azalea amœna*, most showy of very dwarf shrubs.

There is one plant, also of kindred type, for which I must, before concluding, express my admiration, and that is *Azalea mollis*. Of comparatively recent introduction from Japan, it has scarcely as yet gained a foothold on American lawns. At first sight one might fancy it a superior form of the ordinary but choice and lovely hybrid American or Ghent azalea, which, in a general way, it doubtless resembles.

AZALEA MOLLIS.

The foliage is similar, and the general appearance of the flower, at a little distance, of like character, but the bloom appears at least two weeks earlier than that of the Ghent azalea. Moreover, on examining the flower somewhat nearer, we will recognize immediately its superiority to the ordinary form. The petals are twice the size, as large even in some cases as those of the rhododendron, and suffused with the most exquisite tints of orange, saffron, and crimson. Of the type, there is scarcely anything as fine on the lawn.

DEUTZIA GRACILIS.

On beholding the beauty of *Azalea mollis* the remark has been made that the Ghent azalea must be superseded by so effective a flower of similar character, but such a thing as one good kind entirely superseding another good kind does not happen in the intelligent practice of lawn planting.

Azalea mollis blooms so early in May that late frosts in rare instances succeed in blighting its beauty, and when young the plant itself is sometimes killed by very severe winters. Generally, however, the *Azalea mollis* is perfectly hardy after a little protection for two or three years. The

TREE PEONY. (PÆONIA ARBOREA.)

Ghent or American azalea, on the other hand, is one of our hardiest deciduous shrubs both in leaf and flower.

The tree peony should not be forgotten. It is hardy and long-lived, and, unlike the herbaceous peony, it has a solid bush form. The flowers are splendid in color and form, superior to those of the herbaceous kind.

A word in conclusion should be given the lilacs, or *syringas*. Some of them bloom profusely and others do not, but their flowers seem specially lovely in early spring, with their delicate purple and white masses. The odor at such times perfumes the air delightfully. Lilacs' leaves, however, suffer from scale and are often unhealthy. The narrow-leaved Chinese and Persian sorts have been usually, in my experience, the healthiest.

While speaking of the double-flowering fruit trees I failed to call attention to the double-flowering almond, which is a very different plant from the double-flowering peach, though nearly related. It is dwarf with slender-growing stems and erect habit, bearing in early spring wreaths and masses of small white or pinkish flowers. Although an old and well-known shrub, the double-flowering al-

COMMON PURPLE LILAC.
(SYRINGA VULGARIS.)

mond is a gem in its way and has already attained great popularity. Its flowers belong to the time of spring when the Japan quince and *Forsythia* are in their full glory. Only by severe pruning immediately after the bloom can the flowering almond be constrained to bloom freely year after year. In other words, it is a poor plant without pruning, and this remark applies to the *Forsythia* and many other shrubs.

We have thus scanned hastily the charming lineaments of our spring buds and flowers, but in by no means sufficient detail to realize adequately their special attractions, and certainly not enough to secure consideration for all the varieties adapted, at this season, for adorning the lawn. Scattered singly about the place, or massed each kind by itself rather than mixed greatly with other plants, all groups of shrubs should contain on the outskirts some of these spring flowering plants.

In a word, there is nothing more important for the fullest enjoyment of the lawn than the continued presence of flowers throughout all seasons of spring, summer, and autumn, and certainly during no season do we revel in a fuller sense of gladness in the presence of growing nature than during the budding leaves and flowers of spring.

CHAPTER IV.

TREES AND SHRUBS FOR JUNE EFFECTS ON THE LAWN.

DOUBTLESS the poet, in dwelling on the lovely prime of summer days that comes in June, saw through his mind's eye several component parts that made up the charming whole. There is one part, however, that forms so large an element of the fairest scenes of a June day that I shall venture to dwell exclusively on this most interesting feature of their beauty.

Sky and clouds and sunlight and the songs of birds would offer their delights to the eye with half their bounty, if vegetation, *i.e.*, grass and trees and shrubs, were absent. Even the odor of bursting bloom is not only necessary to the fullest effect, but we would feel that an important element had been lost if we should miss the scent of summer flowers. More than at any other season of the year, does the pleasure of odorous bloom characterize the early days of summer, and the number of plants that possess this charm in June we shall find by no means small.

The very ripe and rounded perfection of flower and leaf enthrals the senses in June. Nature seems now to have attained to a deep, profound perfection that, while it communicates rest and peace and absolute satisfaction, does not in any sense enervate. There is nothing slumberous in the air now any more than there was in spring. The senses are alert and keyed to the finest enjoyment of all things in the heavens above and the earth beneath. We look out on this high tide of the year, and with the thought of the Creator when these scenes first were born, declare that it is very good.

And of all this, much, as we have seen, is due to trees and shrubs, to leaves and flowers. The spring is the time of budding beauty, whether of leaf or flower; the autumn, of leaves crimson and green, or brown in final maturity and decay; and summer, late summer, the season of leaves also, but of deep rich green, shadowy leaves.

June, however, and sometimes May even, for the seasons move not entirely by returning months, is the time of *leaves* and *flowers*. It is the best-dowered portion of the year in the way of perfected vegetation. I cannot tell you half of its treasures of tinted flowers and exquisite leaf, and will therefore only attempt to note briefly the attractions of a few of the plants that particularly contribute to the special character of these perfect days.

But what shall I consider first? It is, indeed, a case of positive embarrassment of riches. Perhaps it may be wise to look first at the leaves of certain trees, and then to those of noteworthy shrubs, and so pass to the crowning effort of this gifted time, the flowers of hardy trees and shrubs. I would not be thought disregardful of the supreme charms of hardy herbaceous plants or wild flowers, but trees and shrubs must always form the main body of the effect of lawn planting, and so, in this chapter I propose to restrict myself to the consideration of their peculiar attractions.

The green leaves of June are solid and rich, and produce the main broad effects of foliage in early summer as well as later, but the lawn-planter who fails to employ all the various coloring of leaf that can be secured so easily for the lawn at this season, who neglects to minister in full measure to the universal deep enjoyment of color as displayed in natural associations of June leaves and flowers neglects one half his art.

First and foremost among the hardy plants that minister to our enjoyment of color in June are the maples. Not all the maples are thus highly gifted.

The scarlet maple has borne its flowers and early red leaf-buds, and now looks merely green, and the silver *dasycarpum* has also its usual green color. So likewise the little English field maple, and the sugar, the striped, and the broad-leaved maple *(Acer macrophyllum)*. It is enough, however, that we have the sycamore, Norway, ash-leaved, *Colchicum rubrum (lætum)*, and above all, the several unequalled Japanese maples. The lawn that is ornamented with these trees alone has a rich variety of color even without flowers.

Let us look at these maples. The sycamore *(Acer Pseudo-Platanus)* apparently has its color ready at hand to sport in diverse varieties of silver, gold, and reddish purple. Sycamore maples, in their simplest type, have red veinings and mid-ribs, and especially red leaf stalks. There are several varieties of these variegated and purple-leaved sycamores. The simple purple-leaved is one of the most effective, and is specially peculiar because the strong purple tinge is confined to the under side of the leaf, so that in order to do it justice it should be seen more or less ruffled by the wind. Then there is the silver variegated and golden-tinged varieties, and a fine distinct kind striped and barred with white and red and green. There are other golden varieties variously blotched and suffused with yellow, such as *Leopoldii* or *lutescens*, and a purple-leaved kind more variegated in tint than the one generally termed *purple-leaved*, and which doubtless is the best variety noteworthy for that color.

All these curiously and richly tinted maples are, however, peculiar only for the short time their rich colors continue to be striking. They come almost with June, and generally go with June, for the heat of midsummer dulls them sooner than those of most other trees, although the same heat affects unfavorably the abnormal purple and gold color of nearly all deciduous leaves.

But to realize the effect of rich color in June we must turn to the varieties of Norway maple, *Acer platanoides*, and to *platanoides Schwerdlerii* especially, with its broad red purple leaves. The leaves of the Norway maple, in any case, are massive and noble. They are not, perhaps, larger than those of the sycamore, but they are more numerous, have shorter stems, and are piled together in a more effective manner.

The purple *Acer platanoides Schwerdlerii* glows especially when viewed against strong evening or morning sunlight. At such times, its colors literally flash and sparkle.

June, or late May, again is the season to which this maple confines the display of its charms. Its size resembles that of its parent, the common Norway maple. Usually, however, variegated trees and shrubs are apt to be more dwarf than the parent form. *Acer Lorbergii* is another red-leaved Norway maple of considerable value, but less attractive than *A. Schwerdlerii*.

I must also mention here one of the most interesting of maples, *Acer Colchicum rubrum*, or more properly *Acer lætum*, a true Japanese maple, although sometimes supposed to come from the region of the Caucasus. The great charm of this maple lies in the lovely tints of its young growth in June. Young red leaves and leaf-stalks at this season completely variegate the tree, while at the same time we behold elegant contours and refreshing green tints. Otherwise the tree is of medium size, and, unfortunately, defective in hardness while young in many parts of the United States. *Acer Colchicum rubrum (lætum)* is rare and somewhat difficult to propagate, as well as slightly tender, and therefore deserves a position both prominent and protected.

Maples generally make a most interesting feature in June, whether for their young growths of glowing red or for their refreshing green. I question, indeed, whether the lovely colors of June foliage are not more rich and varied among maples than in any other genus of hardy trees.

But of all maples, the most remarkable, the most gifted in color, are the Japanese maples. Every tint of green, gold, silver, red, and purple meet and commingle on their elegantly and most strangely formed leaves. The many-formed Japanese maple, *Acer polymorphum*, is positively rainbow-dyed with color, but other kinds, like *Acer Japonicum*, with its fine red flowers, and *A. Japonicum aureum* are perhaps more noble with the greater mass and richness of color of their leaves. The subtle beauty of tint and form among these maples all combine to render them (I am tempted to say) the very highest development of complex, delicate beauty among hardy trees and shrubs. And June also is the month wherein we may see the most perfect development of Japanese maples. Later in the season their tints are liable, like those of all variegated-leaved plants, to become dulled by intense heat. Hot summers and cold winters are indeed liable to damage them at times. We regret to acknowledge it, but nevertheless it is an undeniable fact.

JAPANESE MAPLE.

Then there are the leaves of the purple birch, not only noteworthy for their deep purple tints, but also especially effective in combination with the characteristic white bark of the European birch, of which it is a variety. As a single tree this birch is very striking, more so indeed than any other purple-leaved tree, except the purple beech, which in its way stands supreme.

The beeches, indeed, are all *facile princeps* among trees, both for beauty of color and nobility of form. No trees have cleaner-cut and more elegant contours of trunk and adjacent branching, and few more symmetry combined with picturesqueness. As we look at them, the thought at once arises how complete and enduring they look, what a sense of reserve power and noble perfection they convey.

And among them, perhaps among all trees, the purple beech stands pre-eminent for broad masses of rich glowing leaves in June. If we look at the young growth of the purple beech against the evening or morning sun we shall find displayed a peculiarly rich sparkling red, quite indescribable. The finest tints appear on the outer portions of the foliage, where the sun's magical influence can work most effectually. August finds broad, shining masses of more or less purple leaves on this beech when viewed from certain directions, but its prime is past for color, although it still holds high rank for its other excellent qualities.

Another interesting tree for color of foliage is the *Kœlreuteria*. Its ornamental value, though much inferior to that of the purple beech, is considerable on account of the warm, sunny tone and peculiar feathery conformation of the foliage on the outer ends of the branches.

Among shrubs, a fine dark purple- or red-leaved shrub during June is the purple berberry. It is generally richer-colored than most purple-leaved trees and shrubs, but in June the color is particularly fine on the new growth.

Another shrub of as rich color in its way is the dwarf variegated-leaved *Weigelia*. Both have rich, pure golden tints, but the dwarf variegated *Weigelia* is the most useful for lawn-planting, because it forms one of the limited class of shrubs suited for occupying the outskirts of shrub-groups, or some limited space where low, compact-growing plants are specially valuable. It is a thrifty, vigorous shrub, well known, and deservedly popular.

The purple hazel shows very rich colors in June. Its leaves are deep purple, as deep as those of the purple beech, but it is more straggling in habit than the purple beech and otherwise less attractive, although a valuable ornamental shrub. Its main fault is a tendency to winter-kill at the tips, but the effect of this is to dwarf the plant rather than to do it any other harm.

And thus you have briefly, and with scant justice I confess, a rapid survey of the best purple- and variegated-leaved trees and shrubs specially effective in June. It is my desire to gain by means of this consideration a greater and more enthusiastic regard for the rich, subtle tints of the leaves of trees and shrubs, whether used singly or in groups, and certainly nothing can illustrate better these wonderful colors of hardy plants than the phases presented in June by the trees and shrubs just mentioned.

Let us turn now to the flowers of trees and shrubs in June. They make in truth the crown and summit of nature's summer efforts. Full, fresh vigor at this high tide of the year intensifies the loveliness of all vegetation, but flowers are specially lovely now, both for numbers and delightful color and odor. How and where shall I begin? It would seem actually as if all flowers bloomed at this season, and one might easily construct a most attractive lawn of exclusively June flowering plants.

Very numerous and distinguished are the flowering shrubs of June, but the more noteworthy trees perhaps should have our first attention. If the horse-chestnut were as fine in August as June, it is possible we might deem it as valuable an ornamental tree as the Norway maple or purple beech. In addition to finely rounded contours and

HORSE-CHESTNUT TREES, CENTRAL PARK, NEW YORK.

broad light-green foliage, the horse-chestnut has conspicuous flowers in May, which few hardy trees have at any time of the year. And what lovely flowers the horse-chestnut has! There are many varieties distinguished by either peculiar leaves or flowers shaded with various degrees of white and pink, but perhaps the finest of all is the red-flowering horse-chestnut. The odor of the flower is not, in any of the varieties, specially attractive, but the color of the rich red flowers is very beautiful, particularly if the hue of the leaf is light-gold, like several varieties that are by no means rare. Indeed, few more attractive objects can be seen on the lawn than a red-flowering horse-chestnut in full bloom, and its beauty is specially peculiar to the months of May and June.

The catalpa should be mentioned doubtless for its large purple flowers in July. These flowers grow in spikes and are attractive. It is a hardy, large-leaved tree, but straggling and irregular in appearance.

Among summer-flowering trees, however, if not among summer-flowering shrubs, the white fringe *(Chionanthus Virginica)* stands almost pre-eminent, whether we view it as a shrub or tree. The foliage, to begin with, is broad, solid, and lustrous, rich enough to make the fortune of any ordinary plant. Yet in June we forget this attractive foliage as we lose ourselves in admiration of the cloud-like mass of fleecy flowers, which, examined closely, seems veritable lace of the most delicate texture. So numerous are these flowers that I have seen a specimen of white fringe stand out against a background of dark evergreens like a pure white cloud attached to the greensward. The fringe-tree is choice,

RED-FLOWERING HORSE-CHESTNUT.
(ÆSCULUS RUBICUNDA.)

JUNE EFFECTS ON THE LAWN.   63

and by no means common, though a well-known plant. It behaves well during the most trying vicissitudes, whether of winter or of transplanting. It needs little or no pruning, and should occupy the most distinguished positions on the lawn.

The laburnum is a lovely tree of medium size, with June flowers of exceeding beauty, long clusters of yellow blossoms, which often sport remarkably in color, turning sometimes to a deep purple. There are several varieties of both the Scotch and common laburnum, but they resemble each other much, and what differences do exist are somewhat difficult to define in words that would be intelligible to the ordinary reader. The laburnum can hardly ever be a popular tree throughout America, for it suffers from blight in many sections to a degree that is discouraging to the lawn-planter.

WHITE-FLOWERING HORSE-CHESTNUT.
(ÆSCULUS RUBICUNDA.)

Many trees have such beauty of foliage in June as to fairly overshadow the attractions of the flowers. The tulip tree *(Liriodendron Tulipifera)* is a notable instance of this peculiarity. Notwithstanding its flowers are so curiously and finely formed and tinted, we scarcely notice them at first glance buried as they are among the broad, glistening and beautiful leaves. These flowers bear a distinct resemblance to those

CHIONANTHUS VIRGINICA.

of the bulbous tulip, and cannot therefore be other than interesting.

But let us turn again to one of the most important families of flowering plants to be seen upon the lawn. I refer to the magnolias. Few genera show bloom, by means of one or other of their varieties, as long as the magnolias. From mid-April to midsummer we fail not to have beautiful flowers on some one of these plants. In June we have at least eight or ten species and varieties presenting their full glory of inflorescence. Old familiar forms are here, as well as one or two as rare as any plant to be found on the choicest lawn. Nothing should be more familiar among trees than the cucumber tree (*Magnolia acuminata*), but its flowers in June are of moderate size and somewhat insignificant in appearance with their greenish-yellow tints.

A much finer variety than *M. acuminata* is *M. cordata*, an American tree not very unlike the cucumber tree, but far more choice and uncommon. It has a fine pyramidal shape, and a comparatively small heart-shaped leaf, whence the name. *Magnolia cordata* is a strangely disregarded ornamental plant, exhibiting one of those curious instances of the neglect with which we treat our finest native trees.

A better and more widely known June flowering magnolia is *M. glauca*, the common, sweet-scented, white swamp magnolia often sold by boys in our railroad cars. Of all the better-known magnolias, whether American or Asiatic, this has by far the sweetest scent. It is a comparatively low-growing shrub, however, and bears numerous flowers, therein differing greatly from most other summer-blooming magnolias.

There are two or three interesting varieties of *Magnolia glauca*, such as *M. Thompsoniana* and *longifolia*. The first is remarkable for its sweet odor, and the latter for long, ornamental leaves, and also for a harder nature than *M. Thompsoniana*, which is sometimes lacking in this respect. *M. glauca* is generally quite hardy, although I have known winters severe enough to nip its young growth, especially if that young growth was not sufficiently matured during the previous fall.

But of all American deciduous magnolias, the most noteworthy is the great *Magnolia macrophylla* with large leaves two feet in length, and so like in size and general aspect to those of the palm of the tropics, that scarcely any other hardy tree of the North suggests Oriental vigor in the same degree. Amid these huge broad leaves, we find great cup-like flowers, which are curiously monstrous, rather than beautiful. A foot wide the white petals extend, and the cup in the centre would hold nectar for the quaffing of gods rather than fairies, who are usually credited with using flowers for chalices. It is to be regretted that this great striking flower dispenses a distinctly disagreeable odor, otherwise it would be a tree of specially excellent ornamental qualities.

Magnolia tripetala likewise blooms in late May and early June in its home in America. Except *Magnolia macrophylla*, there is no larger-leaved native magnolia than *tripetala*, hence the common name umbrella magnolia. This large foliage lends a grand aspect to a well-grown specimen of *Magnolia tripetala*, and in other ways it proves itself much superior to *M. acuminata*. The flowers are creamy or yellowish-white in color, rather than greenish-white like those of *M. acuminata*.

Turning to the Asiatic magnolias, we find several other varieties that bloom finely in June. There are one or two late-blooming Asiatic varieties, that, long known in this country, have failed to make a favorable impression because, like *M. Kobus*, for instance, they bloom seldom and sparsely and only in late maturity. Two recently introduced magnolias are, however, free from all such objections, and have, besides, very decided advantages peculiar to themselves.

They are termed respectively *M. hypoleuca* and *M. parviflora*, or *Watsonii*, and are rare. We have seen already that few summer-blooming magnolias have flowers that will bear comparison with many other blossoms of June: hence the two magnolias, *hypoleuca* and *parviflora*, become doubly valuable on account of the late season at which their flowers appear.

Let us look at them a moment. They impress us as noble trees, not as shrubs, bearing in this way a certain resemblance to *M. tripetala*. The foliage of *M. hypoleuca* is more like that of *tripetala* than perhaps any other magnolia, although it has also a fine distinct character of its own. Of a bright silver on the under side of the leaf, whence the name *hypoleuca*, the beauty of the foliage is made still more attractive by a distinct flush of red pervading the leaf stem, mid-rib, and even the more complex veining of the leaf. Held up against the light the appearance of this leaf is fine, but the flower, nevertheless, forms the chief attraction of this as well as of all other magnolias. It blooms in June, is large and milk-white, and above all is very sweet-scented, qualities that would render valuable any flower, but joined to the other characteristic traits of the magnolia they become doubly precious.

When the *M. hypoleuca* was first seen in this country, it was believed that the highest development in the way of a June-flowering magnolia had been obtained, but this proved not to be the case. *Magnolia parviflora* has shown itself, even during the short time it has been introduced, the gem of the entire collection of magnolias; finer, perhaps, in the sense of combining the greatest number of excellent qualities, and certainly much the best for the exquisite character of its odor.

In a greenhouse one hundred feet long, the scent of the flowers borne on a young plant of this magnolia is delightfully apparent throughout the entire length of the building. *Magnolia hypoleuca* has certainly a delightful odor, but this odor of *M. parviflora* is more pungent, more delicious and subtle. The petals and their arrangement suggest those of *M. glauca*, but they, as well as the leaves and entire plant, are much larger, and the centre of the flower acquires far greater beauty from a deep-crimson flush that suffuses the very curious and formal arrangement of pistils and stamens. This arrangement and color give the flower the appearance of having a deep-red heart. The foliage and general habit of *M. parviflora* is neat and thrifty.

The purple fringe, *Rhus cotinus*, although somewhat inferior to the white fringe in general characteristics, and to which, indeed, it bears no relation except in name, is exquisitely subtle and lovely in the coloring of its flowers. These flowers come in June and envelop the entire bush or tree in rosy-purple, rounded masses of soft, fleecy clouds. It is well-named the smoke tree, for I know nothing to which the disposition and coloring of its small, numerous flowers can be more aptly compared than a mass of smoke suffused and penetrated with sunlight.

On first turning to the consideration of summer-flowering plants, we are at once attracted to the most splendidly gifted of the entire class, viz. : Rhododendrons and hardy azaleas. They seem intended to be grouped together and are usually employed in that way. The azalea is, in every way, smaller than the rhododendron, and when planted on the outskirts of a group of the latter, shade off harmoniously the outline of a mass of the former.

RHODODENDRON.

The flowers also of these two shrubs serve to perfect each other when associated together. One, the rhododendron, is splendid, glowing and complex in detail; the other, choice, exquisite, simpler in form, and yet most subtly and richly tinted. It is difficult to decide on the comparative excellence of their beauties, because these beauties are so individual and different. For the rhododendron, we can say it has more effective, shining evergreen foliage, but on the other hand, the hardy azalea endures more steadfastly winter and summer vicissitudes.

PINXTER FLOWER.
(AZALEA NUDIFLORA.)

Such plants as these should be employed in favored nooks, on a hillside, if possible, where the eye may look down upon their charms. The employment of both of these attractive plants is rapidly becoming an actual necessity to the well-ordered lawn.

Nor does the fact that the rhododendron occasionally suffers from sudden changes, both in summer and winter, seriously check its growing popularity. Many, in fact, are

BROAD LEAVED LAUREL.
(KALMIA LATIFOLIA.)

already learning that a little protection by planting in the lee of other trees, and a practical consideration of the pedigree of the variety used, considered with regard to the more or less hardy nature of its ancestors, will secure general results of the most satisfactory character. *Azalea nudiflora* is a good example of this genuine American plant of the azalea type.

In this connection, however, I must not fail to offer meet tribute to the excellent beauty of the common laurel of the American woods, *Kalmia latifolia*. While its flowers, perhaps, are not as splendid in form and mass as those of the rhododendron, nor as varied and subtle in coloring as those of the hardy azalea, the curious, quaint construction of its flower-cup is yet quite as distinguished in its way for its exquisite daintiness and charming symmetry. It surpasses the rhododendron, moreover, in hardiness, and possesses the attraction of comparatively large evergreen leaves, which the deciduous hardy azalea does not possess. When grown in the nursery, *i. e.*, transplanted now and then, the *Kalmia latifolia* may be readily moved at any age, but to tear old plants from their native haunts in woodland nooks and plant them successfully on the lawn, has been repeatedly proved to be a difficult operation.

As we give our attention more closely to deciduous shrubs, we are impressed by the number of specially noteworthy genera that distinguish themselves in June either by their foliage or their flowers. What a lovely group, for instance, are the various June-blooming spireas.

There were, as we remember, fine spring-flowering spireas like *S. Thunbergii*, but how lovely, also, are June-flowering *S. Reevesiana, fl. pl.* and *S. trilobata*, a similar but still more attractive species. The branches of these spireas hang during June in the most graceful curves studded to their very tips with lovely rosettes of pure white flowers.

Then there is *S. prunifolia* with upright habit, neat, bright green leaves and numerous white flowers coming in late May oftener than in June. Red-flowering *S. Fortunei* and *Fortunei macrophylla* and *lævigata* are also June-flowering, while among other kinds blooming in the same month may be noted the choice and delicate little spireas *bella* and *ariæfolia* and the more common-looking and larger-growing *chamædrifolia, nepalensis,* and *ulmifolia*.

One of the most striking of all spireas on the lawn, however, is the June-flowering *S. opulifolia aurea*. The leaves of *S. opulifolia aurea* are broader and larger than those of any other spirea, which is generally a small-leaved race, and the colors, especially at this season, are delicate shades of gold. Indeed so effective is this golden color that had the white flowers studding the entire stem been less lovely I would have classed it among the golden- and purple-leaved plants. If we add to these qualities exceptional vigor and hardiness, it will be readily seen that *S. opulifolia aurea* is a shrub peculiarly adapted to lawn planting. Indeed the general habit and the flowers render the common type *opulifolia* almost as fine as the golden variety.

But I must not linger on these interesting spireas too long, while there are other interesting June-flowering shrubs waiting to claim our attention. Every well-planted lawn must have some Philadelphuses or mock oranges, with

June flowers like veritable orange blossoms. *Philadelphus coronarius* is the most sweet-scented and in other ways the best variety, although *grandiflorus, laxus, speciosus*, etc., are larger and more easily propagated. There is a fine dwarf golden Philadelphus that does not receive the attention it should.

A well-known June-flowering genus of shrub is the *Deutzia*, not *Deutzia gracilis* only, but *Deutzia crenata, fl. pl.*, a Japan plant, strong-growing, and bearing masses of attractive pinkish-white flowers, and also the smaller *D. scabra, fl. pl.* There are also *Deutzias Fortunei, crenata* and *scabra*, both interesting, hardy, rapid-growing shrubs. The vigorous bright-green bush honeysuckles are also attractive in June, with the red and white flowers of *Tartarica*, the white of excellent drooping *fragrantissima*, and the yellow and yellowish-red of *xylosteum, flexuosa*, and *Ledebourii*.

GORDON'S MOCK ORANGE.
(PHILADELPHUS GORDONIANUS.)

DEUTZIA CRENATA, FL. PL.

The sweet-scented shrubs *Calycanthus floridus* and *C. lævigatus* likewise offer the spicy fragrance of their

JUNE EFFECTS ON THE LAWN. 73

chocolate-brown buds and broad rich foliage. These are choice shrubs and can scarcely be used too much in the salient points of shrub groups.

Exochorda grandiflora should have been mentioned perhaps among the spireas, where it properly belongs, but it is so different in every way, so specially suited to distinct single positions, that I have ventured to consider it apart from the other varieties. Few shrubs are more difficult to propagate than this spirea, hence its reputation for rarity and choiceness. But aside from these qualities the leaves and flowers of this plant are very attractive, the leaves for their light green, slightly bluish tint, and the flowers for their number and pure white color, wonderfully bright and effective in mass. The general habit of the plant is broad, bushy, and vigorous. In this climate the

EXOCHORDA GRANDIFLORA.

SWEET-SCENTED SHRUB
(CALYCANTHUS FLORIDUS.)

YELLOW JAPANESE-KERRIA.
(KERRIA JAPONICA.)

flowers appear in late May and early June. The pretty, small-leaved *Kerria Japonica* also bears attractive yellow flowers in June and makes an interesting shrub on the outskirts of shrub plantations.

Among the large shrubs specially suited to the centre of a mass of deciduous foliage are the *Weigelias* or *Diervillas*. They are rapid-growing, bearing abundant leaves and flowers, and are generally popular. They form one of our staple plants for the construction of any group of shrubs. Some of the *Weigelias* bear light-red and others striped flowers. *Weigelia rosea* is justly considered one of the best kinds.

Among the most attractive of June-flowering shrubs is *Tamarix Africana*. There are one or two other kinds that bloom during this month, but none better than *T. Africana*. The characteristic feathery habit and great vigor of the tamarisks renders *Africana* specially valuable in a group of shrubs where variety of form and beauty of flower are desired. There are several late-blooming tamarisks, such as *Gallica* and *Indica*, which makes this June-flowering *Africana* particularly valuable. Pruning is absolutely essential to keep the lanky growth of tamarisks in subjection.

RED FLOWERING WEIGELIA.
(WEIGELIA ROSEA.)

We come now to a very noteworthy genus among June-flowering shrubs. The snowball or viburnum genus is a large one, but only half a dozen hardy varieties are thoroughly well suited to lawn planting. The common snowball *(Viburnum opulus)* is, perhaps, one of the most generally useful on the lawn, because it is fine, singly or in mass. It grows vigorously, and is broad, and bears numerous balls of snow-white blossoms. The only serious fault it has is an openness of foliage or nakedness of stem that makes it less effective when planted singly than it would otherwise be.

As a June-flowering viburnum, however, there is nothing like the Japan snowball (*Viburnum plicatum*), already spoken of in the highest terms elsewhere. Dark green and glossy leaves, crinkled and compact, especially if well pruned, and large white balls of flowers, persistently retained on the plant for weeks, are, as we have also seen, its distinguishing characteristics. Good judges have commended this plant as in many senses the best of deciduous shrubs.

VIBURNUM OPULUS.

Another June-flowering shrub of considerable merit should not be neglected. *Lycium barbarum*, etc., is an old plant, but very pretty, especially when trailing over rockwork. The flowers are small and of a purple or violet color. Many of these fine old hardy plants are in danger of being forgotten in the rush for new and rare varieties.

A special glory of June, a glory entirely unequalled in its way at any other time of the year, is found in the several genera of hardy climbing vines. Many of them are, of course, familiar to the reader, and probably none more so than the honeysuckles. They make a numerous family of varieties, with thick, glossy green leaves and abundant sweet-scented flowers. The Belgian, or striped monthly, red and white, is perhaps at once best known and most generally popular. *Canadensis* is pink and straw color, with the straw color predominating. One of the best yellow ones, indeed one of the best of all honeysuckles, is *Halleana* from Japan. This variety is evergreen to a very considerable degree, which much increases its value. Then in June there are lovely clematises, that love to climb over stumps or on a screen or

FOUR GOOD CLEMATISES.

trellis of wood. The prevailing colors of the June-blooming types are purple and white, and these colors are of the purest, richest tint. Open-petalled, large, sometimes ten inches in diameter, star-shaped, these flowers gather in close masses among small, inconspicuous leaves. The best perhaps is *Jackmanii*, for free blooming and general hardiness, but there are excellent varieties among the lighter-colored *lanuginosa* and *patens* type. All these June clematises should be pruned after they have finished flowering, so as to secure a vigorous growth and bloom for the following year.

The curious and rare Japan climbing hydrangea also is a June-flowering vine. It has dark-green, long-stalked, cordate leaves, sharply toothed, and white hydrangea-like flowers in loose clusters. Like ivy, it throws out multitudes of rootlets, and clings well to stonework.

During some seasons the Wistaria is a June-flowering vine, but whether it blooms in May or June, its grape-like clusters of purple flowers, piled among picturesque and tossing masses of light-green leaves and tendrils, are always beautiful. There is a beautiful white variety that is particularly effective. The two colors may be finely contrasted by setting out the two kinds near each other and letting

WISTARIA SINENSIS.

their growths mingle. The illustration on the opposite page shows an arbor in Central Park covered with Wistaria that always exhibits the flowers with excellent effect.

Nor should we pass unnoticed on this occasion the summer charms of the two best climbing roses, Baltimore Belle and Queen of the Prairies. There are other excellent varieties of climbing roses, but they do not surpass, and hardly supplement, the excellent qualities of these two well-known kinds.

Pages might be profitably devoted to the consideration of the June-flowering qualities of hardy roses generally, of the Gen. Jacqueminots, Baronne Prevosts, Mad. Plantiers, and a thousand others, but in the brief way in which we are studying June lawns, we can afford to simply touch on the employment of roses as a class. To their magnificent tints and forms no pen can do adequate justice, and their excellence has moreover become a household word. We may profitably, however, devote a few lines to some brief suggestions for the development of the most abundant and best rose blooms, and for the disposition of rose bushes on the lawn.

In the first place, to get the best roses, the soil where the plant is grown should be a rich sandy loam and not clay, and then the old growth of last year should always be cut back almost to the ground, or, if the plant is already old, almost to the main stem. Rose bugs and blight are apt to make rose bushes, unless carefully tended, somewhat unsightly objects on the lawn in spite of their grand flowers. Of course this need not be so, but we should recognize the danger squarely, and if we cannot be sure of

WISTARIA ARBOR, CENTRAL PARK, NEW YORK.

giving our roses the right amount and kind of attention, at least we should plant them in retired nooks in the sheltering skirts of other plantations.

The *Rosa rugosa* from Japan, however, is an exception to this rule, as its leaves are entirely healthy and hardy in all exposures. The leaves are dark-green, crinkled, and attractive, the flowers single, which is for me an advantage, and the fruit large and showy. It is, in a word, one of the most ornamental shrubs for the lawn.

Up to this point we have been considering hardy deciduous plants, properly so-called, and perhaps as regards their forming any distinctive feature of June we would be hardly justified in mentioning evergreens at all, if it were not for the exquisite young growth of some particular varieties.

Let us then note a few leading varieties of evergreens that exhibit this peculiarity. All hemlocks are lovely in their soft, young growth, and delicate tendrils of June, but there is a variegated form that is touched all over at this season with lighter shades on the young growth in a very attractive manner. This variegation differs in perfection a good deal from year to year. The young growth of most spruces is also fine, and specially noteworthy on the dwarfer forms, such as Gregory's dwarf *(Picea excelsa Gregoriana)*. An extremely dwarf American black spruce has likewise pleasing tints on its young growth, but its form is so striking, that this beauty of the young growth is overlooked in contemplating the compact masses of this most eccentric of evergreens. There is a variety of the American white spruce *(Picea alba)* called Glory of the Spruces, which has a warm golden tint in the midst of its young green.

JUNE EFFECTS ON THE LAWN. 81

Perhaps, however, the most extraordinary spruce in June is the tiger-tail spruce (*Picea polita*) from Japan. And its name seems not inaptly given as we note the

JAPAN RAMANAS ROSE.
(ROSA RUGOSA RUBRA.)

enlarged bright golden tips of the branches bursting forth from the enveloping leaf bud. The general appearance of this evergreen is sturdy, stiff, and intensely individual as well as dwarf and enduring. In color it is generally light greenish-yellow, but the color becomes deepened at the tips, and is changed still more by contrast with the reddish-brown envelopes or scales of the leaf-buds dropping off now from one branch and now from another at this season.

In June we do not look among the arbor vitæs, whether Asiatic or American, nor among the so-called cypresses of Japan *(Retinosporas)* for any loveliness of tint peculiar to that season. The junipers, silver firs, and several of the pines on the other hand are peculiarly and supremely beautiful at this season. To begin with, few evergreens can show more beauty than is found on the young growth of our common Canadian juniper *(Juniperus Canadensis)*. Its low, solid masses are thoroughly penetrated by light soft shades, and where the plant chances to stand among a lot of distinct evergreens the effect is still more striking. Of a similar light tint is *Juniperus oblonga pendula*, the true weeping juniper, and a native of Armenia. It is not altogether hardy.

Then what can be finer than the lovely light green shades of the Irish and Swedish junipers. Such picturesque forms and lovely colors would be invaluable for lawn planting if they were only possessed of hardiness and adaptability to light dry soil. The bluest of evergreens, *Juniperus Virginiana glauca* and *Juniperus venusta*, have also specially lovely June tints.

Not many of the pines are particularly remarkable in June. Perhaps *Pinus excelsa*, the Bhotan pine, is most noteworthy at that season, although the dwarf Scotch is decidedly attractive in its early coat of fresh green. *Pinus monspeliensis* is also fine in June. as well as *Mugho* and the dwarf white pine.

But the finest of all evergreens, I am tempted to say, certainly the finest of all evergreens in June, are some of the silver firs. Nearly all of them are remarkable, but chief among them stand Nordmann's fir, the Grecian (*Abies Cilicica*), and the noble silver fir (*A. nobilis*).

Nordmann's is at all seasons unsurpassed for grandeur, and now the light, fresh young foliage checkers the tree all over in the most delightful manner imaginable.

The Grecian silver fir starts earlier, and is most remarkable of all for an early coating of the lovely young growth peculiar to the silver firs.

Abies Pichta, the Siberian silver fir has also voluminous young growth, and it is remarkable among all evergreens for a soft, silky texture which is delightful to the touch.

NOBLE SILVER FIR.
(ABIES NOBILIS.)

Many think *Abies nobilis* the finest of evergreens, and for exquisite richness of blue coloring and picturesque masses it is, indeed, almost unrivalled. Otherwise it lacks the grandeur of outline and great hardiness of the Nordmann's silver fir. It is not unimportant to note here that *Abies nobilis* displays much variety of coloring and conformation on individual specimens, hence it follows that careful selection of the best varieties and their strict perpetuation by grafting become important to the lawn planter.

The Cephalonian fir, *Abies Cephalonica*, is another attractive evergreen in June, although now and then it suffers from hard winters.

Abies Parsoniana or *lasiocarpa* is one of the rarest and finest species of the genus, and its long, curled, light-colored leaves assume the richest hues in early summer.

Abies concolor is another excellent and similar evergreen.

It is an important fact to remember that systematic pruning of both the leader or topmost twig and of the side branches of these silver firs tends greatly to develop the beautiful June growth on every part of the tree. It is not well, however, to continue this pinching too long or too frequently, for the tree may thus come to lose the essential characteristic form of the species or variety.

Very attractive also are the early tints of the dark and extremely attractive dwarf Hudson's Bay fir, as well as those of the neat and elegant *Abies pectinata compacta*. These last-named forms may be classed among the hardiest of evergreens. Turning to several evergreens which are almost unknown on the lawn and that are at the same time attractive in June, we find the hardy form of *Abies Douglasii* or *pseudotsuga Douglasii*. The particular variety of the Douglas spruce generally employed has been found somewhat tender in the Eastern or Atlantic States, apparently because most specimens have been brought from the lower portions of the coast ranges of California. The Colorado form, however, proves perfectly hardy and is not only attractive to the eye in June, but is deliciously resinous in odor. There is a *pseudotsuga Sieboldii*, from Japan, which is also beautiful in June. The blue spruce of the Rocky Mountains *(Picea pungens)* is perhaps the richest and bluest of evergreens at this season, and has also the high merit of being hardy and vigorous.

But after extolling the beauties of all these evergreens in June, we must turn for the finest evergreen effect in summer to the golden yew. Later its colors are more or less dulled, in comparison, and sometimes it is even browned in winter, though scarcely ever actually killed, but now, in June, its deep, rich gold is fairly luminous in its glow of young life. The golden yew bears patiently any amount of pruning, and may be and is continually distorted by pruning into the most artificial forms. There is a silver-tinted variety of the same English yew *(Taxus baccata)* of which the golden is also a variety, but it is hardly as distinct and striking. It is called *T. b. elegantissima;* why, I cannot say, unless silver may be termed more elegant than gold. It is difficult to do justice to either of these last-named evergreens as they appear in late May or early June. The variety and freshness of tint as contrasted in broadly pervading masses with the darker shades of the mature growth really defy description, while they make decidedly one of the most charming features of the lawn in early summer. The Irish yew is not always hardy, but it is striking and distinct.

In looking over this brief review of the most prominent

and characteristic beauties of the lawn in June, I am impressed with the insufficient justice done their loveliness, but I am also consoled at my evident failure by the consciousness that no ordinary pen will suffice to convey an adequate idea of their subtle charm.

For instance, of the fresh, early summer growths of many trees we can say little more than they are dark green; but how poorly such terms express their delicate gradations of color, soft, glistening, and wonderful. Look at that weeping beech! What words can describe the soft, tender, gleaming color of its young foliage. And so it is with a hundred other trees, the charms of which at this season meet us at every turn on many lawns.

With the knowledge of such lawn-planting riches easily attainable by almost every one, is it strange that some countries deem no time and labor too great to secure that utmost vigor of early growth which can alone produce the highest perfection of June flowers and foliage? Is it not more strange that we in America, with our favorable soil and climate and enterprise and regard for all lovely things, do not seek more to employ the lawn-planting beauties at our command? Perhaps we have been hitherto occupied too much with the engrossing duties of a young nation to look to the permanent adornment of home.

Our increased intercourse with Europe however has been teaching us much of late, and we are learning not only that we should do more artistic lawn planting, but that we cannot conform ourselves servilely to European horticultural standards. After much failure in trying to get something else, we are attaining to the conviction that we must have genuine American lawns adorned with only such plants as suit the special conditions of the country and locality.

We are learning that because an English or Scotch gardener tells us we should have a particular tree which he has grown successfully in England, we are not necessarily to assume that horticultural skill, whether Scotch, or English, or French, must be able to compass, in some occult way, its successful employment on American lawns.

Just as we are developing with active enthusiasm home art in our interior, so we are gaining an increasing realization of the importance of studying personally the needs and capacities of our lawns. During the next few years we may be sure that lawn planting as an art is likely to develop into a most important feature of the home-life of the humblest citizen who owns a spot of ground.

Therefore to those who would keep abreast of the time in such matters, I would say, give every possible chance to the June effects of trees and shrubs on the lawn. These occur on the white days of the year, and all intelligent care in the selection and culture of such plants will be now more than ever repaid in the pleasure thus afforded both our friends and ourselves.

CHAPTER V.

THE FLOWERS AND FOLIAGE OF SUMMER.

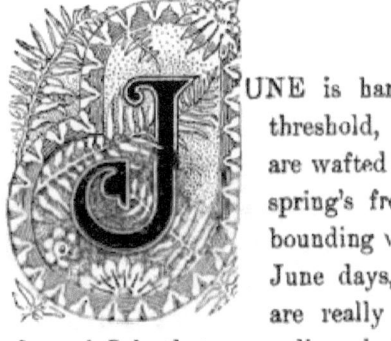

JUNE is hardly summer. It is the threshold, as it were, over which are wafted the odors of spring. All spring's freshness and richness of bounding vitality characterize many June days, and it is not until we are really launched into the full glow of July that we realize what we may fairly consider the genuine climate of summer.

We have doubtless many veritable summer days in June, and so we have in May, for that matter, but even in June there are decided suggestions of spring still lingering in the air.

It becomes therefore very important to the lawn-planter to be able to prolong as much as possible the loveliness of May and June. In America, especially, he has an additional incentive in the fact that July and August are spent largely in the open air by a people who, as a rule, do not spend as much time out-of-doors as most other nations.

A reason for this is not far to find in our changeable climate, but should we not, in a large degree, attribute this neglect of open-air enjoyments to a lack of genuine appreciation of the sweet influences of nature? We are apt to talk much of the beauties of nature after taking homœopathic doses of Ruskin and visiting the White Mountains. As a nation, however, I fear, we are not lovers of the open air, except for purposes of business or of pleasure that hardly involve much direct relation with nature.

Since, however, we are forced to dwell more or less in the open air in July and August, constrained by fashion and the heat of the weather, it is all the more reasonable to make the exterior of the house attractive, and to take the opportunity of making this fashion a means of gradually developing a more widespread love of nature.

Of the three main features of the lawn—flowers, foliage, and grass,—the first, though important, are least so, simply because we can have so few flowers in midsummer. Foliage is, with its shade-giving quality, perhaps the most important, although for those who have realized to what excellence lawn grass can be developed, turf becomes scarcely less valuable.

Maintenance of lawns is not well understood in this country, as a rule, and although it must be acknowledged that the stress of our summer suns is at times terrible, I believe wonders could be accomplished, indeed I may say are accomplished in isolated cases, by skill and untiring labor. When we learn to give as solicitous attention to perfecting our green sward as we expend on the coats of our high-priced horses, we shall begin to realize what kind of a lawn may be made in America in spite of difficulties of climate.

If then shade is most important to make the lawn attractive and lovely in summer, it naturally behooves us to study our summer shade trees. As we undertake this task we find with regret that we must give up the enjoyment of some of our grandest shade trees as having already reached and passed their prime. Horse-chestnuts that formed one of the chief beauties of the foliage of late spring and early summer have probably fallen into the "sere leaf" and become dull and rusty in many places by the end of July. Elms are majestic at all seasons, but their leaves often fade by midsummer. Lindens, except the *sulphurea* and *dasystyla*, and possibly the silver-leaved, are now fading also. Ashes are fresh, and several willows and poplars, but many trees have assumed a mature and even languid appearance, that suggests at once the permanent presence of a more sober stage of existence and a feeling that the tree is resting.

There is scarcely yet much positive decay. Light and life have for them settled down to a consciousness of completed development which, if, on the whole, a satisfactory state of things for the present, suggests quite distinctly the approaching end.

The best shade tree at this season, if not at all seasons of the year, is the beech. This fact was recognized by the ancients, and is still apparent to most tree lovers of the present day. It is true, the beech grows slowly, but did ever any enduring, really fine tree grow otherwise than slowly. The elm and other grand trees may be undoubtedly instanced as capable of the most rapid growth, but they are, it will be found, not positively fine in detail like the beeches.

The broad shining glossiness of the beech leaf sheds a lustrous light and shade of the most grateful character. There is plenty of shadow, but no disagreeable closeness and weight of shade. The pleasant features of this shade pertain to all beeches of whatever species or variety. Their outline and coloring is alike fine in August as throughout the season, and if the purple beech shows a greener tinge on its foliage at midsummer, it still retains its early charm of elegant contour, delightful lustre, and simple grace of leafage.

So well known are the pleasant summer qualities of the purple and weeping beeches, and, for that matter, of the simple, original type of both the American and European species, that the very sound of their names brings back one of the most agreeable and permanent pleasures of deep midsummer—that of lying beneath their boughs *recubans sub tegmine fagi*.

For this purpose, the importance of fostering the most perfect development of the lower branches is at once evident. To do this, it is not only necessary to preserve these lower branches from mutilation by carelessness or unskilful and excessive pruning, but the growth of the tree must be also restrained during youth, where an excessive vigor may tend to diminish the luxuriousness of the foliage near the ground. This applies more especially to the weeping beech, but the suggestion has definite and considerable value in the management of most kinds of trees.

All maples are fine during summer. As a shade tree especially adapted to midsummer, the best of the genus is undoubtedly the Norway maple. Its leaves are broad and shadowy, with a texture and peculiar habit of lying close to the branches that is productive of the most agreeable shade. Broad and massive in general contour and of a rich green color, the Norway maple must necessarily be an agreeable feature of the summer lawn.

For another kind of shade than that of the Norway maple, we turn to the Oriental plane-tree, a near relative of our American button-wood, only a better tree. In this instance we find plenty of shade, under large spreading foliage, but a shade that is far less agreeable than that of the beech or maple. Try the shade of the black walnut and compare it with that of the American chestnut. Something in the texture and set of the leaves makes the difference. Pliny speaks at some length of this difference between shade trees. The shade of the ailantus is not specially agreeable, although its fine large light-green foliage has a delightful Oriental effect on the summer lawn. Practically the ailantus is thrust into Coventry on account of the disagreeable odor of its flowers for a week or two in June.

The American chestnut is a noble tree on the summer lawn. The foliage is shining and elegant in outline, and dispenses a pleasant shade. It grows well, and is nearly always thrifty and vigorous. The flowers, too, that whiten the surface of a great chestnut in summer, add greatly to its attraction.

One of the largest and most conspicuous trees on the lawn is the catalpa. Broad and massive-looking, especially

AMERICAN BEECHER.
(FAGUS FERRUGINEA.)

if pruned properly, it is quite unique in its way. Its shade, however, is not as agreeable as that of the beech or maple. There is a golden catalpa that bears great golden leaves in June, and on its second growth of August and September. These leaves are conspicuous and specially effective at a considerable distance.

The ashes are many of them quite interesting in summer, particularly those that are variegated on their second growth of young leaves. Such a one is the European ash *(Fraxinus concavæfolia)*, so called on account of the peculiar formation of its leaves. The second growth of this variety, as well as the growth of June, has the appearance of a loose bouquet of flowers at a distance, white, red, and green, arranged in an irregular clustered shape.

The white fringe *(Chionanthus Virginica)*, a relative of the ash, has also a fine shining foliage, which makes it a charming plant even after its lace-like masses of flowers in June are gone.

One of the finest summer shade and ornamental trees is the Kentucky coffee-tree. The leaves are acacia-like, light-green, and graceful, but their chief charm lies in the fact that they are set on edge, as it were, so that the sunlight slides or sifts through in a very peculiar fashion. This makes the shade, however, of a most agreeable character, and lends the tree a special charm for the summer-time. A rough, dark bark also gives the Kentucky coffee-tree a still more striking character, from the contrast it makes with the light and elegant foliage.

Of light-green, sunny foliage also is the *Kœlreuteria*—a summer tree in every sense! To a round-headed fine contour is added a light-green color, and a soft green velvety texture suggested rather than felt. In June, its yellow flowers are beautiful, but its foliage alone should obtain for it much employment as a summer tree.

There is again the liquid ambar or sweet gum. We all know this tree, and prize it much for its rich red color in fall. Scarcely less lovely, however, are the summer qualities of its light-green star-shaped leaves and generally unique effect. Indeed, we can hardly employ it distinctively as a summer tree, because of its great ornamental value at all seasons.

Nor would I like to forget in this connection another forest tree, of most excellent and shining qualities in the summer-time, as well as in the earlier days of spring. The tulip-tree is noble at most times, but never more so than when it rears its lofty shining foliage above the surrounding summer greenery. If the tulip-tree were more easily transplanted it would be more widely planted, for it is in every way an excellent shade and ornamental tree. The remedy for this defect or difficulty in transplanting is obtained by setting out in spring young trees four to six feet high. I must not forget before leaving the tulip to speak of the magnificent erect bole its trunk presents. Only corrugated in the bark enough to give it a look of strength, the smooth tall shaft springs up to a great height and makes at all times one of the most attractive features of the tree.

Magnolias generally on account of their flowers belong more particularly to spring, but midsummer should claim at least one species, the American *M. macrophylla*. It is the most tropical-looking tree of the lawn, the great massive leaves assuming the gigantic proportions of three feet long and a foot broad. These leaves are, moreover, rich and shining in color and striking throughout the summer. A conspicuous position and abundant room at some distance from the house should be accorded this magnolia for the attainment of its fullest effect. Its shade is delightful, and as a summer tree its rank is in every way high.

But let us turn to a group of summer trees that rank on the lawn only second to the beeches. There are so many fine varieties in the richly endowed genus of oaks that I am in doubt which to select for special notice. They are all fine summer trees, and the American varieties perhaps most of all. When we lament our inability to grow the perfect evergreens seen everywhere in England, we have only to turn to our grand native oaks and feel compensated by our richness in that deciduous genus alone.

Among American oaks there is the chestnut oak, combining the fine outline of leaf of the chestnut and all the grandeur and shining qualities of the true oak type. For an oak it grows with much vigor and symmetry. Then there is the white oak, also of noble proportions, as well as the red oak. The scarlet oak is somewhat smaller. Among American oaks there is no finer at any time, and especially in summer, than the pin oak *(Quercus palustris)*. Its drooping, yet vigorous and shining foliage make one of the most striking features of any summer landscape. A fine species for this season of the year is the willow oak *(Quercus phellos)*, with light gray, curious, narrow leaves. Originally growing in a more southern climate than our Middle and Eastern States, it yet seems perfectly hardy throughout the North. It is round-headed and small-sized for an oak and is in every way an interesting and valuable ornamental tree. The English oak (*Quercus robur*), and its well-marked variety, *pedunculata*, are noble-looking trees, although they do not succeed as invariably in America as our American species. This oak is fine for both appearance and shade in summer, particularly in one or two of its varieties. The most remarkable is the golden oak (*Quercus robur pedunculata Concordia*). In June, this oak is greenish-gold, but later takes on its full deep golden tint, which it retains until frost. Such bright lively tints are very refreshing and charming during the heat and dull hues of August. No summer lawn should be considered complete without a golden oak planted in some conspicuous position where the yellowish tint will contrast properly with the green of other foliage. This variety grows fairly for an oak, and the foliage, when the tree has been well pruned, lies in thick rich masses of the most attractive character. Indeed, what tree will not judicious pruning improve?

Of the Japan oaks there are few grander and more effective in summer than the royal oak of Japan (*Quercus Daimio*). No oak known on the lawn has larger leaves. For summer ornament it is therefore very effective. The pyramidal oak, a European variety, is also fine in summer with its great vigor and bold outline. Another variety of the English oak, viz., the weeping form, has fine foliage and a remarkable habit to render it conspicuous in summer on the lawn. My space would not of course permit the description of all oaks valuable on the summer lawn; for, indeed, all are fine at that season and the number of the varieties is legion. I have mentioned, however, some of the most remarkable.

The poplars and willows generally seem to belong to an earlier season than midsummer, but there are one or two varieties I must mention in this connection. Many poplars are objectionable on account of an evil habit of suckering and a somewhat coarse appearance, valuable as they are in many situations. But the balsam poplar is in every way a fine ornamental tree. It is clean and healthy and free from suckers, and has a grand outline and size of leaf. The color of the foliage is rich and shining, and well fitting to the summer lawn. Yellowish drab or brown and finely marked, the branches and trunks are likewise attractive.

Resembling the balsam poplar, in its fitness for the summer lawn, there is the *Salix laurifolia* or *pentandra*, the laurel-leaved willow. This plant has been employed with little reference to summer, but few trees have finer foliage in summer, and it continues bright and shining until late in fall. It is strong-growing, however, more a tree than a bush, and inclined to lose its lower branches, and therefore should be planted in the screening masses of other shrubs.

Of a dwarfer habit is the gray, curving, narrow-leaved rosemary willow, the cool, soft tints of which are well fitted to please the eye during the glaring days of August. It suits the outskirts of shrub groups from its compact, round and weeping habit. All the willows, in fact, are pleasant to the eye in summer, and free from the worn-out look peculiar to many trees at this season.

There are two summer trees or shrubs (for they partake of the characteristics of both shrub and tree) which we must not overlook, so beautiful are they, and unique in their own peculiar way. One is *Stuartia pentagynia* and the other *Oxydendrum arboreum*, or *Andromeda arborea*, the sorrel-tree. The first, bearing throughout the season foliage invariably bright and beautiful, is particularly attractive at midsummer for creamy-white, orange-like clusters of flowers. The *Andromeda arborea*, noticed in detail in another place, has during the scarcity of flowers at midsummer the supreme attraction of white, swaying tassels of sweet-scented bloom.

The little *Hypericum*, studded with quantities of bright yellow flowers, is not to be despised at this season, and the delicate, feathery foliage and beaded pink flowers of the hardy *Tamarisk Indica* are in full perfection at about the same time. The rich, effective hues of the *Althea* flowers also pertain properly to summer, although they last into September.

But the now celebrated *Hydrangea paniculata grandiflora*, with its great trusses of white and pink flowers, hardly belongs to summer properly, for its richest and most varied tints of crimson only appear just before the first approach of frost.

Let us not forget either in assembling our summer lawn beauties to employ the old and neglected *Lycium barbarum*, or box thorn, with its curving masses of small, half-climbing foliage, studded in August with little effec-

DOUBLE FLOWERING ALTHEA.
(HIBISCUS SYRIACUS, FL. PL.)

tive purple flowers. It is also valuable because it will thrive in any soil or exposure.

The dogwoods have perhaps no distinctive summer quality, but they are so fine both in wood and leafage throughout the year that I should invariably include them among an assemblage of summer lawn plants.

One of the most effective of our large shrubs in summer is the *Colutea*, or bladder senna, in its several varieties. An acacia-like foliage and great compactness and vigor give it special value for combination in shrub groups, but its yellow or yellowish-red pea-blossom-like flowers in June and July, followed by reddish pods or bladders, are also valuable features for the summer lawn.

SWEET PEPPER-BUSH.
(CLETHRA ALNIFOLIA.)

The *Amorpha*, though more spreading, is somewhat allied to the *Colutea* in appearance, and bears quantities of small purplish flowers in dense terminal flattish clusters during early summer.

For the outskirts of groups, where low-growing shrubs are particularly desirable, the glossy leaves and rounded contours of the *Clethra alnifolia* work in very successfully with the added beauty of protruding spikes of sweet-scented white midsummer flowers. *Andromeda Mariana*, or stagger bush, resembles somewhat the *Clethra alnifolia*, though its white summer flowers are less striking in appearance.

The horse-chestnut for bloom belongs peculiarly to spring, but one there is, *Æsculus parviflora*, of dwarf-spreading contours, which forms one of the most effective

DWARF FLOWERING HORSE-CHESTNUT TREES.
ÆSCULUS PARVIFLORA.

objects on the lawn in July, with its rich spikes of white flowers thrust prominently above masses of the peculiar typical horse-chestnut foliage.

But I must not leave the subject of summer trees without referring with deepest admiration to the elegant, tapering, arrow-like form and tender, strange-looking, pea-green

102 FLOWERS AND FOLIAGE OF SUMMER.

foliage of the Chinese cypress. No member of the *Taxodium* family attains its full panoply of foliage in this climate before July. Cypresses should be employed above all things for their summer effect. Very graceful and impressive are Southern cypresses, with their picturesque masses of feathery foliage, but unique and beautiful, almost above all other trees on the summer lawn, is a good specimen of the strange, foreign-looking Chinese cypress.

CHINESE CYPRESS.
(GLYPTOSTROBUS SINENSIS.)

Most spireas flower in May or June, but there are several that bloom during mid and late summer, and have therefore an important place in such assemblages as we are discussing. *Spiræa callosa alba* is perhaps the most noteworthy, for, although it commences to flower in June, it has an abundant second bloom in July, which, added to the flower's beauty and its rounded, low-growing form, make it useful in different combinations of shrubs. *S. Billardii, Douglasii, salicifolia,* and *tomentosa* are other varieties of spireas that bloom late in summer.

Weigelias generally are valuable June-flowering shrubs,

FLOWERS AND FOLIAGE OF SUMMER. 103

but one peculiar one, *W. Lavallei*, I must mention for its abundant dark-red flowers borne a second time in July and

JAPAN IVY.
(AMPELOPSIS TRICUSPIDATA.)

August. The variegated dwarf weigelia is fresh and attractive in late summer, as well as during all other seasons of the year when it is clothed with foliage.

104 FLOWERS AND FOLIAGE OF SUMMER.

I must not leave the summer lawn without dwelling briefly on the charms of various climbers at this season. The *Akebia quinata*, neat and elegant all summer, is never apparently more so, it may be by contrast, than in August. *Ampelopsis tricuspidata*, with shining leaves and rootlets clinging to stone or wooden walls, is bright as ever, and seemingly more vigorous in late summer. The broad, massive, strange-looking leaves of the Dutchman's pipe are very effective now, and

DUTCHMAN'S PIPE.
(ARISTOLOCHIA SIPHO.)

SWEET-SCENTED CLEMATIS.
(CLEMATIS FLAMMULA.)

several clematises, yellow *apiifolia*, white sweet-scented *flammula*, greenish-white *Grahami*, the old-fashioned *Virginiana*, all clothe during summer their nearest support with thick masses of leaves and flowers.

The honeysuckles are fresh and pleasing all summer, especially when climbing over stumps or rocks and hillsides, and in several instances, such as those of *sempervirens* and *sinensis*, throughout the season. *Menispermum Canadense*, the moon-seed, makes a pretty clothing of foliage throughout the summer; but the most effective of summer climbers is the great *Tecoma (Bignonia)*, or trumpet creeper.

Our common old-fashioned trumpet creeper *(Tecoma radicans)* with its rich crimson trumpet-shaped flowers is splendid both in leaf and bloom when trained over stones and stumps of trees, but *Tecoma grandiflora*, with its broader and larger orange-colored flowers, quite surpasses it. It is not, however, always hardy. Effective shrubs may be made of these strong-growing trumpet creepers by training them over a stump or post, six or eight feet high, where they rapidly assume a perfect bush form.

In considering the valuable summer traits of the plants I have named, I feel that I have given a very brief tribute to their peculiar charms, and I know full well too that many other kinds exist, suitable for like employment, but pause because my intention is to be stimulative and suggestive rather than to exhaust this subject. Moreover, enough varieties have been considered to make, in proper combination, even the most ambitious lawn beautiful throughout the months of July and August.

TRUMPET CREEPER.
(TECOMA RADICANS.)

CHAPTER VI.

GREEN AUTUMNAL FOLIAGE.

DID it ever occur to any one that it would be well to brighten the lawn in fall with more trees that remain green at that season? If it ever has, the evidence scarcely appears. Yet the dull and fading hues of autumn, in spite of the increasing beauty of dying leaves, need some green color to refresh the eye. Perhaps in improving lawns we do not sufficiently consider all the valuable qualities of different plants, failing to recognize the lessons afforded by woodland scenery. It may not, therefore, be uninteresting to touch briefly the fall characteristics of certain trees and shrubs noteworthy in this respect. We might naturally turn to evergreens as especially suited for our purpose, but, with few exceptions, their hues have been dimmed since June. The green does not seem as warm and fresh as it did then, and an evergreen has never that cheerful enlivening aspect presented by the green of deciduous trees.

We propose to include no plants the foliage of which suffers from mere white frost, and even to include some the leaves of which will endure a severe freezing without injury to their beauty. There is doubtless a season in late August and early September, during which the lawn should be carefully supplied with such foliage and flowers as will yet flourish; but we have chosen a later period, which is sometimes deferred until the middle of October, and which is more neglected and needy.

One would think the maples would be valuable for their green in fall and so they unquestionably are. They are healthy, thrifty, and vigorous, but no variety very remarkable for its late green exists among them unless it be the little colchicum maple, properly called *Acer lætum*. The foliage of this tree is pleasing and of curious outline. Delicate red stems support the leaves, and the general appearance is bright and cheerful. It is a choice, uncommon maple, to which I have already referred with respect, and should be more employed as a single specimen on the lawn.

The common catalpa *(C. syringæfolia)*, much spoken of nowadays for its enduring wood, and most valuable to the lawn planter for broad, shadowy foliage, retains its green color well in fall. There is also a dwarf form, *C. Bungeii*, sometimes misnamed *Kæmpferi*, rounded like a hemisphere, with very delicate autumnal greens. The *Aralia Japonica* is drooping and graceful and effective in its autumn green.

Chionanthus Virginica, the white fringe, old, well-known, and choice, is not usually spoken of for its autumnal beauty. The reputation of the exquisite lace-like flowers has doubtless eclipsed the glory of the foliage. It is large for a shrub, lustrous and oval in contour, and the leaves have a dark, rich green in fall.

The American persimmon is a noteworthy tree for its green in fall; but the Japanese persimmon, or *kaki*, shows a richer, glossier foliage, like orange leaves in color. Unfortunately, it is not hardy in the Middle and Northern States.

Few shrubs are prettier in the fall than the evergreen thorn (*Cotoneaster* or *Cratægus pyracantha*). The small glossy dark-green leaves and orange-colored berries, all protected by masses of thorns, characterize the finest foreign *Cratægus* which is thoroughly healthy in America, as it is also attractive in very late fall and even winter.

Cercis Japonica, the Japan Judas tree, has heart-shaped leaves, glossy, tough, and retained late in fall. It is rare and choice, and decidedly attractive both for its flowers and leaves during at least five months of the year. In spring, early pink flowers wreathe the stem, before the leaves put forth.

The best green-leaved spirea in fall is, perhaps, *S. pruni-*

INDIAN BEAN.
(CATALPA BIGNONIOIDES.)

folia, which assumes still richer colors as a late autumnal garb. *Spiræa crispifolia*, rare, and recently introduced from Japan, is a variety of *S. bullata;* a dwarf mass of rounded, curling foliage, it is well preserved in fall.

Salix laurifolia, or *S. pentandra*, the laurel-leaved willow, preserves a shining green late in the season. The ornamental value of this tree is not sufficiently considered. It endures all exposures and soils, even close to the seashore, and is always clean and thrifty.

The elms are remarkably deficient in attraction during the fall, with one or two curious exceptions. The one specially notable is the weeping—so called slippery—elm, or it may be simply a variety of the American, which grows with great rapidity, and has a fine vigorous foliage. So rapid is this growth that grafts made in the spring will attain six or eight feet during the following summer. We see a specimen before us, while we are writing, where a large American elm has been stripped of its branches and grafted at numerous points with cions of this weeping elm. The effect produced after a few years has been most extraordinary. Long, pendent branches, clothed with luxuriant foliage, swing and wreathe themselves about against the sky like gigantic snakes. The most valuable quality of this choice tree lies in the fact that its foliage is frequently green until October, and always green weeks later than most other elms. There is one other elm which is rare —*Ulmus parvifolia*,—that holds its green so late that it might be classed with oaks and beeches for this peculiarity. It is of moderate growth, and has rough, slightly curled foliage, grouped closely along the branches.

So far as we know, the lindens can only boast of two varieties that remain really green in fall, viz.: *Tilia dasystyla* and *T. sulphurea*, golden-barked trees with bright green foliage. All other lindens fade soon, and become almost unsightly in early autumn, so that the green foliage of these varieties seem very curious to behold in October. The effect of the unusual season of such coloring is increased by the strong contrast afforded by a bright yellow bark and a singularly lustrous foliage.

WEEPING BEECH.
(FAGUS SYLVATICA PENDULA.)

But the noblest trees of bright green and other good qualities are the beeches and oaks, rich in color and picturesque in form, always affording grateful shade; other trees may possibly be as fine in some peculiar fashion, but none can be more generally satisfactory. Not specially early in spring in putting forth leaves, they are most beautiful in June, and indeed throughout the summer. In

WEEPING BEECH IN WINTER.

autumnal landscapes, however, their late foliage, almost evergreen during mild winters, performs a valuable part, for the very reason that there is now so much less beauty among trees than earlier in the season. All kinds of beeches are fine in the fall. The cut-leaved, the purple, and the common American and European beeches are all most effective and green until winter; but the noblest of all is the celebrated weeping beech. Its great, gleaming masses of foliage assume all kinds of fantastic shapes, and reveal bowers and recesses until the leaves of almost every other

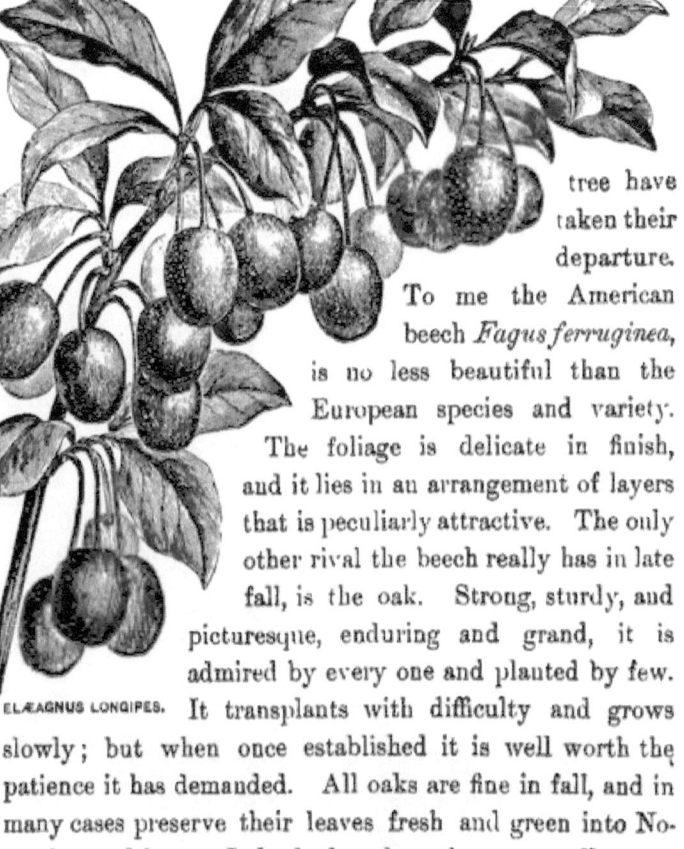
ELÆAGNUS LONGIPES.

tree have taken their departure. To me the American beech *Fagus ferruginea*, is no less beautiful than the European species and variety. The foliage is delicate in finish, and it lies in an arrangement of layers that is peculiarly attractive. The only other rival the beech really has in late fall, is the oak. Strong, sturdy, and picturesque, enduring and grand, it is admired by every one and planted by few. It transplants with difficulty and grows slowly; but when once established it is well worth the patience it has demanded. All oaks are fine in fall, and in many cases preserve their leaves fresh and green into November and later. Indeed, though we have no really evergreen oaks in the North, there are seasons when some oaks, notably the pyramidal, retain a few leaves all winter. The willow-leaved oak, as well as the pin oak, and the rare, large-leaved *Daimio* from Japan, among others, are very beautiful in fall, sometimes even in late November and December.

Did space permit, we should like to dwell on the beauty in autumn of various privets, *Daphne cneorum* of tiny evergreen foliage, and certain of the *Elæagnus* species, notably the gray *E. Hortensis* and the robust *E. longipes*, with large leaves and red berries, as well as the beautiful fall climbers, evergreen honeysuckles, *Akebias*, Virginia silk, etc. All these should be planted with taste here and there about the lawn, supported by occasional masses of rhododendrons, laurels, mahonias, and other evergreen shrubs. Thus adorned, the lawn, in the fine air and lights of autumn and during bright days, may well tempt us to linger amid its yet beautiful foliage, where crimson and gold are mingled plentifully with green.

CHAPTER VII.

AUTUMNAL COLOR ON THE LAWN.

HE supreme point of our enjoyment of lawn-planting is reached when we have compassed in our grounds the loveliest effects of color. Although this is a fact, I fancy we seldom consciously attempt to compass these color effects. A dress pattern is selected, the tints of every part of the room, both walls, furniture, and floor, are studied with the critical eye of genius, but when we come to the lawn, composition of any kind is seldom attempted, much less a harmonious disposition of color.

Indeed, I believe, when any one does more than stand specimens about wherever they may happen to come, form is apt to receive first and almost exclusive attention. A pyramidal tree, a broad-spreading tree, a tall tree, a dwarf tree, secures a certain amount of attention for its proper disposition, but the foliage might be, to all intents and purposes, one shade of green for any consideration color receives in the special grouping and arrangement. Even Central Park, New York, the most notable landscape-gardening essay in America, has always impressed me as defective in studied color effects of foliage. This is doubtless caused in part by a want of sufficient variety in the large masses of the plants employed. Twenty-five years ago, when the Park was planted, there was likewise a much smaller variety of ornamental trees in the nurseries than there is at present.

Yet, notwithstanding this apparent neglect of color in lawn-planting of the present day, I am not inclined to believe that our enjoyment of color in foliage falls at all behind that of our enjoyment of tree form. Form doubtless appeals more to the direct, practical instincts of the gardener or farmer, and in his hands has rested in large part all tree-planting up to the present time. Nay, more, I believe that if women could or would have given as much attention to the lawn as they have to the flower garden, this reproach of baldness of color would not now apply in the same degree to the tree-planting in vogue.

The truth is that color, for almost every one, is a great and positive delight. This delight may be more sensuous and less purely intellectual than that inspired by agreeable form, but it belongs more truly, nevertheless, to the restful physical pleasure associated with the lawn. Indeed the mere mention of the word *color* on the lawn calls up to the memory lovely tints of foliage and flower, and few will perhaps acknowledge that they have neglected color for such purposes. In most cases this erroneous impression comes from ignorance of possible color combinations of this character. People have a taste and regard for beauty of foliage of every kind, but the trouble is their knowledge is defective.

In short, I would venture to assert that if the mass of cultured men and women could realize— that is, see directly before their eyes, as it were—a tithe of the lovely compositions of color attainable by means of foliage on the lawn, fashion would simply declare that an attractive home must include such effects if it would be considered at all complete.

The direct proof of this assertion lies in the falsely directed enthusiasm shown for the Persian rug wrought into the lawn with bedding plants, echeverias, alternantheras, and the like. True, the Persian rug is an admirable thing in its way, an absolute work of art, but then it is not always in harmony with the natural effects suitable to a special surface of greensward. Yet people delight in Persian-rug or carpet gardening from a simple and very reasonable love of color. I contend, indeed, that carpet or ribbon gardening, artistically composed, is both right and proper in its way, only it should be subordinated to, as well as co-ordinated with, other compositions of color throughout the entire system of planting on any special lawn.

With the object of inspiring a due regard for the charming possibilities of color composition in foliage not only during one season but during all seasons, I propose to consider briefly the material that constitutes one of these effects, and something of the methods by which it can be best attained. If artists were all gardeners or gardeners all artists, these effects and their construction would be familiar to us; as it is, we must be satisfied with a suggestive sketch, and hope that the love for lawn-planting may soon grow sufficiently to demand a more exhaustive treatment of color composition in foliage than I can expect to give at the present time.

The foliage which I now choose for consideration is that of late fall, and the part of the season that I specially select as offering the most lovely and varied color of autumn is that which is frequently called Indian summer. We all know it. There is possibly nothing of the kind in the world that surpasses it. The shimmering haze and indistinct view of objects that seem to wave slightly before the eye, the brilliant tints of outlying trees and shrubs relieved against dark foliage and naked branches, all combine to create a picture of surpassing loveliness.

As well might I attempt to explain how to imitate the tints of the leaf itself as to discern the methods by which all these wonderful effects are brought together in field and wood. The brisk, pure air and almost faint stillness often add to the glamour of the scene. In short, the senses simply luxuriate in the feast spread before them, to the entire exclusion, for the moment, of any desire to explain the why and wherefore. Like the lotus eaters we are satisfied "only to hear and see," but, doubtless, like them too, only for a little while, in spite of any intimation of the poet to the contrary. When the time comes to plant—and we have studied the subject—we find, however, that by working on the same principles as nature uses in her favored spots, we can secure something of the same effect on our lawns. It may not indeed have the peculiar charm of true wildwood scenery, but in a more cultured, dignified way, it may be quite as beautiful.

Any lawn can secure more or less of these autumnal color effects, but large lawns where the attainment of distance is possible will compass better their employment. The colors may be thus seen toned down to their loveliest shade, and that wonderful Indian summer atmosphere attained which, during some, not all seasons, produces such magical effects. Doubtless smaller lawns can and should supply charming color combinations peculiar to this season; I only allude to the superiority of large lawns for the purpose.

Let us see how we must go to work to build up these effects. In the first place, we must see that we have dark-green or brownish backgrounds and recesses against which to construct our most brilliant features. In fact, some of these tender grays and browns of autumn are truly wonderful, and, moreover, a part of the picture we are apt to overlook, although if they were left out we would at once miss them. Of what then are these backgrounds composed? First we must remember that the autumnal pictures on the lawn and in the woods can never be exactly alike. One is cultivated and the other wild nature. While therefore the general composition is constructed on like principles, the material and spirit of the two scenes, if I may use such an expression, must be of necessity different.

Thus in both we find a background, in the main of heavy green, brown, or gray, varied in the widest and subtlest manner within certain limits, but the material used must and will be greatly different. Hickories and pepperidges, for instance, are practically ruled out from lawn planting of any kind because they are so difficult to transplant and grow. On the other hand, the lawn may employ many foreign varieties of trees which will go far to make up for any lack of the wild beauty of native trees unsuited for the purpose. Such an arrangement of trees will be characterized by dignity and a choice and elegant charm, suggesting even in solitude the fitness of the place for human occupation. It is therefore no mere imitation of nature we should attempt on our lawns.

The very first and best tree, for instance, to use in the massed and green part of our autumnal lawn effect is the Norway maple. This may seem a little strange to those not familiar with trees, for maples are generally looked upon as capable of distinguishing themselves in fall chiefly by means of color. But the Norway maple holds a dark-green color late, and finally its leaves wither and drop without making any special exhibition of red of any shade. Otherwise, the Norway maple is considered the most generally valuable of lawn trees, alike for fine rounded contours, rich coloring, and healthy long-lived vigor. It occupies therefore a fitting position in forming the mass of the background of a plantation made for autumnal effect. If some pool or stream happens to be near this grouping the effect will be greatly enhanced by appearing the second time in the watery mirror of its surface.

Having secured the background of dark green, in front of which to build up other elements of the picture, we must be careful not to destroy its broad loveliness by constructing small mixed-color effects after the Persian-rug type. There may and should be, doubtless, variety in even the background, but in the main the mass effect must be in this case dark green. Variety may be obtained by white-stemmed birches, and the branches even of deciduous trees that have lost their leaves. Deciduous trees, by the by, should make up the major portion, if not all, of our autumnal effect. Evergreens, except as they may be used here and there very sparingly to punctuate, as it were, the mass of the background, should not be employed, because, as a rule, they do not look well associated with deciduous trees.

Now and then great variety of form may be attained in the background by using in the immediate outskirts of the grouping, rigid-looking, grotesque, naked branches, like those of the Japan *ginkgo* and pyramidal oak.

The Kentucky coffee-tree shows in this background delicate, pleasing outlines, early denuded as it is of foliage. Indeed it is one of the most attractive of deciduous trees, with its peculiar trunk and branches, and its light, feathery, graceful foliage. Wide-spreading branches of the curious weeping elm, lately referred to, standing well forward in the mass, serve to vary the effect with partially naked limbs, for the leaves of this elm hang on late.

The broad, rounded contours of that loveliest of deciduous trees, the *Cladrastis tinctoria*, *Virgilea lutea*, or yellow wood, increase this variety with curious branching and beauty of yellow fading foliage. The background is thus subtly shaded, and yet broad and massive. Dark-green color characterizes the bulk of the plantation, while all sameness of color is relieved by browns and grays of other foliage, and

KENTUCKY COFFEE-TREE.
(GYMNOCLADUS CANADENSIS.)

occasional naked stems and branches. These other colors are subordinated, as well as softened, into due sympathy with the autumnal characteristics of this particular part of the season. After all, the background should be employed mainly as a foil for the brighter beauties of autumn. It is common to think of red tints as the noteworthy colors of autumn foliage; yet there are many others which are very attractive, as even our brief consideration of a proper background has already shown us.

We must come now to consider the higher notes or chords of our symphony of color. The most brilliant effects are reached in the red or crimson tints. Scarlet is a color almost unknown to the normal foliage of hardy plants. The most familiar example of this rich chord of color is found in the autumn tints of the swamp, or falsely named scarlet, maple, *Acer rubrum*, and in the common sugar maple. Of all the forms of maples, except the shrubby *polymorphum* from Japan, these are the only species remarkable for their red color in fall. How beautiful they are, thousands can testify who have stood entranced before the sugar maples of the hills of Vermont or the scarlet maples on the banks of the Delaware. Sugar maples sometimes color grandly, especially on hillsides.

On the lawn, these reddish tints often fail, or simply serve to warm the rich golden-yellow which is apt to take their place. For that matter, who has not often seen as fine a yellow on the tulip poplar! We should, therefore, plant the tulip poplar in the background, where its colors will blend agreeably with the greens and browns of the other trees. The sugar maple, also, does not generally make the richest points of color in the landscape, but must be contented to heighten very materially the quieter tints of the background. Since, moreover, it is elegant and symmetrical in outline, one of our very choicest shade trees, it should stand well forward in the mass or background.

The scarlet or red maple is the richest in autumnal color of all maples; I was about to say of all trees. It seldom fails during any autumn to change more or less splendidly; and therefore deserves to stand out a single flaming monument in the van of all autumnal color. There is something quite indescribable in the glow and intensity of tint often displayed by this maple. Is it ignorance or the want of seeing eyes that causes its lack of employment on the lawn? It is true, the scarlet maple is slower-growing than the sugar maple, of less regular and pleasing outline, and certainly less beautiful and satisfactory at other seasons of the year. But in fall, it simply reigns supreme.

Scarcely less beautiful than the scarlet maple are some of the oaks. Many of them, like the Turkey, English, and pyramidal oaks, are grandly effective in the background with their solid dark-green tints. But the white, red, and scarlet oaks—American species all—take on the most distinct and glowing autumnal colors. All oaks are too much neglected in lawn-planting. Whether for color, form, or rugged longevity, they are invaluable for ornamental purposes on the lawn. Here, too, while speaking of oaks, I should again mention the golden oak *(Quercus Concordia)*. This tree serves as an instance where—although it too is apt to lose its beauty somewhat before the Indian summer—another color than red becomes, by its intensity, almost the brilliant feature of the scene. Its special peculiarity appears in the fact that it becomes more and more golden all summer until in mid-autumn it stands a bright yellow flame of health and vigor amid the dull and fading tints of fall. It is one of the choicest of recent introductions, and holds its foliage late.

Turning again to the consideration of reddish autumnal tints, we find the liquid ambar presenting the deepest, darkest crimson on its more or less star-shaped leaves. This tree is of smaller size than maples, tulips, or oaks, but is one of our half dozen thoroughly excellent autumn trees. It is round-headed, has a straight rough stem, and is altogether a very characteristic American tree. In this arrangement of color it should be continually remembered that we want striking, prominent points of interest on which the eye may rest with pleasure. There must be generally no confusion, no mingling in the case of these interesting points of red color. The group of red trees look better standing quite away from any general green mass, a flaming forerunner or standard-bearer at the head of the retreating hosts of autumn.

Before proceeding to dwell on beautiful shrubs, we must look a moment at a plant that is almost a shrub in habit, but which merits a most distinguished position on the lawn. This plant is the new and rare Chinese sumac *(Rhus Osbeckii)*. I know of no richer red than that which suffuses its large leaf. It is crimson, changing almost to scarlet in certain spots. The large wing or prolongation of each leaf on either side of the stem makes it still more

LIQUID AMBAR.

curious and effective. In habit it is somewhat straggling and open, but the color is positively unsurpassed.

Andromeda arborea, or *Oxydendrum arboreum*, the sorrel tree, is another most excellent plant in the foreground of our autumn picture. The leaves hang on late, and assume lovely variegations of mottled green and red, turning later into fine reddish crimson. Though a native plant, this shrub is rare. It should certainly be as common as its slow growth and difficult propagation will permit.

Cornus florida, the white flowering dogwood of early spring, has also glowing red autumnal tints on its leaves, which compose themselves in broad stratified masses.

All this color, however, in the case of shrubs intended to carry out the general design, should be backed up in the same manner as the colors of trees were treated—that is, with plants of similar size and solid green foliage like the California privet and laurel-leaved willow. Both are large and rapid-growing, well calculated to make a pleasing contrast among the larger contours of the trees which constitute the true background. A partial mingling of shrubs and trees, moreover, gives the scene a natural appearance. The stems of the trees are clothed by these shrubs much as they are wont to be in woodland glades. For this purpose the evergreen thorn comes in well with its dark-green or bronze-red foliage, neat, beautiful, and compact, with that picturesque irregularity of outline peculiar to thorns generally.

Few shrubs clothe these autumn tree trunks more attractively than many of the olive or gray-green willows. They put forth leaves, moreover, early and hold their foliage

EUROPEAN OLEASTER.
(ELÆAGNUS HORTENSIS.)

late. Even the weeping willow does this. But the rosemary willow, with narrow, waving leaves, is better suited for the purpose. Its blue green produces in fall that charmingly cool tone so pleasing along the edge of a mass of trees, especially when the entire scene lies on the banks of a pool or stream of water. The effect is repeated on the water in still more delicate combinations, and affects one like a subdued distant musical note reverberated or echoed on waves of air. Most lawns can have a pool of water. It is certainly desirable as a means of displaying autumn colors with peculiar and striking effect on its mirror-like surface.

But do not forget the willows of many species. They form a notable instance of what may be accomplished by the grays and greens of fall. The shimmering atmosphere of Indian summer suits wonderfully the glowing crimson and sparkling green foliage of that season. Yet even during that season there are different days which are to me more lovely still, being almost solemn with their pure air, clear and buoyant and yet devoid of brightness—like the interior of some great cathedral. It is for these autumnal effects that I wish to secure proper employment for alders, birches, oleasters, and willows.

Do you know the oleaster or *Elæagnus*, especially *Elæagnus hortensis?* It is a vigorous, easily grown plant, and has that whitish or grayish-green so attractive in many combinations of foliage. All the oleasters, in fact, have more or less of these whitish tints, but *Elæagnus hortensis* is one of the best.

For delicate, lovely variegations at all seasons of the year except winter, I know of nothing finer in its way than

Spiræa Thunbergii. Its small golden green leaves have throughout spring and summer the most exquisite coloring. In fall, however, there is added a wonderful flush of pink that seems to me fine above all the tints of autumn. Such a plant should scarcely stand out on capes and promontories of foliage among flashing reds and crimsons. Its delicate tints harmonize better with more neutral surrounding colors, and accord generally with a more retired position.

We find a more brilliant autumn shrub and therefore one to be planted more prominently in the *Spiræa prunifolia*. The leaves of this plant are small and of a shining green, and hang on late in fall when they assume a deep-red color. It is a rapid-growing shrub and should be planted well in the foreground about the base of some brilliant scarlet maple.

Then the sumacs! We all know them in fall by the roadside with their crimson leaves and great erect bunches of velvety, purple, and crimson seed vessels. Central Park, N. Y., has masses and territories of them planted in the most effective manner. All around the brilliant capes and headlands of our autumnal picture these plants prove invaluable for strong red color. There is nothing neutral about them. They are steeped in one deep pervading luxuriance of tint. But we need not content ourselves with even their excellent beauty, for have we not their grander relatives, near cousins, more deeply crimson, if possible, and of finer form and aspect? I refer to *Rhus glabra laciniata* and *Rhus Osbeckii*. One of these, the former, is a well-known though choice lawn plant, curiously and distinctly cut-leaved. The latter, the most effective of all, *Rhus*

Osbeckii, the Chinese sumac, has already been mentioned incidentally. It is as much of a tree as a shrub, and may very properly head a mass of shrubbery thrown out here and there from the general grouping of trees.

Nor must we forget to use in our groupings for autumn effect, the rich crimson wood of the red-stemmed dogwood amid the soft browns and grays or brilliant greens of other foliage.

The yellow of the golden willow is also brilliantly effective in such combinations. The importance of tints and forms of naked branches in producing lovely effects in fall must never be overlooked.

For characteristic strength and rigidity of outline the purple berberry is also one of these plants remarkable on the lawn in fall for other qualities than color. The purple berberry, however, has much rich color on its leaves in fall. For more delicate and exquisite variegations of red among shrubs, however, we must turn to the Japanese *polymorphum* maples. Nothing can be more lovely than their tints in autumn, except the tints of the same plant in June. As an effective feature on the point of some shrub group intended for autumnal effect, few plants can equal and none surpass these Japanese maples.

Yet variety of effect in lawn-planting for autumnal beauty need not stop here. There are whole genera of red- or yellow-berried plants which are very striking and effective even at a little distance. First and foremost are the *Euonymuses*, with brilliant scarlet four- or five-hooded seed-vessels that hang on far into November, and even December. A good specimen of *Euonymus latifolius*, for instance, presents one of the most splendid sights of the year, with its dark-green foliage literally studded with scarlet or crimson fruit. The European *Euonymus* and its varieties display the finest masses of color, although the American kinds bear very attractive fruit. Both countries have sorts that turn purple in fall notwithstanding the fact that the prevailing hue of the genus is green until very late.

There are also bush honeysuckles, mountain ashes, the black alder, *Ilex verticillata*, and the snow-ball, *Viburnum lantana*, all remarkable for their brilliant crimson or orange berries. Very remarkable, too, is the snowberry or *Symphoricarpus racemosus* bearing clusters of snow-white waxen fruit. The dark-purple berried Indian currant, *Symphoricarpus vulgaris*, is less remarkable though very attractive. *Callicarpa purpurea*, with steel-blue bead-like berries, is also very pretty in autumn. Mahonias have small bright-blue seed-vessels in autumn, and such broad, shining, picturesque foliage that no well appointed shrubbery can afford to neglect them. The little broad picturesque *Berberis Thunbergii* has also charming autumn tints and bright-red berries.

Nor should we forget the lovely effects accomplished by climbing vines in fall. Most remarkable for color and vigor is the Virginia creeper or *Ampelopsis* in all is forms. The crimson garlands it wreathes about the naked or dead trunks of prominent trees are very effective, because so concentrated and so distinctly contrasted with adjacent sombre coloring. More beautiful, if possible, than our Virginia creeper is its near relative *Ampelopsis Veitchii* or *tricuspidata* of Japan. This vine is unquestionably the finest of all climbers in fall. The outline of its leaves and the lustre of its tints at all seasons of the year are very beautiful, but in fall its subtle hues of red and green are positively unsurpassed in their way.

Celastrus scandens, the common bitter-sweet, is well worth planting for autumn effect at the base of dead or naked trunks. It is often brilliantly crimson and grows vigorously, bearing rich orange-colored berries.

In thus dwelling on certain plants suitable for producing fine autumnal colors, I have not attempted to describe the entire list. It is enough that those enumerated constitute a rich collection of lovely colors. Autumnal nature leaves us splendidly. Her falling robes are gathered about her in such a regal fashion, and amid such pure airs and tender skies, that it hardly seems right to mourn for her. The sadness of her passing away is forgotten in the effect of her proud splendor and the certainty of her resurrection in a few months.

Is it not somewhat strange that these effects and combinations are seldom attempted on the lawn. An army with banners on the greensward could hardly be more impressive than such scenes if approached for the first time. I think, moreover, the magnificence of these effects is intensified by the uncertainty that attaches itself to their yearly recurrence. No one has fathomed the laws that regulate their development. It is not frost, nor dry weather, nor rain exactly that favors their greatest brilliance. Doubtless maturity and decay are the main factors in their production, yet some years we hardly find them at all, and again the glow will burst upon us when we least expect it, and when the character of the maturity and decay would lead us to look for prevailing dulness.

Enjoyment of bright color in peculiar combination I believe to be the keynote of the bulk of all this autumnal pleasure found in the changing hues of trees. No painter, therefore, should prize color effects more highly than the lawn-planter, nor seek to compose more artistically the tints at his command. The limitations of his picture are perhaps broader, more subtle, and less defined than those of the painter, but very much the same in kind. He cannot perhaps count on results years hence, as the painter can on the effect of the strokes of his brush, but nature helps him more generously in the management of his material. The lawn-planter may place himself implicitly under the control of nature's wonderful processes, and by simply working on natural principles he will attain the most delightful results. They will not be exactly woodland scenes that have at times startled him by their solemn, luxuriant grandeur. Yet, consisting as they do of cultured and dignified specimen plants congregated together on the same principles as those of the woods, they will suit better the association of the home circle. If we could have the bit of attractive autumn woodland transferred entire just as it was to our very doors we would not like its unkempt condition. The more artificial scene referred to would suit us, very properly, far better. We must remember that good lawn-planting must be founded only on nature's methods of accomplishing similar effects; in a word, the spirit of our new work, as already remarked, though ever so natural, must be cultured and dignified, in proper accord with that of our best homes.

134 AUTUMNAL COLOR ON THE LAWN.

To sum up, we do not want a Persian rug on our autumn lawns, nor a hap-hazard, inartistic dotting about of plants. Much less do we want a wild wood about our doors at any time. But we do want solid backgrounds of greens, and browns, and grays, intermingled with naked branches. The richer colors we need on outer boundaries, and flashing bits of red or yellow, singly or on prominent points, and beyond all, up to the very house, broad stretches of greensward.

CHAPTER VIII.

LAWN-PLANTING FOR WINTER EFFECT.

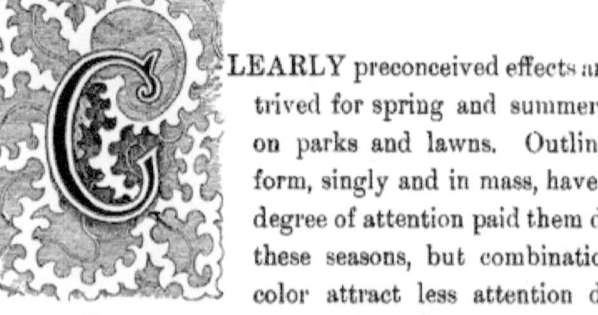

CLEARLY preconceived effects are contrived for spring and summer, both on parks and lawns. Outline and form, singly and in mass, have a fair degree of attention paid them during these seasons, but combinations of color attract less attention during even the "perfect days of June." Later on, as summer hues fade, still less thought is given to securing renewed beauty of foliage and flower by employing such plants as are specially fine in August and September. Such plants may indeed be set out, but this is seldom done with a conscious intention of prolonging the season of beautiful foliage, or of producing distinct compositions. In autumn, finally, two specially charming objects may be and sometimes are sought in the use of plants. One looks to the retention of a rich, healthy, green foliage as late as possible by means of certain oaks, beeches, elms, and golden and green conifers, while another employs the wonderful crimson and gold tints of maples, liquidambars, sumac, etc., to construct the lovely pictures naturally peculiar to the season.

I am sorry to say, however, that we find the last essay made in the most tentative manner. Most people who attempt the experiment are satisfied with a scarlet maple or two, or a liquidambar. It seems hardly to have entered their minds that in thus combining on the lawn unrivalled autumnal color they have at hand possible mass effects of the finest character. They look with pleasure in fall at glades of oak, pepperidge, and maple entwined with blood-red Virginia creepers, and never think of analyzing the composition of the charming effect, much less seek to develop the same thing, as it were, on their lawns. It is this apathy in regard to a thousand natural charms that ask for recognition at our very doors that impels me to consider briefly one department of this subject, namely, the production of domestic winter landscape. I choose it because, after the varied attractions of June, lawn-planting for winter effect seems to me worthy of more distinct treatment than that of either of the other seasons.

A portion of the lawn which can be seen as a picture through the frame made by the outline of a certain window should be so planted that it will always be sure to present a delightful scene during the varied changes of winter, when one is necessarily kept within doors more than in summer. Nor need there be any detriment wrought to the general character of the lawn by this limited operation, if only a broad, systematic treatment be maintained everywhere on all parts of the place.

Let us, then, look out upon our lawn, and see where and

how we can best produce the desired result. I assume that most of us possess lawns of limited dimensions; in the case of the larger lawns, their treatment may be considered by regular experts. The small landholder, however, with his few hundred square feet of land, must generally bestow such treatment as he can give himself, with the help of inferior labor. Moreover, a thousand are interested in small holdings where one possesses or cares for the grand estate.

Most houses have several windows, any one of which may be selected for the frame of our winter picture. Other things being equal, the window should be chosen that looks out on the bleakest part of the lawn, or in some direction where objects would otherwise be visible which it is desirable to screen. In either case, it will be found that evergreens, of which all artificial winter landscapes should be more or less composed, serve to modify and render cosey bleak places, as well as to hide unsightly details. Frequently this point lies on the northwest part of the grounds. Complete unity, however, must exist between the treatment of this and other sections of the lawn; otherwise everything will have a loose, straggling, semi-detached look, as if the plants had happened together by chance, and were not at all sure that they were worthily treated or comfortably situated.

The general outline of the masses of foliage will naturally be made coincident with the boundary lines of the property, except as glimpses without are desired; so that when we use the larger evergreens they will very properly occupy the background of the picture. In other words, their rich, solid mass will make a bold and suitable foil, both summer and winter, for the more delicate tints and outlines of smaller evergreen and deciduous plants. For this, indeed, is one of the peculiar features of our winter lawn: that it uses deciduous plants, plants devoid of foliage, as freely as evergreens, in the winter picture.

Nothing in the woods can surpass the sweeping grace of fold on fold of snow swathing the dark, drooping branches of the hardy spruces that make up the mass of the background. Pine and hemlock may alternate now and then with Norway spruces, and vary the charm of this background with the bright green or bluish tints of the former and the peculiar light bluish-gray of the latter. The pines, especially those of the *mughus* species, stand firm, rugged, and strong, and the long blue needles of the white pine lend just sufficient variety of tone to satisfy the eye. For grace nothing can surpass the hemlock, which readily retains in its folds sweeping wreaths of snow or diadems of icicles.

Rich mass, firm outline, and evergreen tints of the greatest variety characterize the view thus far considered from the window. But we have only begun to analyze the many possible and varied effects. Broad spaces of grass slope up to the house in front, and, although not green, serve to establish a sufficient distance to permit the arrangement of a middle-ground as well as a foreground and a background. This middle-ground is always to me the most charming part of any section of the lawn. Elsewhere, mass or extreme detail obscures one's best conception of any beautiful plant. In the middle-ground, the really choice plant offers itself to the eye with the most inviting effect. Its weak points are thus somewhat hidden, and its charms are enhanced twofold by the distance that here just suffices, not only to lend enchantment to the view, but to give an adequate impression of the plant considered as a whole. The plants that stand nearest the evergreen background are evergreen also, both because they are allied by nature, and because they appear most bold and characteristic seen at a little distance from the house. One exception to this arrangement may be effectively made by interspersing among the evergreens white birches, the value of which can hardly be overestimated in any lawn-planting, and in winter, ornamentally considered, they are almost indispensable. Notice the striking effect of the delicate, gleaming white stems placed here and there directly against the dark background of evergreens, and surrounded, perhaps, by fields of snow and ice. See how the contrast brightens the whole scene, and how curiously the white trunks and graceful drooping branches bear snow wreaths or icicles, each in its own characteristic way. A solid background of evergreens presents much variety of rich color, blue, green, and silver, but the whole effect is, as it were, punctuated by these white birches. Nature uses the birches most delightfully in many a woodland winter scene, and our lawn is, we find, greatly improved by the free use of this artistic resource. But our attention is specially claimed by the specimens occupying the middle-ground. Here, too, we find a fair admixture of evergreen trees advisable. The evergreens disposed near the foreground are of medium, and in some cases of dwarf size, but always of interesting character, well fitted to make single features on the lawn.

First and foremost is the Nordmann's silver fir, broad and massive, with shining silvery leaves,—in every way a hardy, slow-growing evergreen, of noble outline and special symmetry. Though grand and impressive, it needs intelligent pruning, and for successful transplanting, a fibrous condition of roots that can be secured by frequent removal in the nursery and systematic root-pruning. The same remark applies to all silver firs, which are in many senses the finest evergreens for producing winter pictures. There is the silver fir *(Abies amabilis)*, lovely, both by name and nature, and the still finer *(Abies nobilis)*, of unsurpassed blue tints. Hudson's Bay silver fir, of the same genus, is one of the darkest, hardiest, and most dwarfed species, specially fitted for the outskirts of groups, or for dotting here and there in isolated positions. Parsons' silver fir *(Abies Parsonsii)* has wonderful leaves, always curling upward, long, and of a delicate bluish-green color. The so-called dwarf silver fir *(Abies compacta)*, an intermediate form between Hudson's Bay silver fir and Nordmann's fir, is especially noteworthy for hardiness, symmetry, and compact elegance. It should be one of the most popular of evergreens.

Then, among the larger forms, we note the Grecian silver fir, very fine and lighter-colored. The weeping silver fir is the type, perhaps, of the statuesque in the family. Intelligently pruned, it develops into a solid weeping column of dark green. But here, as with all silver firs, if we are to get a compact growth below, the leading or top shoot must be pinched off from time to time during May or June. If possible or, rather, if not incongruous with the

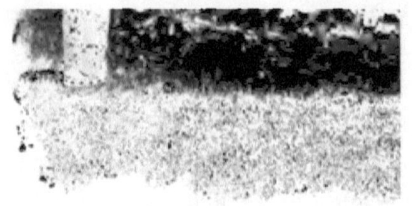

ORIENTAL SPRUCE.
(PICEA ORIENTALIS.)

remaining part of the composition, it is well to place each of these species, firs, spruces, and the like, by themselves. Spruces we used to make up the mass of the background; but then there are spruces not only adapted for this purpose, but suitable for general planting in the middle-ground, and even for the most distinguished positions as objects of special interest in the foreground. Any one looking at the dense round or hemispherical shape of the Gregory spruce, and at the taller though slow-growing columnar form of the weeping spruce, would scarcely believe that this and the common Norway spruce are so closely akin. The blue tint of the Colorado spruce (*Picea pungens*) shows capacity for varying color that is most invaluable for winter effect. Alcock's spruce, from Japan, has also lovely variegations of yellow, silver, and green, and the tiger-tail spruce (*Picea polita*), from the same country, is rigid, yellow, and characteristic, and hardy and fine in many ways.

The Oriental spruce is perhaps the most desirable of all the spruces for both winter and summer landscape. Its shining dense masses are remarkably hardy and striking. It belongs rather in the background, as somewhat larger in habit than the others. Nor should we neglect the beautiful American white spruce, hardy, dense, and richly colored. It grows more slowly than the common Norway spruce, but eventually attains sufficient size to associate it more or less with that evergreen. The most noteworthy spruces, however, for winter-landscape effects are the weeping hemlock spruce and the weeping Norway spruce. The former is a charming evergreen, graceful and picturesque, with soft curving lines. Its light color and delicate tendrils give it an almost feminine appearance. The rugged, strong outline of the weeping Norway spruce, on the other hand, offers the greatest contrast to the habit of this hemlock, and delights the eye, especially in winter. The long branches of this slow-growing evergreen droop and hug the stem in most persistent fashion, now and then curling up eccentric shoots, which afford convenient lodgment for the snow. Both these striking evergreens should occupy the middle-ground of the picture in specially effective positions. A cedar of Lebanon, where a cedar of Lebanon can be coaxed to grow, is also a prize on the winter lawn.

WEEPING NORWAY SPRUCE AND DWARF PINE.
(PICEA EXCELSA INVERTA AND PINUS STROBUS COMPACTA.)

Among the pines we find, perhaps, our most lovely and refined winter colors, but to establish pines upon the lawn is not always easy. Unless transplanted frequently in the nursery, pines develop naked roots, hard to remove with safety. The spruces and arbor vitæs act better, but silver firs and pines are, to say the least, troublesome in this respect. The most lovely pine, to me, in winter is the

Bhotan pine (*Pinus excelsa*). It presents such picturesque open masses, and the leaves are so long and delicately green that the eye dwells on its varied outlines with exceeding pleasure.

Then there is the Swiss stone pine (*P. cembra*), bluish-green, and extremely striking in winter, as well as extremely hardy. Among the dwarf pines such forms are noteworthy as the dark *mughus* and *mughus compacta*, the finely tinted light-blue dwarf white pine, and the more yellow and rounder dwarf Scotch. *Mughus uncinata* is also striking, and, although dwarf, quite erect in habit. The large-growing pines massed in the background among the other large spruces are peculiarly varied in color and form, and often very beautiful, laden with snow and ice. Dark, massive Austrian pines should have their forms displayed somewhat more prominently than the rest, while the delicate-hued and more sparsely-branched white pines should be grouped directly with the Norway spruces, for the sake of artistic breadth combined with interesting variety.

CEDAR OF LEBANON.
(CEDRUS LIBANI.)

Hemlocks also mass well in the background, their lighter colors and more graceful forms relieving the sombre character of the adjoining spruces.

In the outskirts of groups and rather in the foreground, we should find choice plants, such as the rare and exquisite golden Japanese or sun-ray pine (*Pinus Massoniana variegata*), with its rich and permanent yellow, so striking in fall and winter, and the slow-growing and extremely rare Japan parasol pine (*Sciadopitys verticillata*), a highly prized and strange-looking tree, with dark green foliage growing in distinct whorls. Nor should we forget to plant in such positions the lovely Japanese *retinosporas*, of delicate, fern-like appearance and unexcelled hardiness of habit.

BHOTAN PINE.
(PINUS EXCELSA.)

Such plants form the intermediate shadings or half tones of the picture, presenting as they do in winter the most delightful tints of brown, green, and gold. It should be remembered that the winter coloring of evergreens is very different from that of summer. In many cases, like that of the arbor vitæ, these winter tints are dull and uninviting, for which reason, in spite of the custom to the contrary, I do not much fancy their employment for winter effects. But the *retinosporas* are, if anything, more lovely in winter than in summer, especially in their mingling of brown and gold. The really golden *retinosporas* have a pure yellow color in winter, very delightful from the fresh contrast it affords to the neutral tints of the surrounding scenery.

Of like character is the bronze gold of *biota elegantissima aurea*, a Chinese golden arbor vitæ. There is a kinship in the appearance of *retinosporas* and arbor vitæs, in which the former have greatly the advantage in varied beauty; but we will do well to employ the golden bronze of the *elegantissima* arbor vitæ whenever we can give it a little favoring protection from cold, which is fortunately not needed for the *retinosporas*. There are exquisite bluish-tinted junipers, also, erect and torch-like in shape, the graceful lines and forms of which can be ill spared from any part of the lawn planted for winter effect.

The regular evergreen shrubs cannot, of course, be neglected. Rhododendron foliage is broad, massive, and shining, one of the most effective features in winter on any lawn. The mahonias, though very different in many ways, have the same general effect, and should be employed, though always with the knowledge that they will frequently winter kill, that is, become deciduous, for they *rarely* die from cold. Masses of these mahonias shine and glisten in winter, and are altogether so fine that we must have them, notwithstanding their weakness. The tree box is also rich, solid, and very attractive during the cold

MUGHO PINE.
(PINUS MUGHUS.)

months, although not always very hardy in the Northern States. It is an old plant, but merits, especially planted singly, the very highest consideration.

Cotoneaster or *Crataegus pyracantha*, the evergreen thorn, whether used for hedges or as a single plant, is always

GINKGO TREE, IRISH YEWS, AND WEEPING SOPHORA.

peculiarly beautiful in winter. Its low, dense masses of red bronze leaves, small and regularly formed, present a diversity of contour of the most pleasing character. Sometimes a large mature plant lives through many winters with its shining, bright-green color unreddened by the faintest touch of frost.

JAPAN PARASOL PINE.
(SCIADOPITYS VERTICILLATA.)

The Irish yew, in a sheltered place, is also invaluable for winter effect.

I have far from exhausted the list of evergreens suitable for our picture, but have mentioned enough to give rich and abundant color and form to a landscape otherwise dead and lifeless. We must take care not to forget, in this analysis of the constituents of charming winter effects on the lawn, to consider the many beautiful forms and even colors of naked stems and bare branches of deciduous trees. It has been already noted how finely white-stemmed birches contrast with the background of evergreens, not only in color, but in delicate variety of form.

In like manner we have effects produced by other deciduous plants standing singly or in groups by themselves, or, under certain circumstances, in the immediate neighborhood and outskirts of evergreens. What can be richer in color, for instance, than the numerous crimson shoots of the red-stemmed dogwood *(Cornus sanguinea)?* Then we may have intermixed with it, or at least planted in close neighborhood, the golden willow, contrasting yellow stems with crimson ones. The red-twigged linden has fine reddish tints in winter on every portion of its current year's growth of wood, and the golden-barked linden is useful in color as contrast to the golden willow and red-stemmed dogwood.

The trunk of the striped maple *(Acer Pennsylvanicum)* is also very beautiful in winter for its pink and green. This is not hardy everywhere in the United States, although attractive in all places where it will live. It is unnecessary to press the point on observant lovers of trees that the *forms* of deciduous plants are very attractive in

OBTUSE-LEAVED JAPANESE CYPRESS.
(RETINOSPORA OBTUSA.)

their winter guise. They look cold and poorly clad, it is true, but the broad solid tints of evergreens readily relieve this bleak effect. And how grand and exquisite they are according to the nature of the tree, whether it be oak or birch, elm or beech! Two of the finest oaks for our purpose are the over-cup and pyramidal, although of the numerous varieties none fail to be effective in their winter habit. But the over-cup oak is specially striking on account of its rugged, grotesque twigs and branches, and the pyramidal for its bold, regular form and rapid growth. Elms, too, with their intersecting Gothic lines, must not be forgotten in planting for winter; neither the cork-barked variety nor wide-reaching weeping elm.

The Japan *ginkgo* also throws out great arms or branches against a clear blue winter sky in the most eccentric manner. No less eccentric, but far more charming, are the noble masses of curled and drooping branches and twigs of the weeping beech. No tree is more picturesque in winter, and no evergreen more grand and striking. The tossing shapes and forms it assumes are myriad, and the play of color on the icicles it at times supports, is a wonder to behold. Its silhouette cut against the sky is remarkable for grace. The weeping sophora is also fine in winter, regularly curving downward, more dwarfed and less odd than the weeping beech. Both of these last-named trees merit the choicest and most conspicuous positions on the lawn, and perhaps the middle distance, a little to one side, suits their proper exhibition best. The strange, far-reaching branches of the weeping larch, especially when laden with snow, are picturesque in the extreme.

LAWN-PLANTING FOR WINTER EFFECT. 153

We must be careful always to keep open considerable stretches of turf, endeavoring rather to flank than to cross with plants the direct line of vision through to the back-

PARSONS' SILVER FIR, WEEPING NORWAY SPRUCE, AND WEEPING LARCH.

ground. It should be our object always to compose a pleasing landscape for winter by means of intelligently combined color and form, but never to forget the homely needs of particular plants in the way of shelter and congenial soil. Fifty feet square, or less, will enable one to have a lovely winter picture, provided the composer can give due consideration to each plant's physiology and possible artistic capacity, while fifty acres in the hands of even a genius, who is untutored, can hardly help producing abortive or overgrown effects at any season of the year. All this means, in short, that an artistic eye, sustained by a thorough knowledge and sympathetic management of plants, can make an inexpensive paradise of the smallest home lot even in mid-winter.

CHAPTER IX.

GARDEN FLOWERS.

THE lawn we have defined as including trees, shrubs, rocks, etc., and, above all, as specially essential, we have included mown or closely cut grass. We do not, therefore, find on the lawn a proper place set apart for flowers. They doubtless bloom here, there, and everywhere on existing trees, shrubs, and plants of all kinds. Forming a very perceptible element of our enjoyment of the lawn, they do not, however, make an actual part of our lawn composition. It is the arrangement of foliage, of trees, and shrubs, and grass that should compose and characterize the lawn. Flowers there will doubtless be everywhere, on the trees and shrubs and along the bases of masses of foliage, where the hardy herbaceous plants will complete and accentuate the charming junction of tree and shrub foliage with lawn grass.

But I believe in making a distinct and comfortable

abode for flowers—in a word, a flower garden, and an old-fashioned one, if you choose to call it so. It should be one where everything conspires to favor the growth of flowers, so that one may gather them without stint. To look only at a tree or shrub satisfies the observer, but flowers, to be enjoyed to the full, must be plucked, their fragrance inhaled, and their beauty of detail admired at leisure.

It would seem best, at this point, to explain what plants I mean to indicate as specially suited to a flower garden. They are what may be somewhat technically termed "hardy herbaceous perennial plants," herbaceous because their growth dies down during the winter and starts up the following spring, and perennial in contradistinction to annual and biennial, because they continue to live for years.

It is, of course, easy to name shrubs and bedding plants that bear plenty of flowers, and there is certainly no valid objection to planting them in the flower garden. Herbaceous plants, however, can be so arranged as to furnish bloom from March to Christmas, and an abundance of it; hence it seems to me that I am justified in recommending them, for the most part, to supply the flower garden. There need be no hard and fast rules controlling the selection, as there are many plants suited for the flower garden, such as hardy rose bushes, that we could not well do without. It is indeed the proper place in which to grow them.

The method of growing herbaceous plants differs but little from that which applies to trees, shrubs, and bedding. Well-drained, rich, and mellow soil is alike congenial to all.

As to the best method of arranging herbaceous plants and the most suitable site for a flower garden, I shall take the liberty of leaving that for consideration in a subsequent chapter. Suffice it to say that, as a rule, the flower garden should be arranged somewhere by itself, masked by trees and shrubs, so that it may not interfere with the unity, breadth, and simplicity of effect of the lawns and tree and shrub plantations. The number of the species and varieties of hardy herbaceous plants is legion. I could not in one chapter, of reasonable length, begin to discuss all that are worthy of mention. Since, however, the object of this writing is rather to suggest and stimulate to farther research than to exhaust the subject, I will content myself with describing a few of the best known and most easily obtained kinds. As one of the chief requisites of a flower garden is abundant bloom throughout the season, I purpose to consider briefly the spring, the early summer, the late summer, and the autumn flowers.

One of the greatest surprises and delights of the year is the first discovery of a wild flower in March. It should be understood, however, to prevent disappointment, that the season of blooming gets much mixed during some years. Early kinds will not appear until well-known later ones have arrived, but the general relation of the bloom will be in the main as I shall give it.

There are few plants in the border that show bloom earlier than the winter heath *(Erica herbacea carnea)*. It is an old plant, but unfortunately one that has been little used in this country. The habit is low and spreading, and the flowers appear in March with the first budding of vegetation. Red flowers hang on their branches in racemes. A lovely little plant that also comes in March during many years is the bluets *(Houstonia cærulea)*. It is common enough in the fields and woods of many localities of America, but is none the less well deserving of cultivation. In height it only reaches about four inches, and the flowers are small, light blue, pale lilac, or often almost white, showing a yellowish eye. It is a dainty flower, and does well in the front part of the border or in rock-work. *Saxifraga cordifolia* (heart-leaved saxifrage) is one of the

HEART-LEAVED SAXIFRAGE.
(SAXIFRAGA CORDIFOLIA.)

earliest of plants. Indeed, it sometimes blooms so early in March that the flowers are injured by late frosts, but to this danger all very early flowers must be more or less exposed. It is a curious-looking plant, this saxifrage, when in bloom. The thick, fleshy roots bear a cluster of large heart-shaped, thick evergreen leaves, from the centre of which arises, in early spring, a large naked stem, bearing at the top a spreading cluster of bell-shaped, rose-colored flowers. In height it is sometimes a foot.

Few plants give more delight on their first arrival in spring, and afterwards until October, than the violets, the bird's-foot violets of the United States *(Viola pedata)*. They are much prized in Europe, and should be equally valued here. The dark-green leaves are handsomely cut, and the pale or deep blue flowers, an inch across, are very abundant and showy, although only four or five inches high. The pansy bird's-foot violet *(V. pedata* var. *bicolor)* is a rare and showy variety, and bears flowers an inch and a half across, and of the deepest velvety purple. Very charming in early spring are the dwarf phloxes *(Phlox subulata)*. It is like moss, no higher than the budding grass, and has myriads of small pink flowers with darker centres. Great masses on the rocks at Central Park along the east and west drives make for visitors one of the most delightful surprises of early spring. One valuable quality of this phlox is that it will flourish on the smallest amount of soil directly on the edge of rocks. There is a fine, pure white flowering variety, *nivalis*, that also deserves general employment. *Phlox amœna* is another fine pink species that grows somewhat higher.

MOSS PINK.
(PHLOX SUBULATA.)

The hardy columbines in the season of bloom are all specially attractive. In early spring we have the Canada columbine *(Aquilegia Canadensis)*, showing abundant red and yellow flowers. This is a showy and effective plant, and should be planted in every arrangement of bedding plants. It is particularly effective on rock-work. It grows one to three feet high. Some of the anemones, or wind-flowers, come early in the spring, bearing blue and white flowers six to eight inches high, like *Caroliniana* and *nemorosa* of the United States. *A. patens* var. *Nuttalliana*, a native American plant of considerable value, is one of the largest flowered blue varied species. *Anemone Pulsatilla*, European pasque-flower, has finely cut leaves and solitary dark

EUROPEAN PASQUE-FLOWER.
(ANEMONE PULSATILLA.)

shaggy, purple flowers. *Anemone sylvestris*, snowdrop wind-flower, has pure white flowers, two inches across, and blooms in April and May, and sometimes all summer. It is only a foot high and is charming. All these species grow about eight to ten inches high. *Alyssum saxatile* (golden tuft), a close relative of rock-candy tuft, comes very early in spring, has curious gray-green leaves and quantities of bright yellow flowers. It comes from the mountains of Southern Europe, and grows about a foot high. Its low compact masses are excellent for rock-work. *Adonis vernalis* (spring adonis) is a showy early spring-flowering plant with yellow flowers two or three inches across and finely cut leaves. It comes from Europe, and grows from ten to twelve inches high.

There is a class of herbaceous plants that grow in close, low tufts that should be used throughout a mass of such plants as a kind of carpet. Dwarf phlox and alyssum are such plants, and performing this office in a still more marked degree, comes *Arenaria verna*. It is the spring sandwort, a low tufted plant, two to four inches high, with numerous white flowers in early spring. Rough usage has little effect on this plant, and a turf might be made of it that would stand much better than grass the wear and tear of passing multitudes. It would, moreover, endure unharmed almost any droughts. *Arabis alpina* (alpine-rock cress) is a spring-flowering plant about six inches high that would also make a good carpet in a group of herbaceous plants. Its small flowers are white and profuse, and there is a variegated-leaved form that is also attractive. The foliage of the ajugas is also suited for the carpet effect, although some of them when in flower are nearly a foot high. The blue flowers are not nearly so valuable as the dense mat of foliage. There is one species—*reptans albu* and *rubra*—white- and red-leaved bugle—that is particularly valuable on account of its dark purple mats of leaves four to six inches high.

The aubrietias are valuable low-growing plants that bloom in early spring. There are half a dozen or more kinds having dwarf-tufted habits that more or less fit them for the carpet effect. The flowers are generally of a bluish-purple shade, except *A. Leichtlinii*, which has a bright rose-colored bloom. Aubrietias look well planted in masses among rocks. Another pretty spring-blooming plant, suitable for carpet effect, is the mouse ear *(Cerastium Bieber-*

STEMLESS GENTIAN.
(GENTIANA ACAULIS.)

steinii). It forms dense mats of bright green foliage, six to eight inches high, and is covered with white flowers in early spring. *Cerastium tomentosum* is still better suited for a carpet plant. It is a very dwarf, woolly plant, growing one to three inches high, and bearing small white flowers. The pretty stemless gentian *(Gentiana acaulis)* is an alpine plant, one to three inches high. It forms a mass of leathery leaves, and bears in early May flowers of a vase form, two inches long and blue in color, as no other flower but a gentian can be. It is admirable for rockwork, makes a good carpet, and is altogether a charming plant. A very pretty dainty plant, six to eight inches high, is the *Epimedium*, blooming in May. It is hardly, however, suited for carpet purposes. The foliage is neat, but not massive enough, and does not grow in tufts or mats. The airy clusters of purplish and yellow flowers of quaint shape also unfit it for a carpet. It should be planted among rocks or by itself, where its charms will be a little protected. Its common name is barrenwort, and it is an alpine plant.

ALPINE BARRENWORT.
(EPIMEDIUM ALPINUM.)

The best species of the genus is *macranthum*, from Japan, bearing pure white flowers. This species grows ten to fifteen inches high.

A well-known plant in May and June is *Astilbe Japonica*, incorrectly called *Spiræa Japonica*. It has interesting dark-green foliage, and quantities of upright growing spikes or clusters of creamy white flowers. It grows ten to twelve inches high, and is very attractive.

ASTILBE JAPONICA.

Corydalis nobilis is one of the finest ornamental herbaceous plants. The flowers, which appear in early spring, in large heads on stout stems, are of a rich yellow color. It disappears altogether soon after flowering. Deep sandy loam suits it, where it will not be disturbed. It comes from Siberia.

The wild pink, or Pennsylvania catchfly (*Silene Pennsylvanica*), is to be commended as a spring flower. It grows four to eight inches high, bears numerous pink flowers, and is decidedly attractive.

NOBLE FUMITORY.
(CORYDALIS NOBILIS.)

Every one has heard of the common wild English primrose (*Primula vulgaris*), which produces sulphur-colored flowers in spring. Its beauty and associations naturally make it valuable to us, although it is seldom grown. It seems to stand our winters well, and if planted in half-shaded spots along banks and moist spots will doubtless stand our summers.

Dicentra spectabilis, sometimes called *Dielytra spectabilis*, is one of the bleeding-hearts that appears in spring and blooms on into early summer. It is one of the best-known and most charming of herbaceous plants, with graceful, drooping racemes of heart-shaped flowers of rosy crimson and silvery white. It grows one to two feet high, and comes from Northern China. There are some pretty spring-blooming irises,—*cristata*, the crested dwarf iris, is one of them. It is a little native plant growing only three to six inches high, with large pale-blue flowers. Then there is *Iris pumila*, a little taller, six to nine inches high, with yellow, white, and blue flowers in early spring. *Iris verna* (vernal iris) is another dwarf species, three to eight inches high, from the South, with violet-blue flowers in May. It is very fragrant, and is a rare and desirable sort. All these little spring irises are well fitted for planting in rock-work. The spring meadow saffron (*Bulbocodium vernum*) is perhaps the earliest-flowering hardy bulb, and bears purple

BLEEDING HEART.
(DICENTRA SPECTABILIS.)

crocus-like flowers in March and April. Like all early-flowering kinds, this bulb should be set out in the autumn. *Anemone Hepatica*, or *Hepatica triloba* (liver-leaf), is another early-blooming plant, that bears beautiful deep-blue flowers. It does particularly well in shaded rock-work and half-shaded spots in the border. It is hardy and enduring, and well deserves employment.

The genus narcissus has been for a long time well known and useful for spring blooming. The bulbs should be set out in fall, from September to December. Usually they will bloom satisfactorily for many years, in which case it will not, of course, be necessary for a long time to lift, divide, and re-set them. The cheaper sorts may be used effectively for naturalizing among shrubs, or planting in the grass, where they succeed better uncultivated than most other bulbs, on account of their hardy, enduring nature. There is something specially attractive in the use of bulbs in this fashion, and particularly the early daffodils, "golden daffodils," as Wordsworth says, "tossing their heads in sprightly dance," but after all, flowers really satisfy us better, and do better in the garden, where we can coax and tend them a little. Even the hardy daffodil in the sunny garden border, carefully tended, grows better, and certainly looks well associated with congenial friends. It is, moreover, not only the old and common kinds which we may establish, but a great variety of other kinds no less beautiful, and distinct

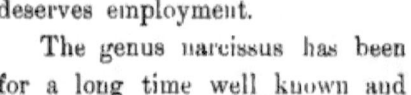

SPRING MEADOW SAFFRON.
(BULBOCODIUM VERNUM.)

from the common one. They will prolong the season of bloom, and give a fine variety of form. Of the bolder kinds suited for striking effects we should name *Narcissus maximus*, *N. incomparabilis* and its forms, *N. poeticus* and its varieties (they succeed each other in blooming), *N. odorus* (the larger jonquil), *N. bicolor* and the form nearly allied to it, *N. cernuus*. Not a few others would do, only avoiding the Italian kinds and the alpine and Spanish species.

Of the types named, I will describe *maximus*, or trumpet *maximus*, as large, bright yellow, single, and very early; *incomparabilis*, single orange phœnix, with large primrose-colored flowers having a sulphur crown; there is another *incomparabilis* which called butter and eggs, bearing flowers double, yellow, or sulphur with a

POET'S NARCISSUS.
(NARCISSUS POETICUS.)

TRUMPET MAJOR.
(NARCISSUS MAJOR.)

crimson nectary; *poeticus* (poet's narcissus or pheasant's eye), flowers pure white with distinct red crown; *odorus* (campernelle or fragrant jonquil), golden-yellow flowers; *bicolor*, very large white flowers, with golden-yellow perianth; and *pseudo-narcissus* (daffodil or daffodowndilly).

GARDEN FLOWERS.

A well-known and valued bulb for spring effect is the crocus. Members of this genus bloom in the fall, but I shall only speak of the spring-flowering kinds.

They come so early in the spring, out of the very snow sometimes, that they are a surprise and delight to us. When the crocuses appear, spring seems to be actually at hand. They are white, purple, and yellow, but to me the yellow is most pleasing. There are several species in use in gardens, but they are variable and not to be depended on, so that it is as well to buy the mixed sorts and let them come up white, yellow, or purple, as they will. They should be planted two or three inches deep and close together, even an inch or two apart, to get their best effect. Every three or four years they require to be lifted and reset. They are charming planted in the growing grass of greensward, but they run out in a few years, having a much less robust constitution than the daffodils, which often linger here and there in grass for many years. The best so-called

DAFFODIL.
(NARCISSUS PSEUDO-NARCISSUS.)

FRAGRANT JONQUIL.
(NARCISSUS ODORUS.)

species are *Crocus Susianus*, yellow and brown; *C. vernus*, blue, purple, and white; *C. versicolor*, white, lilac, purple,

CROCUS VERNUS.

and gray-striped. Hyacinths look well in the flower garden during the spring, and last for years often, if well manured and cultivated. The species, *H. orientalis*, is the parent of the innumerable and brilliant varieties so largely imported from Holland to meet the demand for it in this country. Holland, we may say, furnishes bulbs for the world, whether tulips, crocuses, or hyacinths, or for that matter lilies too. There are special selections of unnamed sorts of hyacinths in different shades of blue, white, red, and yellow, made by nurserymen and seedsmen, and they may be procured in mixture or in separate colors, the mixed roots being less expensive. The different colors of hyacinths do not all bloom at one time, and for massing in mixtures, it is necessary to plant the bulbs at different depths, in order to have the display as nearly as possible simultaneous in all its variety. Blue generally comes first, and next in order, red, white, and yellow. Blues should therefore be planted deepest, say seven or eight inches, and the others propor-

WINTER ACONITES.
(ERANTHIS HYEMALIS.)

tionately shallower in their order. Usually about six inches apart is suited to their growth.

The glory of the snow, *Chionodoxa Luciliæ*, is a bulb from the mountains of Asia Minor. It grows from four to eight inches high, and in early spring is covered with spikes of the most beautiful sky-blue, white-centred flowers. Winter aconite *(Eranthis hyemalis)*, also bears beautiful bright-yellow flowers in early spring. But the earliest of all these early bulbs is the snowdrop, *Galanthus nivalis* and *G. Elwesii*, bearing large bell-shaped white flowers, which often peep out

THE SNOWDROP.
(GALANTHUS NIVALIS.)

in January. All these very early-blooming bulbs are specially attractive planted in the greensward, where their charms are relieved by the first green of spring. Yet the border in the flower garden is the most congenial after all, the place where the best flowers bloom.

Many of the irises are beautiful, but there are none more

SCARLET TURBAN LILY.
(LILIUM POMPONIUM.)

delicately and daintily beautiful than the bulbous and tuberous-rooted species. Chief among these are the golden-netted irises *(Iris reticulata)*. The flowers are deep violet-blue, netted with fine golden-yellow lines. It is early blooming, fragrant, and hardy. *Iris Iberica* (Chalcedonian iris) is a showy species with large rich purple flowers, beautifully veined, and spotted with a black spot on each petal. It blooms somewhat later than *Iris reticulata*. There is a well-known pomponian lily, *Lilium*

Pomponium, that blooms comparatively early in June. The flowers are pendulous, scarlet, and attractive. The plant comes from France and grows about three feet high. *Crucianella stylosa* is an ornamental plant, diffusively tufted with a profusion of weak, straggling, procumbent stems clothed with whorls of six or more narrow lance-shaped leaves growing about a foot high. The flowers are borne in small but handsome terminal heads, and are bright rose or pink, with long styles protruding conspicuously beyond the corollas.

CRUCIANELLA STYLOSA.

I propose now to consider some of the summer-flowering plants, the plants that commence to bloom in June or early July, and oftentimes continue in flower throughout the season. There are many, but we shall attempt to consider only a few. *Achillea tomentosa* (downy yarrow), different from most herbaceous plants, displays striking and attractive foliage, but the flowers are pretty, and of a bright-yellow color. It is only six or eight inches high. The *Aquilegias* or columbines are always quaintly beautiful, and there are none more so than the summer-blooming ones. *A. chrysantha*, the golden columbine, is probably the best, because it produces golden-yellow flowers all summer. Like all *Aquilegias*, the flowers have curious long spurs. *A. cærulea* (Rocky Mountain columbine) has charming blue and white flowers, and is only less valuable than *chrysantha* because it does not bloom all summer. Both of these columbines grow two to three feet high. *Aquilegia vulgaris* (Munstead giant) is of garden origin, robust, growing three feet high, and producing pure white flowers in abundance. *Armeria maritima*, one of the sea pinks or thrifts, bears attractive rose-colored flowers and broad foliage about a foot high.

Asperula odorata is the common woodruff of Northern Europe. It grows six to twelve inches high in dense tufts of slender stems with leaves mostly eight in a whorl, and has flat clusters of small white flowers in summer. When wilted this plant has the odor of new-mown hay. The *Campanulas* or harebells are of course well known for their dainty beauty. They are all summer-flowering, but perhaps *Campanula rotundifolia* blooms somewhat earlier than some of the others. It is a beautiful native species, with numerous deep-blue flowers. It grows only six to twelve inches high.

LILY OF THE VALLEY.

To speak of the lily of the valley in praise, or dwell on its charms, would be superfluous, for all the world knows them. The dainty bloom pushes its white bells from the sheathing leaves during the latter part of May into June.

And the no less dainty maiden's pink *(Dianthus deltoides)* comes in early summer also. It is an humble plant, six to nine inches high, and the bright-pink or white flowers, with the dark or white circle in the centre, grow out of dense tufts of grassy leaves. Then there is the sweet-william of the gardens of earlier days, *Dianthus barbatus*, with deep crimson flowers, and a height of one to two feet. Finally, there is *Dianthus plumarius*, the garden pink or the cushion pink, forming broad tufts and bearing flowers with beautifully fringed petals and a delightfully fragrant odor. It grows only six or eight inches high. *Dicentra eximia* (plumy bleeding-heart) is a plant from the Alleghany Mountains, nine to eighteen inches high, with leaves as graceful as those of a fern. The flowers are rose-colored, and appear all summer, hanging in graceful racemes. The *Dicentra spectabilis*, scarcely less beautiful, comes earlier. *Iberis corræfolia* (corris-leaved perennial candy tuft) is a beautiful dwarf evergreen shrub, with large pure white flowers.

THE MAIDEN'S PINK (DIANTHUS DELTOIDES), AND THE NIEREMBERGIA RIVULARIS.

The summer-flowering irises are also important. I mean those that bloom in early summer. The Florentine iris, or the orris root, belongs to this time. It bears large fragrant white flowers with a tinge of blue, and a bright yellow-white tinged with pink or lilac when they have been open for some days. There are generally many flowers completely covering the stem. The Siberian iris is tall with narrow leaves, and white and blue and delicate-veined flowers. *Iris Siberica*, var. *hæmatophylla*, is a very dark-leaved early flowering kind that often blooms the second and third time during the season. *Linum perenne*, the perennial flax, is attractive all summer, with its tufts of narrow foliage and its bright blue flowers, an inch or more across, which seem, on their slender stalks, semi-detached and floating.

No garden would, of course, be complete without its peonies and tall phloxes. The herbaceous peonies present every shade of white, pink, rose, red, crimson, and dark purple among their scores of varieties. Their flowers are perhaps the largest and most showy of any we are likely to plant in our garden, and make a great display at a distance. I will mention one kind because it is so unique. *Pæonia tenuifolia, fl. pl.*, is different from

HERBACEOUS PEONY.
(PÆONIA OFFICINALIS.)

all others on account of its abundant finely divided foliage, from the midst of which peer out large double brilliant dark-red flowers. The tall phloxes to be seen in gardens are usually the annual kinds, but the herbaceous kind, *P. Carolina*, bears beautiful pink-purple flowers, more than an inch across. It grows about a foot high and blooms all summer. *Phlox stellaria*, starry phlox, is a similar free-blooming summer kind of about the same height that bears white flowers.

SLENDER LEAVED PEONY.
(PÆONIA TENUIFOLIA, FL. PL.)

The bachelor's-button (*Ranunculus speciosus, fl. pl.*), grows a foot high, and displays large golden-yellow flowers, invariably double. *Silene Virginica* (fire pink) is one of the finest catchflies, and produces brilliant scarlet flowers, an inch or more in diameter, from June to August. It grows about a foot high. Statices are among the best and most desirable herbaceous plants. Their flowers are of long duration, and when cut and dried are effective for winter decoration, as they retain their color in a dried state. One of the best is *Statice latifolia*. It bears in June immense panicles of bright blue flowers, often two feet across. Its native place is Southern Russia, and it only grows about a foot high. The familiar name of this type of plant is woundwort. Meadow-rue or *Thalictrum*, bearing large panicles of flowers in summer, presents one of its best effects in *speciosum*, a fine large yellow-flowered sort

SEA LAVENDER.
(STATICE LATIFOLIA.)

with handsome leaves which grow three to five feet high. Other meadow-rues bear purple flowers, and still others white. One of these white species comes from Japan. The spiderwort (*Tradescantia Virginica*) is a native plant, valuable chiefly for its continuous production during summer of its peculiar deep violet-blue flowers. *Trollius Europæus*, European globe-flower, is a pretty plant with large lemon-colored buttercup-like flowers, one to one and a half inches across, on long stems. It grows two feet high, blooms from June to August, and comes from Arctic Europe. There is a large double orange-colored species from Japan that blooms in the spring. *Tunica saxifraga*, rock Tunica, is a delicate spreading dwarf plant that bears all summer a profusion of small rosy-white flowers. It grows six to ten inches high and is excellent as a carpet plant. *Viola cornuta*, horned violet, commences to bloom in spring and lasts all summer. It is not unlike the common violet, and its prevailing tints are blue, purple, white, and yellow. It is a valuable violet for this special quality of continuous flowering.

ROCK TUNICA.
(TUNICA SAXIFRAGA.)

Among the flowers that bloom still later in summer and even in early fall, I will mention the beautiful *Achilleas*, or yarrows or milfoils. The Egyptian yarrow has silvery fern-like foliage and yellow flowers. It grows twelve to eighteen inches high. *A. fillipendulina* is a more vigorous showy species that displays golden-yellow flowers in dense, flat corymbs and has attractive foliage. It grows two to three feet high and blooms from July to October. *A. millefolium roseum*, rose-colored milfoil, blooms all summer. The leaves are finely divided. It grows one to two feet high. *A. Ptarmica, fl. pl.*, sneezewort, is a showy species bearing pure white double flowers. It grows about a foot high.

ACHILLEA PTARMICA.

Anthemis tinctoria, the yellow chamomile, is one of the most desirable and showy hardy herbaceous plants. The flowers are golden yellow and one to two inches across. It grows from twelve to eighteen inches high and blooms from July to November. *Anthericum liliago*, St. Bernard's lily, grows one foot to one and a half foot high. The leaves are narrow-channelled, in considerable tufts. It produces lengthened racemes of pure white flowers all summer. The flowers are open and spreading. *A. Liliastrum*, St. Bruno's lily, differs from the last chiefly in producing larger flowers that are not spreading but bell-shaped. The *Asclepias*, butterfly weed, or swallow-wort, is showy and effective in masses. It comes from North America. *A. tuberosa* is one of the best. It grows one to two feet high. The

YELLOW ASPHODEL.
(ASPHODELUS LUTEUS.)

stem is branched above, and bears numerous umbels of the most brilliant orange flowers in summer.

The asphodels were always favorite plants with the ancients in the earliest days of gardening. They have

YELLOW CHAMOMILE.
(ANTHEMIS TINCTORIA.)

received deserved attention within a few years, after having been wellnigh lost to gardening. They come from Southern Europe, have fleshy bundled roots, narrow leaves, and tall, simple, or branching stems which bear a great number of white or yellow lily-like flowers. *A. luteus* is one of the best varieties. It grows two to four feet high, and has a dense, very long spike of fragrant yellow flowers which last a long time in summer. The asphodel luxuriates in rich, deep, moist soil; and the stronger-growing species are fit subjects for naturalizing in open moist woods, and by the banks of streams and pieces of water.

There are many asters, and most of them flower from September to November, and contribute largely to the beauty of the American autumn landscape. One or two species, however, bloom earlier. *A. amellus*, var. *Bessarabicus* (Russian starwort), one of the best and largest purple-flowered species, blooms in late summer and early autumn. It grows about eighteen inches high. *A. ptarmicoides* is a white-flowered species, one to two feet high, also blooming in August and September.

Baptisia australis (blue false indigo) is from the Southern States, and grows two to five feet high. The foliage is handsome, and its dark-blue lupine-like flowers hang in racemes one to two feet long. A large clump is very fine, and lasts at least two months in summer. *Callirrhoë involucrata* (crimson mallow) is one of the most showy of crimson flowers. It is spreading in habit, and bears its large flowers throughout the summer. The dainty harebells or bell-flowers *(Campanulas)* must not be forgotten. *C. Carpatica*, from the Carpathian Mountains, is one of the best. It is a handsome tufted plant about nine inches high. The leaves are heart-shaped, and toothed on the margin, and the flowers, growing on long slender stalks, are large, broadly bell-shaped, and bright-blue. It flowers from June to September. *C. Carpatica* has also a beautiful pure white variety. *Cassia Marylandica* (American senna), growing three to four feet high, is a native plant well worthy of a place in the garden, where it should have abundant room, as it forms very large and showy clumps. The light-green foliage is attractive, and the bright, yellow, oddly shaped flowers grow in abundant clusters throughout July and August. Most of the clematises are climbers, but there are bush forms that make very attractive herbaceous plants.

AMERICAN SENNA.
(CASSIA MARYLANDICA.)

C. Davidiana bears large clusters of fragrant blue hyacinth-like flowers; grows three feet high, and is quite erect in habit. It blooms a long time during summer. *C. integrifolia* is another erect species, one to two feet high, with blue, very fragrant, solitary, nodding flowers one to two inches across, and blooming in July and August. *C. recta* (upright virgin's bower) is an old, well-known species, two to four feet high, with numerous white summer flowers.

When any one speaks of larkspurs, my memory always carries me back to a charming old flower-garden that I knew long ago in an old New England town. The larkspurs, or *Delphiniums*, make a numerous group, clearly marked and not easily confounded with either of their nearest relatives, the columbines, or monk's-hoods. A large number of rather variable forms are comprised among them. Their style of growth is bold and striking, and blue and purple, purplish-red, and white comprise the sum of their colors. These colors, however, are so bright in most species and varieties that when considered along with the noble plume-like mode of flowering some astonishment may be fairly expressed that they have received so little employment.

Delphinium elatum, tall larkspur, grows five to six feet high with strong, erect stems and five-lobed leaves.

GAS PLANT.
(DICTAMNUS FRAXINELLA.)

The flowers are blue, and appear in July, August, and September. This is one of the oldest species, a native of Siberia, and is very striking and handsome. *Delphinium formosum*, beautiful larkspur, however, is finer. It grows only three to four feet high, with stems of medium strength and straggling, and produces graceful racemes of bright gentian-blue flowers. It blooms freely from June to September. The flowers are often an inch across. There are some fine improved double-flowering varieties of *D. grandiflorum*. They are of all shades of blue, with large very double flowers on spikes often two feet long. These plants grow four to five feet high, and flower throughout the summer and fall.

Dictamnus fraxinella (gas-plant) grows from one to two

feet high, bears spikes of curiously shaped, showy flowers in summer. The plant on a warm evening gives off a gas so abundantly that a lighted match applied to the flower ignites it and produces a bright flash. *Digitalis purpurea* (common foxglove) is a well-known and very ornamental plant. The quaintly shaped flower and color, varying from white to dark purple, combine to produce this excellent effect. It grows three to five feet high. *Dracocephalum Ruyschianum* (hyssop-leaved dragon's-head) is from Europe, and grows from twelve to eighteen inches high. It is very showy in summer, bearing purplish-blue flowers in closely whorled spikes an inch long. This is the best of the species of dragon's-heads.

GAILLARDIA GRANDIFLORA.

Eryngium alpinum is a very pretty plant two feet high, looking something like the thistles at first sight, owing to the peculiar character of the leaves surrounding the usually dense, compact, bluntly spike-like heads of flowers. It blooms in July and August. *Euphorbia corollata* (flowering spurge) is a tall branching plant two to three feet high, bearing pure white flowers in heads all through July and as late as October. The *Gaillardias* (especially *Gaillardia grandiflora*) are a fine, showy family from the Western States that have been much improved recently. *Gaillardia grandiflora* bears bright yellow and red flowers on stout, erect stems one foot high. They continue in bloom all through July, August, and September.

GERANIUM SANGUINEUM.

Geranium sanguineum, blood-red geranium, is from Great Britain and grows one to two feet high, with spreading, almost trailing, and much intertwined stems—forming in well developed plants finely rounded masses about two feet wide. The leaves are roundish and much and deeply divided. The flowers, one and a half inches across, grow singly on long, slender stalks, are large, dark red or purple, and appear in greater or less profusion throughout summer and autumn.

Gillenia trifoliata, Bowman's root, is a native plant twelve to eighteen inches high. The reddish stems bear handsomely-cut foliage and at the top a loose open head of white flowers, sometimes tinged with rose. The branches of the head of flowers are so slender that the long-petaled flowers look light, floating, and very graceful.

BOWMAN'S ROOT.
(GILLENIA TRIFOLIATA.)

Funkia subcordata is an early plantain lily and so is *F. ovata*, both blooming in midsummer. Its flowers grow in racemes or clusters and are white and very fragrant. The leaves of these plantain lilies are large and showy, egg-shaped, and slightly heart-shaped at the base, and the flower stems rise about eighteen inches high. *Gypsophila paniculata* comes from the Caucasus and grows about three feet high in a mass, as broad as tall, of thread-like stems bearing abundant small white flowers. It is a very graceful and delicate plant, blooming from midsummer to early autumn.

PLANTAIN LILY.
(FUNKIA OVATA.)

The little *Helenium Hoopesii* is a neat Western plant twelve to fifteen inches high, that bears large orange-yellow flowers, which continue blooming a long time in summer. *Hemerocallis flava*, day lily, is a beautiful plant that bears sweet-scented lemon-yellow flowers on stems two and a half feet high. It blooms in midsummer.

One of the finest old garden flowers is the hollyhock with cup- or rosette-shaped flowers studded along stems six or eight feet high. The colors vary from white to red, dark purple, and bright yellow. The double varieties are much prized, but I confess to a special liking for the old single cup- or wineglass-shaped kinds. There are some shades of these old kinds that are also very attractive, ruby- or wine-colored and pure white. The growth of a renewed regard for the simple and often lovely old forms of single flowering plants is a promising sign in horticulture. Heresy though it may seem to suggest it, I am sometimes inclined to think the double flower essentially a monstrosity. Strong plants of hollyhocks will only bloom the second year after planting.

GERMAN IRIS.
(IRIS GERMANICA.)

The irises are perhaps the most beautiful of the flowers of summer. Of those that flower in summer the German iris should be named first, being first in order of bloom. The ordinary form has violet-blue, very large flowers, but by hybridization fine varieties with a great range of beautiful combinations of color have been secured. The blue changes into purple and bronze and rose and yellow and white. Some of these varieties grow three feet high and have flowers four inches across. The gem of all the irises, however, is *Iris Kæmpferi* from Japan, growing three to four feet high. The flower is like some great orchid of the quaintest form and differs from any of the ordinary kinds of iris, being specially broad and flat. These flowers are both single and double and display the greatest variety of color from the purest white to the darkest shades of royal purple, through pinks and blues, with gold and other markings. The introduction of many of the finest of these kinds from Japan we owe to Mr. Thomas Hogg.

LILIUM AURATUM.

Of no less value than the summer-blooming irises are the

lilies of July and August. The finest of these is, perhaps, *Lilium auratum*. It is a grand lily with white flowers, spotted with maroon and a gold band through the centre of each petal. It is sometimes a little difficult to grow. *L. Batemanniæ* is also a beautiful summer lily from Japan, with flowers of a clear orange-apricot color, unspotted. *L. speciosum* is another favorite Japanese lily of easy growth and general adaptability. There is a beautiful white form and also a white tinged and spotted with rose. One of the best native species is *Lilium superbum*, Turk's-cap lily, with flowers of a bright orange, marked with purple spots and beautifully recurved. This kind is very hardy and tenacious of life, and is particularly effective and successful planted among rhododendrons and other similar shrubs.

LILIUM SPECIOSUM.

TURK'S-CAP LILY.
(LILIUM SUPERBUM.)

The tiger lily, *L. tigrinum*, is very showy and stays in bloom a long time during summer. There is a grand variety of this tiger lily *(tigrinum splendens)* that has tall stems and fiery scarlet flowers. *Lilium Canadense* is a showy summer blooming species, with nodding yellow or orange flowers spotted with brown. There is also a deep-red variety of *Canadense*. *Lilium pardalinum*, leopard lily, is a summer-blooming species bearing numerous large orange-scarlet flowers. It is one of the best and easiest grown of the Pacific-coast species. *Lilium Pyrenaicum*, yellow-turban lily, is a fine showy species with yellow flowers spotted with black. Most, if not all of these lilies are easy to cultivate, and simply require good garden soil.

BUTTON SNAKEROOT.
(LIATRIS SPICATA.)

The *Liatris*, blazing-star, or gay-feather, is a genus of very showy plants from the Western and Southern States. They have tuberous roots, straight stems two to five feet high, and generally very narrow leaves, the upper part of the stem being crowded with flowers that form a long, dense spike of some shade of purple. *L. pycnostachya*, Kansas gay-feather, comes from the prairies of the far West, and grows five feet high, with a very dense spike of flowers ten to twenty inches long. It flowers in summer later than *Liatris spicata*.

Lychnis Chalcedonica, scarlet lychnis, or Maltese cross, comes from Russia, and grows two to three feet high. This is one of the oldest as well as one of the most brilliant of hardy garden plants. It has been neglected for much less showy summer flowers.

DOUBLE SCARLET LYCHNIS.
(LYCHNIS CHALCEDONICA, FL. PL.)

Lythrum Salicaria, purple loosestrife, is a beautiful plant. It grows about three or four feet high during July,

August, and September, with numerous square, stout, woody stems branching a little at the top, and terminating in long spikes of rosy purple flowers. *L. Viscaria splendens*, German catchfly, is a dense tufted species twelve to fifteen inches high, with brilliant scarlet flowers in summer. *Monarda didyma*, bee balm, grows about three feet high, with erect stems clothed with large egg-shaped leaves. The flowers are in close head-like whorls at the extremity of the stem, and are deep red,

PURPLE LOOSESTRIFE.
(LYTHRUM SALICARIA.)

appearing in June or July, and lasting a couple of months. It is sometimes called the Oswego tea, and comes from North America. One of the most showy and interesting flowers that bloom all summer is the evening primrose. Many bloom for a very long time, and have unusually large flowers of striking and attractive appearance, and are besides pleasantly fragrant. *Œnothera Missouriensis* is perhaps the most showy of the group. The plant produces many prostrate stems, branching freely about a foot high. The leaves are large and lance-shaped, and the flowers are very large, several inches across, and bright yellow. It grows luxuriantly in warm, sunny aspects and light rich soil, but in soil that is not exactly favorable it soon dies off and needs to be replanted every year or two, like an annual or biennial.

Opuntia Rafinesquii, Western prickly pear, forms curious broad mats six to ten inches high. It is a hardy cactus, with round, very spiny stems, and yellowish flowers, often with a reddish centre. It blooms in summer, and is excellent for rockwork. Among the best garden flowers of summer are the poppies, I mean the hardy herbaceous poppies, not the annuals, which are also very pretty. The hardy type of these showy poppies is the Oriental poppy *(Papaver orientale)*, of which there exist several showy varieties, such as *P. bracteatum*, etc. *P. bracteatum*, great scarlet poppy, is a splendid tall-growing species, producing dense rounded masses of long leaves roughish to the touch above and below. The flower stems are almost leafless, very rough and shaggy, and three or four feet high, supporting each an enormously large bright orange-scarlet flower marked, at the base of petals and sepals, with a large intense dark crimson spot. It is a native of Siberia. Other kinds come from Greece and the Pyrenees. *Papaver nudicaule* var. *croceum*, Iceland poppy, is an entirely different plant from the last. It is a pretty dwarf-growing plant, with bright saffron-colored flowers growing on stems one foot high. It is excellent for rock-work.

PURPLE FLOWERING RASPBERRY.
(RUBUS ODORATUS.)

Rubus odoratus, purple flowering raspberry, is an old well-known plant of the highest excellence. Its large massive foliage is effective, and it grows in the shade and in the most unpropitious places. The flowers are an inch or more in diameter, and a deep purple.

Pentstemon cobæa is an early variety blooming in summer and also *Pentstemon barbatus*, var. *Torreyi*. It is somewhat rare. The foxglove-like flowers are two inches or more long in a spike of purple striped with white. *Petalostemon decumbens* is one of the prettiest prostrate plants with stems a foot long, on the ends of which are borne dense spikes of deep violet-purple flowers. It commences to bloom in summer and lasts till frost. *Platycodon grandiflorum*, large bell-flower, is the same as *Wahlenbergia* and *Campanula grandiflora*. It is the largest of all the bell flowers. The buds, before opening, become inflated like a balloon. The flower is a shallow bell, two inches or more across and deep blue. It blooms all summer and is very attractive. *Salvia pratensis*, meadow-sage, is twelve to eighteen inches high, comes from Europe, and bears long spikes of rich blue flowers all summer. *Scabiosa Caucasica* is a handsome plant only a foot high. It grows vigorously and bears freely beautiful soft lilac flowers, that, when cut, last a long time in water.

PENTSTEMON BARBATUS.
(VAR. TORREYI.)

LARGE BELLFLOWER.
(PLATYCODON GRANDIFLORUM.)

There are several herbaceous spireas that merit well a place in the flower-garden. *Spiræa Filipendula, fl. pl.*

dropwort, grows three feet high, has fern-like foliage and numerous double white flowers in summer. It is an old

MEADOW SWEET.
(SPIRÆA ULMARIA.)

and favorite plant. Then there is the red flowering and fragrant *S. lobata* or *venusta*, queen of the prairies, and meadow-sweet, *S. Ulmaria*, from Great Britain and Northern Europe and Siberia, with fragrant white flowers and from three to four feet high, loving moist places and water-courses. There is a pretty speedwell blooming long in the summer-time. It is *Veronica amethystina*, a better kind than *gentianoides*, twelve to eighteen inches high, and bearing showy amethyst-blue flowers in pyramidal clusters. *V. longifolia*, var. *subsessilis*, is, however, the best of the speedwells, bearing a larger flower-spike and larger individual flowers of a brilliant amethystine blue, which contrast finely with the rich green foliage. It is one of the Japanese acquisitions. *Yucca filamentosa* belongs to the summer season, with its tall spikes of bell-like flowers and strange tropical-looking leaves suited for rockwork. This plant is hardly an herbaceous plant, and yet it seems to belong here rather than among shrubs on account of the appearance of the great spikes of flowers.

GENTIAN LEAVED SPEEDWELL.
(VERONICA GENTIANOIDES.)

We come now to the fall-blooming, hardy, herbaceous plants, which give us so much enjoyment during the decadence of the plant-life of the year. Their colors supplement and perfect, if they do not enliven, the charming tones of "the melancholy days," and as long as they last we seem to have about us still a remnant of the special loveliness of summer. The autumn monk's-hood, *Aconitum autumnale*, is one of the best, with dark-blue flowers on stems three feet high, lasting a long time in perfection. It associates itself well with *Anemone Japonica*, and bears bold racemes of dark-blue flowers, is very robust, and has large, deeply cut leaves, and is a native of China and Japan.

The best-known and appreciated, perhaps, of autumn flowers are the asters, starworts, or Michaelmas daisies. In this country we know the New England aster the best, *A. Novæ-Angliæ*. The large violet-purple flowers appear in great profusion along our roadsides. Every park and flower border should have them. They grow four or five feet high. *A. longifolius*, var. *formosus*, is more showy and grows in the form of pyramidal bushes completely clothed with bright rose-colored flowers blooming all the fall until frost. *A. Shortii* is a tall-growing species and bears in fall large bright-blue flower-heads. Chrysanthemums generally bloom late, on the edge of winter, but there are some kinds that come earlier in autumn. Among these are *lacustre* and *maximum*, much alike, with large flowers three or four inches across. The first grows four to five feet high and likes moist soil, while *maximum* is of a dwarf habit, only one foot high.

There are few more showy and satisfactory plants during summer and early fall than *Coreopsis lanceolata* often mistaken for *grandiflora*. Its large lemon-yellow flowers bloom very freely on long stems two to three feet high. *Gentiana Andrewsii*, closed gentian, is a pretty, late-flowering species with fine blue flowers an inch long. It likes a good garden soil, especially if it be sandy and moist. Some of the sunflowers bloom late in fall, notably *Helianthus Maximiliani* which grows six to eight feet high. It is very free-flowering and large-growing, and should have plenty of room. It comes from Texas. The finest sunflower is perhaps *H. orgyalis*, graceful sunflower, also hailing from Texas. It grows six to ten feet high, has great flowers three or four inches in diameter, and has narrow leaves that give it a very graceful habit. The sunflower is splendid in inflorescence, but coarse in general effect, and should therefore be planted somewhat in the background or in the midst of large shrubbery. Standing alone it suggests a coarse, greedy plant that seems inclined to seize upon and exhaust all the ground around it without regard to the rights of other plants.

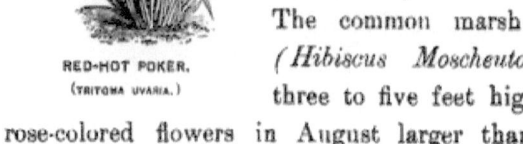
RED-HOT POKER.
(TRITOMA UVARIA.)

Hemerocallis Thunbergii is a fine late-blooming day-lily that bears yellow sweet-scented flowers on stems four feet high. One of the most splendid of fall blooming herbaceous plants is the rose-mallow. The common marsh rose-mallow (*Hibiscus Moscheutos*), growing three to five feet high, with light rose-colored flowers in August larger than hollyhocks, and continuing long in bloom, is the best known. *Hi-*

GARDEN FLOWERS. 193

biscus Californicus is, however, the largest, growing five feet high, and bearing white flowers four to six inches across, with purple centres. Among the best fall plants, especially when mixed with grasses, such as the *Arundo*, etc., are *Kniphofias* or *Tritomas*, the red-hot poker plant. Like the *Arundo*, it is better, although it sometimes winters well, to take it up and winter it in a cellar.

It blooms splendidly in autumn until frost. There is no more strange and intensely colored flower than that borne by this plant. It is like flame partially at white heat. *Tritoma aloides*, often called *Uvaria*, is a well-known kind that grows three or four feet high. There is a variety, *grandiflora*, that grows five feet high, and there

CARDINAL FLOWER.
(LOBELIA CARDINALIS.)

is also a smaller species, *corallina*, that grows only eighteen inches to two feet, and bears bright coral-red flowers.

The *Lathyrus latifolius*, everlasting pea, is an unjustly neglected plant, looking well trailed over bushes or on the ground, where its pretty rose-colored flowers last nearly all summer. There is also a pure white variety. Most of the everlasting peas have large roots, and if left undisturbed improve with age. *Lobelia cardinalis*, the cardinal flower of New England woods and waters, displays one of the brightest scarlets among herbaceous plants. It grows three to four feet high, and is easily cultivated. *Malva Alcea*, garden mallow, is a rosy-purple flowering plant that blooms in late summer. It grows two to three feet high, and has flowers two inches across.

M. moschata alba is a similar species, with pure white flowers. *Œnothera speciosa*, a late-blooming, evening primrose, with large, fragrant flowers, the white petals of which become rosy purple when fading. The garden phloxes, derived from *Phlox paniculata*, *P. maculata*, etc., have been much hybridized and crossed. The height varies from one to four feet, the foliage from narrow and shining to broad and dull. The flowers grow in a broad, pyramidal head, often six inches across, and continue in bloom in late summer and autumn for two or three months. There are colors, shades, and markings innumerable. Among the self-colored —*i. e.*, all of one color, we find pure white, cream, salmon, rose, lilac, carmine, purple, violet, and crimson. In some varieties two colors combine, either beautifully shaded, or with a distinct centre of one color and the rest of the flower of another. There are also beautifully striped varieties. This is truly a magnificent group of flowering plants, and should be planted among deciduous shrubs or among other large herbaceous plants where there will be other foliage to support and mask the lower portion of the phloxes.

LEADWORT.
(PLUMBAGO LARPENTÆ.)

Plumbago Larpenta is a beautiful blue-flowering plant of a dense spreading habit, six to ten inches in height. The flowers are in terminal clusters, fine bright blue at first, but changing afterwards to deep violet. They appear in August, September, and October. *Pyrethrum uliginosum*, giant daisy, is a fine, effective, fall-blooming plant, growing five feet high, and bearing large white flowers with yellow centres. *Rudbeckia maxima*,

STONE CROP.
(SEDUM ACRE.)

large cone-flower, is also a striking plant four to six feet high, with large glaucous leaves and bright yellow flowers with brown centres. The *Sedums*, live-for-evers, are excellent plants for poor, shallow soil, and especially for rockwork. *Sedum acre*, the common stone-crop, is one of the best, as it is low-spreading and moss-like. It is particularly good for carpeting, and displays numerous yellow flowers in summer.

There are two excellent Japanese stone-crops or *Sedums* that grow in large tufts, with thick glaucous leaves and rosy-purple flowers in clusters. They bloom in late fall. The two species are *Sieboldii*, *spectabile* or *Fabaria*, of which the last is the larger

SEDUM SPECTABILE.

and perhaps more showy. *Senecio Japonica*, a little-known groundsel, belongs to the same family as the ragweed, one of the most extensive in point of species to be found among plants, having, it is said, nearly a thousand different kinds known to botanists.

Senecio Japonica is one of the handsomest members of the family. It is of striking habit, grows five feet high, with leaves nearly a foot across, divided into nearly a dozen divisions. The flower-heads are about three inches across with the narrow outer florets of a rich orange color. It is a moisture-loving plant, and should be grown in rich, moderately stiff, loam.

The *Silphiums* are large-growing coarse plants, with sunflower-like blossoms, in summer requiring places in the background with plenty of room. *S. laciniatum* is the largest and most showy of the family. Dr. Asa Gray writes of this plant: " On the wide, open prairies the leaves are *said* to present their edges uniformly north and south, whence it is called the compass-plant." The *Solidagos*, golden-rods, present one of the most characteristic and familiar flowers of the United States, and should be planted in clumps like the *Silphiums* where their graceful habit and masses of yellow flowers will display their beauty effectively. In the eyes of most they are weeds, but in cer-

COMPASS PLANT.
(SILPHIUM LACINIATUM.)

tain parts of the flower garden few more striking plants can be set out for autumnal effect. The species *rigida*, *Shortii*, and *Canadensis* are among the best, the last growing fully five feet higher.

Stokesia cyanea, from the Southern States, is one of the rarest and handsomest of native plants. The flower-heads, three or four inches across on strong plants, are a fine sky-blue, somewhat like a large China aster. It blooms till frost. *Vernonia Noveboracensis*, New York

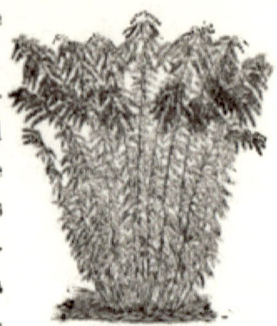

GOLDEN-ROD.
(SOLIDAGO CANADENSIS.)

iron-weed, grows two to six feet high, with dark-purple clusters of flowers at the end of straight stems. It should also be given plenty of room and kept rather in the background.

There are of course plants suited for carpeting portions of the flower garden and rock garden that are not used for their flowers, which are generally insignificant. Such are most of the *Sempervivums*, or house-leeks. There is *S. arachnoideum*, cobweb house-leek, an alpine plant, with its small rosettes covered with cobwebby hairs; *tectorum*, the common house-leek, and, one of the finest and largest of all, *S. calcareum*. The last named has regular bluish leaves tipped each with a purple spine.

NEW YORK IRON-WEED.
(VERNONIA NOVEBORACENSIS.)

Before closing this brief list of hardy herbaceous perennials I must refer to the Christmas roses, *Helleborus niger*,

CHRISTMAS ROSE.
(HELLEBORUS NIGER.)

which I cannot exactly term autumn flowers. They bloom so late that, by using a frame over them and thus securing a little protection, their beautiful white flowers may be had at Christmas. They should be planted in a shady position and moist soil, as they are impatient of dry weather. *H. niger altifolius* is one of the best varieties, with pinkish white flowers and the characteristic dark-green foliage.

COBWEB HOUSE-LEEK.
(SEMPERVIVUM ARACHNOIDEUM.)

The magnificent Japanese and Chinese chrysanthemums should be given liberal space, but my excuse for not considering them is their lack of hardiness. They may live and thrive with some protection, but there is no certainty. The proper way to grow them is to cultivate strong plants in pots and set them out in early fall, just before they bloom, with the expectation of lifting them when the flowers have gone.

Colchicum autumnale, common meadow-saffron, is known as the autumn crocus, and is one of the latest flowers to appear in our beds and borders out-of-doors. The flowers appear alone without leaves, and consist of six lance-shaped somewhat spreading petals, rosy purple in color, and supported only an inch or two above ground. The leaves begin to grow after the flowers cease, and reach their fullest development the following spring and early summer. They are lance-shaped, dark olive-green, and about nine to twelve inches long.

AUTUMN CROCUS. (COLCHICUM AUTUMNALE.)

SINGLE DAHLIAS.

The dahlias constitute a well-known class of late flowering-plants, and present a rich variety of color at a season when flowers are scarce. Their forms, however, are stiff and artificial looking, and the more they are "perfected" by cultivation the stiffer they seem to become.

These objections, however, do not apply to the single dahlias, that have been deservedly increasing in reputation of late. Their colors are quite varied and their single petals graceful.

Notwithstanding the great beauty of many double flowers. there is much to be said in favor of the more humble single-blooming kinds.

The employment of herbaceous plants in the woods or in grass is a charming method of displaying their most characteristic beauties; and for natural effects in connection with rockwork very many varieties are invaluable. Within the limits of the garden, however, and in the soil that can be there readily prepared, hardy herbaceous plants will thrive and grow as nowhere else. It may be somewhat less natural, and perhaps less artistic, but it is human, and it suits the flowers. I believe that the suggestion of any diagram arrangement of herbaceous plants will be hardly profitable. One would as easily suggest an arrangement for a bouquet of flowers. It should be irregular, and so disposed as to prevent one plant from obscuring the beauties of the others. The large ones should come, as a rule, somewhere at the back, and the next size nearer the front, and so on to the smallest. It is simple enough. A knowledge of the habits of the plants and good natural taste will do the work well if the above general rule is followed. These herbaceous plants may be planted effectively on the lawn in connection or in front of the shrubberies. First trees, then shrubs, then herbaceous plants or wild flowers, and finally grass. This is the natural arrangement of such lawn plantations.

CHAPTER X.

GRANDMOTHER'S GARDEN.

URING early boyhood, I paid long visits at the home of a dear old grandmother, in one of the most thoroughly crystallized towns of New England. Grandmother was a Quaker of the old school, and a pillar of the meeting, consequently everything about her was of the approved old-time sort. The garden, certainly, was no exception to the rule. I think I see now, the sober, dignified Quaker ladies, attired in suitable dove-color, pacing the garden walks or daintily plucking flowers. Surely finer flowers never grew than were reared in that garden, for the maintenance it received was exquisite. What sunny hours we children spent in it. And it was truly a charming spot, though something must be allowed for the glamour of boyish freshness and spirits. I feel, indeed, after seeing all the modern inventions, that I could cheerfully forego

the most blazing effects that we behold nowadays on expensive lawns, for the privilege of enjoying once more the old garden behind grandmother's house. I wish you could see the quaint old place as I recall it after the lapse of many years. It was, I confess, a somewhat formal and prim affair; but there was nothing commonplace or vulgar about it, as in the baser sort of what is now called ribbon gardening. On the contrary, there was a distinct flavor of individuality in the character of its appearance. The designer, being either a practical housewife, or inspired by one, had thought of many things besides mere ornament, and even the ornament had a distinct difference, which gave this garden a special suggestiveness of its own.

The paths were laid out with entire regularity, and marked with long rows or borders of dwarf box; but there the regularity and sameness ceased, unless we count as regular the scrupulously kept gravel of the walks, bedded with white pebbles. Such a garden naturally had its grape-vine, trained on some suitable supports, which, in this case, happened to be the stable wall. The next-door neighbor, I remember, had an arbor for his grape-vines, that began, as it seemed, nowhere in particular, and ended twenty feet off with the most delightful neglect of any why or wherefore, except that it existed for the grape-vine; that was evidently enough for Deacon Jones. Nowadays such an arbor must have done duty alike as a place for seats, for a promenade, and also for the display of architectural ornament in the Queen Anne style. Not that such a triple performance of duty is not proper enough, but only it was not the way of gardens of those earlier days.

For the economies of the house, there were all sorts of fragrant herbs, such as thyme, sweet-marjory, sage, mint, and half a dozen other sweet-smelling and savory plants, that were on this account, however, none the less attractive as ornaments of the garden. They were not only delightful in themselves, but delightful because they reminded us of grandmother's wonderful store-closet, from which issued so many good things.

GARDEN PINK.
(DIANTHUS PLUMARIUS.)

But grandmother's garden was, before all things, a productive flower garden. Unlike modern gardens, created for external show alone, it was a real storehouse of color and odor, out of which one could, day after day, gather rich treasures, and yet leave its beauty apparently undimmed. Everybody about the house, boys included, was welcome to pluck a flower occasionally without let or hindrance. The flowers, indeed, seemed actually to enjoy being plucked. They were not, of course, specially rare, and yet I am sorry to say that it might be difficult to find some of them nowadays. Their simple charms have, in fact, been almost entirely obscured by the glittering novelties of the modern horticultural world. For instance, there were those rich old damask roses. They are seldom if ever seen now; and yet what

SWEET-WILLIAM.
(DIANTHUS BARBATUS.)

masses of them there were in grandmother's garden, and how well I remember their rich color, and the delightful odor they exhaled when the dew was resting on their petals. Where shall we find now such beds of sweet-scented pinks,—not carnations, but real hardy pinks,—and such sweet-williams? In few places; for they are out of fashion now. Tall clusters of phloxes stood here and there. Blue larkspurs, tall, quaint, and lovely, nodded above carpets of portulaca vine, studded with scarlet flowers. Broad patches of the gorgeous herbaceous peony were striking in effect, close by the straggling foliage and flowers of the sweet-pea. Great hollyhocks were there, too, with richly colored single petals, the pure outlines and decorative appearance of which fail not to charm the eye even now, amid the multitudinous resources of the modern gardener.

FALL LARKSPUR.
(DELPHINIUM ELATUM.)

SINGLE HOLLYHOCKS.

Snowdrops, crocuses, and other bulbs used to spring up as if by magic, year after year, in secluded spots of grandmother's garden. Evidently no definite arrangement had been applied to any of these plants, but somehow they were seen to be greatly to the advantage of the general effect. All stood together, just as they happened to come, behind the borders of box, in the rich, weedless brown earth. How fresh that brown earth smelled as it was dug up in early spring! Of other climbers than the grape-vine there were few. Wistarias, clematises, and the long list of similar plants of the present day were little used then. Filling their place in their own attractive way, were delicate morning-glories and graceful cypress vines, trained with some formality and with almost reverential care.

These reminiscences may and should have a distinct purpose and effect on present landscape gardening undertakings. Let our circumstances and intentions be what they may, we can certainly build up for ourselves once more some genuine development of these quaint old garden recollections. We can, I think, do it all the better if we are poor and have only a half acre or a scant 25 x 100-foot lot.

In that case we should make a pilgrimage to Sunnyside (Irvington, N. Y.), and see how Washington Irving did, by fine instinct alone, for he was hardly a landscape gardener, what few landscape gardeners would have the simple self-control to attempt. A plain rambling house set on the banks of the Hudson with one walk winding from the picturesque lane to the porch and door-step, half a dozen or more elms and maples, a few simple flowers, blue and white, along the base of the dwelling, and you have literally all there is of the lawn. Not a coleus bed, not a shrub, nothing but exquisitely kept turf and a few stately old trees.

The repose, the dignity, the quaint simplicity, and unconscious self-restraint of Sunnyside is my ideal of what a small place should be with a grandmother's garden behind it.

COREOPSIS LANCOLATA.

But the reader will say, perhaps, I have my acres of land with drives, rhododendron groups, shrubberies, green houses, beds of cannas and coleuses, and yet why cannot I too have my grandmother's garden? You can have it, without doubt, but since it will be necessarily out of keeping with the general scope of your place, you will have to isolate it and shut it from view with large trees and shrubs, so that it will be a surprise when discovered, and not count in the general effect of the lawn.

In order to explain what I mean, I have introduced a plan of a place near Orange, N. J., where just this arrangement for a grandmother's garden was undertaken. It is not, of course, exactly what we remember our grandmother's garden to have been, *other times, other manners*,—but it is built on the same plan, amplified and perfected in accordance with the richness of our modern list of perennial garden plants. It is less quaint, I acknowledge, less

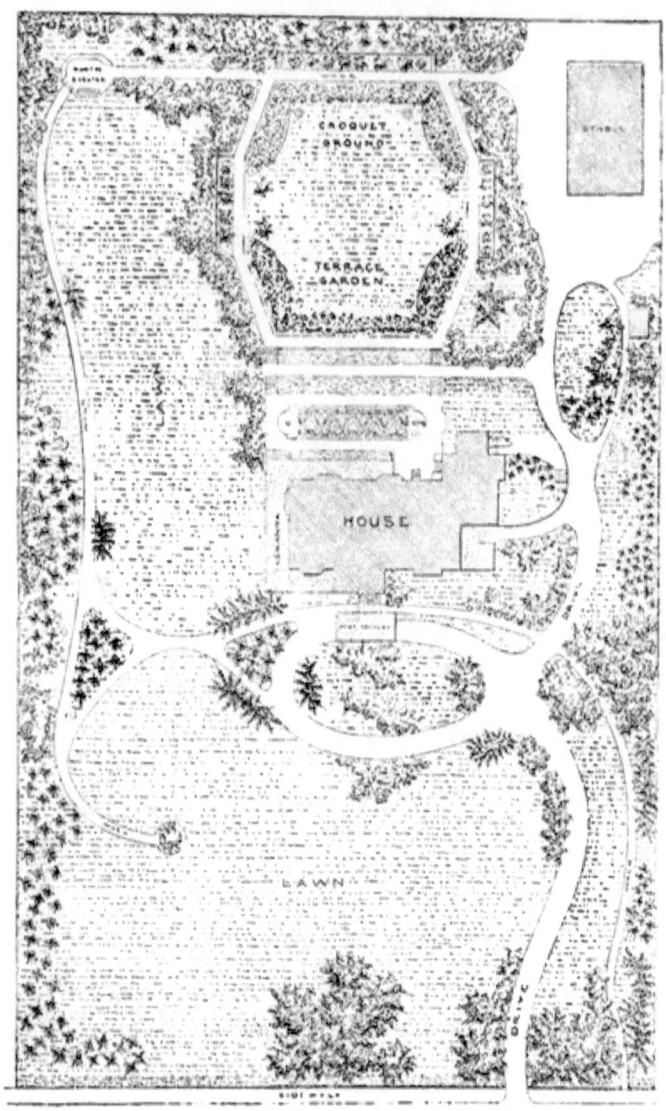

207. PRIVATE PLACE AT ORANGE, N. J., AS LAID OUT BY VAUX & CO.

old-timy, but it has as much quaintness as the old rooms with the grandmother's furniture seen in modern houses, and is quite as much in keeping.

Let us look at the plan. It represents a place of three acres. There is a broad drive that sweeps up to the front of the house and then turns and passes out to the barn. All along the sides of the

CANADA COLUMBINE.
AQUILEGIA CANADENSIS.

place are planted continuous borders of mixed trees and shrubs intended to secure a sense of seclusion, while in front are left two openings to give a view of passers-by and a glimpse of outside life and companionship.

ERIANTHUS RAVENNÆ.

On the left of the house a walk winds from the front door to a fine old shade tree with a seat around it, and so along the outside border of shrubbery to a summer-house in the rear. At the back of the house the ground originally sloped up rapidly so that it became necessary to form a terrace in order to manage the drainage successfully.

Between this terrace and the house, shut in by shrubbery on both sides, was arranged a mat of carpet bedding carefully designed with *Alternantheras, Echeverias, Pyrethrums,* and *Gnaphaliums,* so as to secure an artistic arrangement of vivid green, yellow, red, and white. The spot is isolated, and part, as it were, of the architecture of the house. In such places only, on country places, do we consider planting of this kind admissible. In any other spot, away from the house, such designs are artificial and out of key.

FESTUCA GLAUCA.

Passing up two flights of stone steps that ascend to the terrace with their intervening terrace walk, we come to the terrace garden, or to what comes as near to the grandmother's garden as we ought to expect to get on such a place.

It consists of a plat of green turf with the corners cut to an octagonal line, and then a border of eight feet for the regular hardy garden flowering plants, lined on the farther side by clipped walls of California privet.

On either corner of the grass plat are tall urns for flowers, and still farther in are tall clusters of grasses, making four keypoints of effect. One of these is made of the dazzling white variegated bamboo (*Arundo Donax variegata*), sometimes called ribbon grass, mingled with a blazing spike or two of the red-hot poker plant or *Kniphofia alceoides* (*Tritoma Uvaria grandiflora*). These plants are not entirely hardy, and need protection in a cellar during winter. Another of these groups is made up of a tender but splendid-looking grass, *Gynerium argenteum*, pampas grass, with graceful foliage and long silvery plumes. The third clump consists of the hardy *Erianthus Ravennæ*, resembling pampas grass, and growing ten or twelve feet high. *Eulalia Japonica variegata* and *zebrina* constitute the fourth and best clump. They are entirely hardy and very ornamental with their leaves striped and banded with white, and their stalks four to six feet high, bearing curly-feathered plumes. *Festuca glauca* and *Stipa pennata* have also their places as attractive grasses.

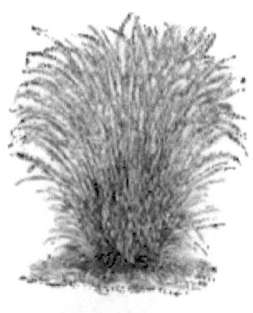
STIPA PENNATA.

And now we may indicate the special points of resemblance in this design to the grandmother's garden. They are to be found principally in the border of plants eight feet wide that skirts the walk and grass plat. Each angle of this grass plat is cut off, making a large eight-sided figure with four long and four short sides. A strip of turf two feet wide is first left, and then comes the mixed skirting border of hardy perennial plants, relieved against the dark green clipped wall of privet. Here, as in the grandmother's garden, there is plenty of color and odor scattered about in somewhat promiscuous fashion, and ready to the hand for plucking or not, as the passing mood may determine.

In a general way, the large-growing plants are placed at the back, beyond a row of lower habit, and next the path we

HAREBELL.
(CAMPANULA TENORI.)

find the smaller specimens. Taken as a whole, however, the appearance of the plants, one to two feet apart, would be called entirely irregular, and instead of bare spaded earth, generally considered necessary in such places, the entire surface beneath the plants is covered with varieties of hardy creepers, such as moneywort, periwinkle, sedum, sandwort, mountain everlasting, arabis, or rock cress, not forgetting the pretty creeping forget-me-not, and the turfing daisy, with its lovely little flowers.

LIVER LEAF.
(HEPATICA TRILOBA.)

All the plants in this border are entirely hardy, and will last for many years without being renewed. Any one may enjoy here abundant color and odor of the most charming kind, for the greater part of the year. First, in early spring, peep out flowers of the lovely blue hepaticas, of the trailing arbutus, the dainty New England mayflower, and certain of the anemones or wind-flowers. The bloodroot, *(Sanguinaria Canadensis)* too, very dwarf, is always eagerly looked for in early spring, on account of the delicate charm of its pure white buds tenderly enfolded with leaves; later on, a clump of its opened flowers are very showy.

Then in May come still more, and, if possible, lovelier flowers, many of which last on far into summer. Such are

larkspurs, garden pinks, the exquisite stemless gentian
(*Gentiana acaulis*), candy tuft (*Iberis*), the asphodels, favorites of the ancients; several beautiful species of violets,
and charming species of anemone, still blooming on into summer. Strictly summer-blooming kinds of herbaceous plants
there are, of course. Here, in summer, are bright yellow

JAPAN WIND-FLOWER.
(ANEMONE JAPONICA-HONORINE JOUBERT.)

Achilleas, the quaint and exquisite blue and yellow *Aquilegias*, or hardy columbines, with strangely formed petals, the
dainty harebells, showy *Coreopsises*, day lilies, certain lovely
species of gentian, the wonderful scarlet cardinal-flower,
brilliant red poppies, rich blue and scarlet foxglove like
Pentstemons, *Veronicas*, white *Astilbe Japonica*, the
garden phloxes, *Liatris* or blazing star, and the purple
foxglove.

Autumn flowers are not forgotten. Masses of goldenrod *(Solidago)*, and orange-colored milkweed *(Asclepias)*, and purple asters are scattered throughout the border; the blue *Aconitum autumnale*, or autumn monk's-hood, the curious chelone, or turtle's head, and the dwarfer kinds of sunflowers.

BLUE VIOLET.

Last, but not least, just before winter sets in, we dwell with delight on the brilliant yellow and purple flowers of the chrysanthemums and Christmas roses. Your attention has been directed in this description to only a few of the plants in this border of mixed hardy flowers. More than a hundred and fifty varieties are used.

Before leaving the subject, it seems worth while to dwell for a moment on the Japan irises, planted in distinct lines within three formal recesses of the California privet, arranged for their reception. They appear in the

PURPLE FOXGLOVE.
(DIGITALIS PURPUREA.)

WHITE VIOLET.

spring, and present, with their curious forms and hues—as strange and beautiful in their way as any orchid—one of the most unique and charming effects in the entire garden. The broad, straight paths that run past all these flowers, and the grass plat and croquet ground make a worthy frame for our border, and everywhere the eye meets, at almost any season of the year, objects of interest.

ORIENTAL POPPY.
(PAPAVER BRACTEATUM.)

This place has, therefore, an attraction that is related somewhat to the charm grandmother's garden possessed for us in early days. There is, first, the neatness and perfect keeping that suits the level space adjoining a terrace and the architectural lines of a house, and then there is all the profusion, and far more than the variety, that characterized the floral treasures of the old-fashioned example. More than that, we have individuality of beauty, which is, in one sense, the best of all beauty, fostered in the highest degree. One's economical instincts are satisfied with the idea of possessing flowers that need no re-setting year by year, and one's instinct for beauty can certainly ask for no more abundant feast than is here spread out.

JAPAN IRIS.
(IRIS KÆMPFERI.)

CHAPTER XI.

BEDDING PLANTS.

HE terms flower bedding, color bedding, or carpet bedding are familiar to every one who gives flowers the slightest consideration. Farm door-yards and Newport lawns alike disport themselves in the gay but unfortunately often garish colors of the coleus and geranium. No need to advocate their use. They have achieved a foothold that is not likely to be soon shaken. The universal delight in rich color is satisfied by their employment and the expense of their employment is comparatively small.

They have long ago come to stay. It therefore behoves us carefully to consider here how they should be employed in any definite attempt at a harmonious arrangement of a well-appointed lawn. As we find them presented on many grass plats, their appearance is vulgar, inharmonious, and barbaric. The discord of color shocks one like an accumulation of false notes in music. So common, moreover, has this bad composition grown, that some of the most refined and enlightened spirits among landscape gardeners have declared unqualified war against all color and carpet bedding whatsoever. It seems to me, however, that this is a prejudice and a narrow one.

The reasonable view, the artistic instinct, would be, I am sure, to consider each coleus and geranium as a single beautiful plant and therefore deserving employment in artistically conceived designs and appropriate surroundings. It is a great mistake to consider the employment of a coleus or geranium as requiring any different general principle of landscape-gardening arrangement from that of shrubs and trees. The coleus is taken up in the fall— though there is nothing peculiar in that—and new plantations of it made in the following spring, but lack of hardiness should affect not at all the necessity for applying the artistic principles of landscape gardening to all branches of the art. Color and form are given to the artist to use, whether it be in the shape of a coleus or an elm tree, and it is his business to see that the color and form are arranged in the composition in the most effective, harmonious, and pleasing way. The principles governing their arrangement are, moreover, the same in both cases.

Now all this is doubtless evident as soon as we give the subject reasonable consideration. Why, then, the prejudice against the use of bedding plants, as evinced by persons of unquestionable taste. It must be mere thoughtlessness; for if they would only think for a moment, they must see that the arrangement of an oval bed of coleuses and centaureas into a glaring combination of stripes and formal bands of red, white, and yellow, like some gigantic pastry cook's tart, does not prevent a better method being employed by a better designer.

When we have drawn a well-designed bed on paper, however, we have only commenced to solve the problem of good designing for bedding. The scheme must be made to fit a certain spot, and must be harmonized and adjusted to its surroundings. For instance, a certain decorative bed around the fountain at Union Square, New York, may look

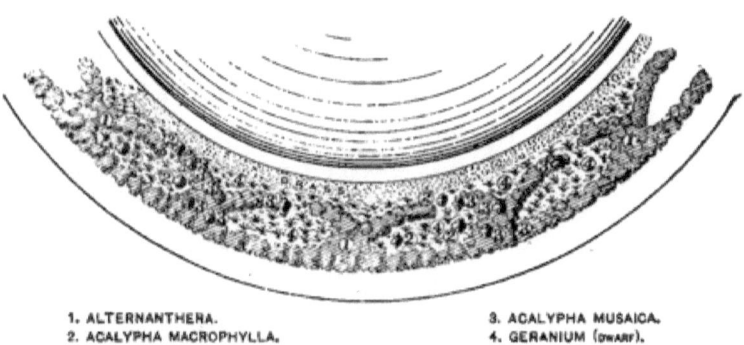

1. ALTERNANTHERA.
2. ACALYPHA MACROPHYLLA.
3. ACALYPHA MUSAICA.
4. GERANIUM (DWARF).

all right, while a similarly arranged bed on a Central Park meadow would shock the sense of harmony.

Let us consider for a moment this arrangement of bedding plants around the Union Square fountain. It is one typical illustration. In good work of this sort, as I have mentioned, there must be a definite recognition of all the general principles of landscape-gardening art. Properly adjusted emphasis must be secured, and the treatment approximated in miniature to that of the ordinary lawn. Consequently we find in the Union Square illustration the grass of the lawn represented by the dwarf, close-set alternantheras, the shrubs by the coleuses and geraniums, and the trees by the larger forms of the acalyphas.

The relations of these parts are, it will be seen, unlike those of the different features of the lawn, but they are carefully studied, so as to bring them into artistic and effective relations with each other and with the gleaming water and the floating pond-lilies. The higher parts of the bed are not so high as to obscure the effect of the water-plants, and the lower parts have a sufficient expanse in places to afford the eye, although in miniature, a little of the pleasure of grass spaces. The eye is attracted from afar by the jewel-like effect of brilliant color, and yet when the fountain is reached all parts are so nicely adjusted to each other that the gaze, dwelling for a moment with delight on the bedding, passes at once to the superior charms of the water-lilies and fountain spray. When we compare such a fairly adjusted and artistic arrangement of bedding as that around the Union Square fountain with the ordinary coleus bed found in many front-door yards, we begin to see why bedding is sometimes severely condemned.

I think the main difficulty with most bedding is that the designer frequently fails to recognize the value of proper emphasis of parts in arranging his flower and foliage beds. He uses cannas alone or he uses coleuses and geraniums alone. Out in the grass he sets a strange and intricate design of rosette-like echeverias and calls it a carpet-bed or rug, and thinks he is artistic. The plants are attractive individually, and the arrangement perhaps curious and interesting, but it is out of place, out of key, and improperly related to its surroundings. They seem unhappy for lack of the congenial company they find in nature.

As a rule, it may be said that ornamental planting of this character, namely, bedding, should be restricted to the immediate neighborhood of architectural structures and to small city squares or greens, where the rigid lines of the

BED OF CANNAS, COLEUSES, AND ACALYPHAS.

neighboring masses of houses are inevitably, to the eye, associated with the semi-artificial-looking bedding.

A favorable arrangement for bedding plants will be found directly against the wall of a large building. A solid background always enhances the attraction of a mass of bedding. First come the cannas, solanums, or other large-leaf plants against the wall, then acalyphas, coleuses, geraniums, and last pyrethrums and alternantheras.

STUDY FOR BEDDING OF FOLIAGE PLANTS AGAINST A WALL.

There is one feature of the flower or foliage bed that is apt to look stiff and inartistic, and that is the extreme edge or border. This is usually too sharply cut in outline. The plants do not blend with the grass, and the sharp transition line is not agreeable. To overcome this stiffness of outline, single plants of the coleus or geranium size should be set out in the grass just beyond the actual border of the bed. Then at various points throughout the bed the pyrethrum or alternanthera edging the masses of coleus or geranium should be brought forward close to the low border, and here and there several of them should be allowed to get over the border and establish themselves in the neighboring grass. This will create a properly related emphasis of outline, a pleasing variety, and irregularity enough to just escape formality. There must be necessarily a certain precision of lines, but the treatment should all the time bear a distinct and well-defined kinship to that employed by nature in our fields and pastures.

I have now considered two common types of bedding, one a narrow border around the stone coping of a fountain, and another the frequently recurring case of a plantation against the wall of a building.

There is another and still more important one, in the small city parks for instance, where there is no building or fountain around which to mass the bedding. In that case the bedding should be arranged as foreground to the shrub groups, leaving the main lawn space undiminished. An illustration of this arrangement may be seen in the half-acre lawn of Jeannette Park, on the East River, near the foot of Broad Street, New York, where belts of glowing coleuses and pyrethrums wind in and out in front of the irregular masses of shrubs and border their confines. At irregular intervals in the belts of coleuses and gladioluses appear masses of cannas and acalyphas.

The effect thus obtained is almost tropical-like in appearance, and yet in a certain sense subordinates itself to, and blends with, the masses of trees and shrubs. It is, moreover, bright and cheerful, and decorative, in a region full of dull brick and stone buildings, where such relief is particularly grateful.

There is again the effect of bedding with a minimum of greenward at Jackson Square, Thirteenth Street and Eighth Avenue, where the open available centre for grass space was so small after the walks and boundary plantations were made, that it was deemed better to fill nearly all the central space with a bouquet of foliage plants of many colors. The bed was an irregular star-shape, with cannas and acalyphas in the centre, and coleuses and geraniums and pyrethrums and alternantheras on the outside.

SWORD LILY.
(GLADIOLUS.)

Masses of bananas, cannas, acalyphas, geraniums, etc., are made to produce excellent effects by planting them in irregular masses up and down a steep bank, with single specimens of acalyphas and geraniums standing outside the main groups. I question much indeed whether coleuses and geraniums should be planted anywhere without such large plants as cannas and acalyphas to emphasize and relieve anything like a flat monotonous effect. Even in the park at the foot of Canal Street, New York, one of the roughest and dirtiest of neighborhoods, where green grass is a priceless boon, a bit of massed cannas, acalyphas, coleuses, and geraniums have been introduced effectively without injuring the open centre grass effect.

Shade is of course all important to the small city park, and the shade of large trees is entirely destructive to the growth of bedding plants, which need sun and air in abundance.

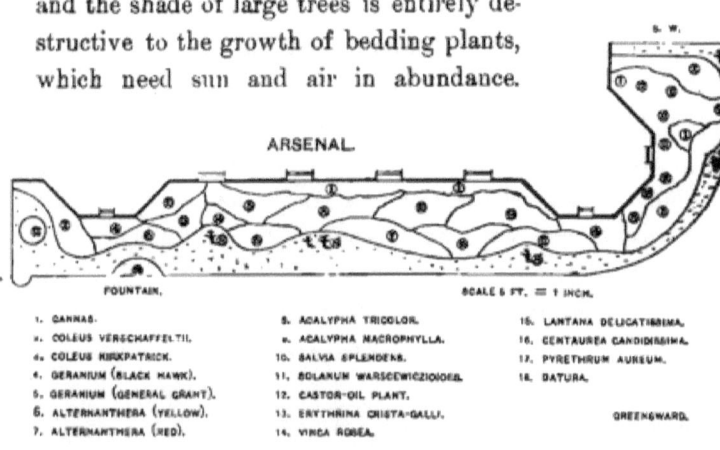

1. CANNAS.
2. COLEUS VERSCHAFFELTII.
3. COLEUS KIRKPATRICK.
4. GERANIUM (BLACK HAWK).
5. GERANIUM (GENERAL GRANT).
6. ALTERNANTHERA (YELLOW).
7. ALTERNANTHERA (RED).
8. ACALYPHA TRICOLOR.
9. ACALYPHA MACROPHYLLA.
10. SALVIA SPLENDENS.
11. SOLANUM WARSCEWICZIOIDES.
12. CASTOR-OIL PLANT.
13. ERYTHRINA CRISTA-GALLI.
14. VINCA ROSEA.
15. LANTANA DELICATISSIMA.
16. CENTAUREA CANDIDISSIMA.
17. PYRETHRUM AUREUM.
18. DATURA.

GREENSWARD.

There are plenty of nooks, however, for bedding plants in small city parks that are not shaded, where they may be planted with excellent effect, adding much to the pleasure of many people.

The system of bedding adopted around the Arsenal in Central Park shows the frequently recurring example already mentioned of a wall bordered with grass and decorated with bedding plants. The large kinds, like cannas, castor-oil plants, solanums, etc., are naturally arranged against the wall, and then the acalyphas and amarantus and geraniums and finally the pyrethrums and alternantheras. This is all regular and in due form, and so is the waving line of the border of bed both on the inside and out.

The peculiar part of this arrangement of bedding lies in the way the large plants, such as cannas, etc., are brought forward nearly to the front of the mass. Then across the border to the very grass are carried narrow clusters of acalyphas, geraniums, etc. These promontories of color are thrown out where the border of grass is narrowest, and in the bays of the bedding single specimens of geraniums and acalyphas are set in the grass opposite the same plants growing in the mass; the whole arrangement being intended to impress the eye as a continually changing effect of recesses and bays and promontories and valleys of the richest color.

The illustration, on the following page, of varying ellipses or discs, superimposed one over the other, makes an excellent and artistic effect of broadly massed colors in bedding.

The illustrations of bedding I have thus far discussed briefly have been carefully designed in the following manner: Measurements were taken of the exact spot the proposed bed was to occupy, and the figure was drawn out on a sheet of paper, showing at the same time any adjoining buildings, walks, or shrub groups. A list of plants to be used in the bed was then made and their heights and colors at maturity written out. It then became a question of combining colors and various heights of plants into a single artistic effect. The outlines and proportions of the various masses of plants were carefully sketched out in pencil and then the colors used were painted between the lines. When this original study had been carefully worked out, tracings on muslin, including color, were taken from it and given to the engineer. It was his duty to mark out the boundaries of the various parts of the bed with stakes. Then the

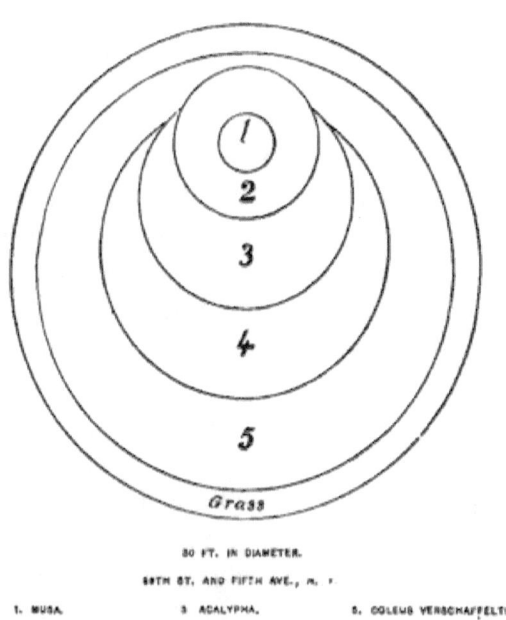

30 FT. IN DIAMETER.
59TH ST. AND FIFTH AVE., N. Y.

1. MUSA. 3. ACALYPHA. 5. COLEUS VERSCHAFFELTI.
2. CANNAS. 4. COLEUS.

gardeners took the map, with its colored pattern and key or list of plants, and proceeded to execute the work of planting out the geraniums, coleuses, etc., in accordance with the design.

Nor did the work of intelligent management end here, for from time to time throughout the summer it was the business of the gardeners not only to water and cultivate the bedding plants, but also to prune them with intelligence and art. It is usually the practice to pinch back coleuses and other plants in order to make them look even and thick, simply a broad, flat mass, but in this way all due emphasis of parts is lost.

In fact no pinching whatever should be practised except here and there where a single plant grows awkwardly, or where too even a surface appears. In some cases, even, as in Union Square, the acalyphas have been trained for a time on sticks to secure the strongest contrast possible between the tree effect of the acalypha and the grass effect of the alternanthera. Pruning plants of all kinds, it should be remembered, means in its proper acceptation the development of natural and characteristic beauties. It means perfecting the special individuality of the plant. Judging from the style of pruning we often see, the object of the art might be readily supposed to mean obliterating as far as possible all individuality.

Having thus defined and illustrated briefly the main principles that should apply to the construction of a color or foliage bed, it would seem proper to consider some of the leading plants suitable for work of this kind. Taking them in the order of their employment, from the lowest to the highest, we have among the grass type the alternantheras. They do not grow ordinarily over five or six inches high, and have close-set leaves not unlike those of grass. Their marked peculiarity is found in their coloring. Each leaf is variegated in irregular fashion with green and red or green and yellow, the foundation color being green. The best of the red kinds are *versicolor*, *amœna*, and *paronychioides*; and of the yellow, *aurea* and *aurea nana*.

Where these alternantheras do not appear as a grass effect throughout the mass of bedding, their proper place is on the extreme edge of the group. Such borders should never be of regular width, but should swell in and out of the general mass. The illustration of the bedding adjoining the Arsenal, Central Park, indicates this method of using alternantheras on the outskirts of the plantations.

Belonging to the same grass type and blending the larger plants of the bedding with the greensward, are the centaureas, pyrethrums, and nasturtiums. The echeverias do not blend with a general mass of bedding. They are too dwarf and too stiff and formal in appearance, and should therefore be always used in designs by themselves. Indeed, to me their strange, rosette-like shapes are not altogether attractive, although they are certainly interesting and curious. Echeverias form the greater part of the famous carpet-beds and rugs constructed with so much art on many lawns. Two excellent echeverias are *metallica* and *secunda glauca*.

Pyrethrums, sometimes called fever few, or golden feather, are also well suited for border bedding-plants. They are somewhat larger in growth than the alternantheras, but their contour is soft and agreeable, and blends well with the general mass. The kind best suited for bedding is *aureum*, on account of its bright yellow color and its dwarf habit. The same irregular treatment of a border arrangement applies as well to pyrethrums as to alternantheras.

There is one plant for which I desire to ask special attention, on account of its fitness for border planting. It is an excellent and charming bedding-plant in every way. I refer to the well-known old plant, the nasturtium vine. There are some kinds more dwarf and less vine-like in habit, and therefore preferable for bedding. The leaf of the nasturtium, with its slightly formal outline, round rather than oval, and its delicate shadings, is decorative individually. When we come, however, to mass a lot of these leaves in the irregular picturesque fashion in which they naturally grow, their full charms appear. These charms are specially effective as a border to color beds, especially if the arrangement is on a slope or bank. The tendrils of the nasturtium push out over the turf, and break up the more or less stiff outline of the bed in the most attractive manner possible. A certain restraint of this creeping nature will be, of course, necessary, to prevent the nasturtiums from overrunning the greensward on one side and the bedding-plants on the other.

I have not spoken of the yellow and orange flowers of the nasturtium, although they are very attractive, because in color- and foliage-bedding the leaf is of prime importance, not only on account of the leaf lasting longer than the flower, but on account of the broad effects of color on the mass, which must be derived from the leaves. The flowers will undoubtedly increase the attraction of the bed, but they cannot be counted as one of the essential elements of the color-bedding design.

An important part of all bedding is the clearly defined solid and distinct colors that can be used in combination with each other. The collection of the variegated and mixed colors may be attractively arranged in an irregular manner, but such kinds will rarely make that flashing, jewel-like effect that is exhibited by the solid self-colors of silver, red, and gold.

The most perfect type of the silvery or white effect is that of *Centaurea candidissima*. It is almost pure white, and forms in combination a clearly marked contrast with the red and yellow of the other plants. The two objections to it are: firstly, that it is not bushy enough, does not grow thickly on the ground; and secondly, that it is hardly tall enough to use as a shrub form of bedding-plant and too large for the alternanthera or grass type. Where the combination will admit it centaureas should always be arranged as an irregular border outside of the geraniums or coleuses. They may be streaked through the coleuses, but if set in large patches within the mass the coleuses are apt to obscure them.

The combination, side by side, of centaureas and geraniums is difficult to manage well. The pyrethrums look better with geraniums, but geraniums, as a rule, look well grown in large masses together, with a few points of the mass accentuated with acalyphas and amarantus. These groups of geraniums can be greatly varied by using the many distinct varieties that are now grown.

The main types of geraniums, however, that are specially useful in this kind of color- or foliage-bedding are the large yellowish green-leaved sorts with showy flowers, of which the General Grant variety is a well-known and popular instance. The second is the horseshoe geranium, with its distinct and lovely leaf shadings and less conspicuous flowers. Third and last comes the silver-leaved, well represented by the variety Mountain of Snow. This variety stands the sun well.

Geraniums are excellent for bedding throughout the summer until frost comes, and are comparatively free from disease. Their forms are picturesque and compact-growing, covering the ground well, while few bedding plants will grow in dry sandy soil better and continue to resist the effects of drought so long.

DOUBLE GERANIUM.

The colors of the different kinds of geraniums mentioned above are so distinct that, on experiment, it will be found that the most effective combinations can be made of their various tints. It is not a generally accepted statement, but I believe it to be nevertheless true, that every geranium bed should have a border round it of pyrethrum, alternanthera, or similar plants of the grass type. This is, of course, simply following out the principles of bedding design I have already laid down.

SINGLE GERANIUM.

We come now to the most important plant for color effect that we use in bedding. The coleus is widely known and appreciated. It has been propagated and varied by cultivation until its wonderful capacity for sporting has given us an astonishing number of the most diverse-looking sorts. The leaves are spotted, shaded, and striped with every conceivable tint of red, yellow, brown, purple, and green. For the best designs of bedding, however, I am satisfied that the most valuable coleuses are those exhibiting nearly solid self-colors of red or yellow. The best examples of these are probably *Verschaffeltii* and golden bedder, red and yellow kinds. The first is, I am tempted to say, the best single kind of coleus we have for color-bedding, if not the best among all plants. There is no plant, I believe, that presents a more brilliant jewel-like effect in a bedding combination of colors than *Coleus Verschaffeltii*.

There is no coleus that I know of which has solidly green leaves, but *Kirkpatrick* does duty fairly well in a green effect, its foliage being only slightly mottled with yellow. Coleuses are not as generally successful as geraniums, especially in dry weather, and in early autumn disease is often liable to attack them.

An excellent plant for a small tree effect in bedding is the *Amarantus salicifolius*. It is weeping and graceful in habit, and glowing with red tints. Its height at maturity is about three to four feet.

A far better plant, however, of the same type is the Acalypha. This plant is apparently little used in this country, but its large, rich-looking, variegated red and green leaves and its weeping habit combine to give it a splendid effect in a foliage bed. I hardly know a bedding-plant except *Coleus Verschaffeltii* that presents such a glowing red as the acalypha, and the acalypha has the advantage of being a much larger and more graceful plant than the coleus. The place for the acalypha in a bed is next to the cannas where cannas are used. It cannot be associated effectively adjoining either geraniums or coleuses, being taller, two to three feet high, and growing much larger leaves.

Salvia splendens is also an effective bedding-plant, growing two or three feet high. Its foliage is attractive and thick-growing, and the flowers are specially attractive, because they glow with a rich red late in autumn.

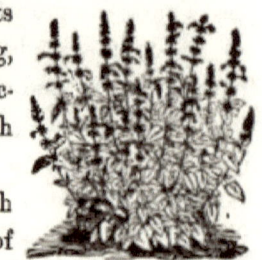
SALVIA SPLENDENS.

Vinca rosea may be also used with excellent effect in this shrub type of bedding. Its rich green glossy leaves are its chief attraction. The last and most important feature of foliage-bedding is the employment of the tree type of plants. First and most important of these are the canna effects. The well known *Canna Indica* has many varieties, but their general appearance exhibits on the lawn great solid leaves extending from the ground six or eight feet high. Their tints of green run in some kinds into rich red and purple hues. One of the best of these is *Canna Ehmanni* of comparatively recent introduction. The foliage is not as large as that of some other cannas, but it is solid and massive and banana-like, and the crimson-scarlet flowers hang in heavy clusters from the top of the plant, and continue in bloom throughout the season. The value of the canna in bedding lies chiefly in its leaves. Masses of these leaves seen even from some distance have a specially tropical and pleasing effect, and

CANNA INDICA.

add greatly to the beauty of any part of a bed that they emphasize. Cannas should be always used in considerable masses.

They are tuberous-rooted and not hardy, and these tubers should be taken up and kept through the winter in a dry cellar or greenhouse where the frost can be kept out. It is a good idea to start cannas in early spring, in pots, so that when they come to be set out they will be a foot or too high. In this way their full effect will be obtained early in the season. cannas should be set out about a foot to fifteen inches apart, to secure their best effect in masses.

BANANA PLANT.
(MUSA ENSETE.)

A grand plant to associate with cannas, because it serves to greatly develop and perfect their special foliage effect, is the banana plant (*Musa ensete*). The leaves are enormously high and broad — eight to ten feet high and two feet broad,—dominating and yet resembling those of the cannas. Nothing can be more tropical-looking, —and the reddish tint of the midrib and adjacent veinings and the prevailing tint of green of the leaf is charming.

The plan of associating the *Musa ensete* with a mass of cannas is also valuable, because the *Musa* is thus enabled by the support of the canna leaves to resist high winds which are apt to beat it about and tear it. *Musa ensete* is the stiffest-growing of its race, but the support of the cannas is nevertheless valuable. These banana plants can be wintered like the cannas in a warm cellar or cool greenhouse, and then potted for May planting.

Other great massive plants suited for the tree effect in bedding are the solanums. The leaves are large, thick, and deeply and picturesquely cut, and hang in drooping masses. It is altogether a massive-looking plant.

SOLANUM WARSCEWICZIOIDES.

The castor-oil plant is another excellent instance of the tree type for bedding. It is the tallest, perhaps, of all the plants used in bedding, and specially picturesque in growth and tinting. Its place, however, is among other plants, such as solanums, where its somewhat naked stem will be properly clothed and supported. The well-known elephant ear, *Caladium esculentum* may be also used effectively in similar associations.

ELEPHANT EAR.
(CALADIUM ESCULENTUM.)

I wish to say a word before closing about the use of tulips, pansies, and daisies for spring bedding. It is really color-bedding with flowers, rather than leaves, for the leaves at the early season when tulips bloom have hardly yet developed. The contrast of the pansies and daisies set out in the same pattern as that of the succeeding summer bedding is attractive and effective, but they are modest in the extreme in the presence of the tulips.

By employing the red, yellow, and white tulips in the summer-bedding patterns the most splendid effect of clear, pure, glowing color can be obtained. The large round bed at the entrance to Central Park, at Fifth Avenue and Fifty-ninth Street, is thus planted in varying ovals that make broad masses of color, first white, then yellow, and then red next to the green grass. Red color forms a striking and pleasing contrast with the green of the grass, and is therefore generally arranged next to the greensward as shown in the diagram on page 226.

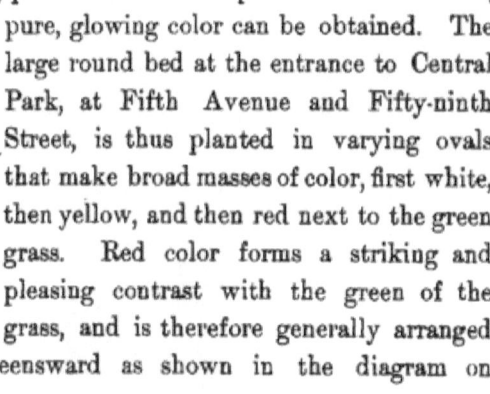
NEW SINGLE TULIPS.

The effect of tulip and pansy bedding is necessarily somewhat flat and monotonous in contour, but this naturally comes from using flowers, as it were, alone for producing a color-effect. In only this way, however, can we secure early spring color-beds, because foliage plants such as cannas, coleuses, etc., cannot generally be planted out with safety in the climate of New York before May 20th. At that time tulips are, as a rule, done flowering, and pansies past their prime.

Pansies are planted out in March and early April, being almost in bloom when set out, and tulip-bulbs are planted late in the fall of the year previous to that of blooming. Two excellent red kinds of tulips are *La Belle Alliance* and *Artus;* among white kinds I would name white Pottebaker; and among the yellow kinds I would select Yellow Prince and Canary Bird. Duc Van Tholl is a splendid red variety, but it is too dwarf, and blooms at a somewhat different time from those mentioned above. I do not insist on these varieties, but take them because they have clean, pure self-colors, and because they are of the same height and bloom at the same time. These are essential qualities for tulips to possess that are intended to be associated together in the same color-bed.

CHAPTER XII.

THE ORNAMENTATION OF PONDS AND LAKES.

DID the reader ever have a place in the country? If he has and does not want to grow sick of it, or if he has none, but hopes to have one, and does not want to be forced to give it up in disgust, let me give him a piece of advice. Don't undertake too much. Have only five hundred square feet of grass and one tree or half a dozen shrubs, but have all of the best. Dig deep, fertilize liberally, plant the best grass-seed and plenty of it, set out the largest trees and shrubs that will be likely to grow, and care for them tenderly, year after year. Dig about them and prune them and spare no pains to make them the best of their kind; or, let me say at once, that the reader's delight in nature and his desire to imitate her effects will not prevent the failure of his lawn-planting. All this is said in advance, because it applies as well to water-plants as to ordinary lawn-plants.

I propose now, in a few words, to tell the reader how I came to attempt to grow, and to succeed, after much tribulation, in growing, a good collection of water-plants, and how reasonably satisfactory water effects were contrived on my lawns. At a comparatively early period in life, having a comfortable fortune, the desire took possession of me to have a country-place.

With my country-place came the usual failures and successes that are incident to the construction of lawns and gardens in the hands of amateurs. The failures, I am frank enough to confess, much outnumbered the successes. I shall, however, content myself with giving a brief account of my lily-pond work. The soil on my place, of one hundred acres, was gravel and sand, and a stream or pond on one side of it had a clean pebbly bottom and water that flowed rapidly down a decline. The water was only a few inches deep in many places. I thought it would be a good plan to dig out the bottom a bit, and in this way lost much valuable fertilizing material. However, I did not mind that, as I expected to dig a hole for each water-plant and to fill it up with good soil from the neighboring field. At this early period of my lawn-planting I unfortunately gave little thought to the quality of the soil. A charming magazine article had fallen into my hands and completely fascinated me with its dainty, fanciful description of lilies grown in a pond-hole or ditch. It all seemed so easy: just a few water-plants set out in what appeared the easiest and simplest fashion, and lo! you had a feast of lilies and lily-pads. The plants seemed to have just grown themselves, like Topsy in "Uncle Tom's Cabin." At this time I was greatly impressed with the idea of planting the lawn with trees and shrubs from the woods, sweet fern, sumach, sassafras, dogwood, red cedar, pepperidge, hickory, etc. Of course, such plants frequently died, and if they did live assumed a stunted form. As an old farmer of the neighborhood subsequently expressed it: "Well, I knowed them things you set out would die. I could have told you beforehand that crowded woods plants have poor roots. But then, you would n't have believed me if I had. Your plants just up and died because a full dose of sunshine did not suit their shady constitutions." Considering this mania, you will not be surprised to hear that I visited a pond in the woods near by and dug up and transplanted to my own pond a large number of roots of white water-lilies. Other water-plants were naturally secured subsequently in the same way. I need hardly say, after the above remarks of the farmer, that my water-lilies did not specially thrive. The lily-roots had not been grown for transplanting and were not, in most cases, young and thrifty, and the soil of the bottom of the stream or pond was not rich and suited to water-plants. However, among the numerous water-plants I set out, many lived. They were strung along a straight, monotonous shore that I had dug out to a line to secure a neat appearance. I learned in after days that this arrangement was about as bad as could be imagined from a good lawn-planter's standpoint. The lilies and other water-plants grew slowly and the flowers were small. I had finally to acknowledge that my lily-pond and stream was not a success. As a result my interest in the plantation soon flagged, and except to gather a few lilies I seldom visited it. Weeds sprung up to its surface and drifted material made it untidy and unhealthy-looking.

Besides, about this time I sold this country-place and so cannot say what the lily-pond finally became, as I never revisited it. Much like any natural lily-pond in the woods, I fancy. Returning to the city, I continued to live there most of the time for several years. Yet I never at any time wholly lost my interest in lawn-planting. Now that I had no country-place to absorb my attention, I went about at home and abroad and saw how other people succeeded and failed in their landscape-gardening efforts. An important source of information existed, I found, in the different nurseries. I did not take so much to the woods now as aforetime. Concerning the construction of ponds and streams and the ornamentation of their surface with aquatic plants, I did not, however, secure as much information as I had hoped. At last, one day, I again met my fate and bought another country-place, only instead of a hundred acres as before it now contained less than ten. The soil was of excellent quality, and there were on either side of the house some grand old native oak, elm, and tulip trees, and I planted a few large shrubs on the outer boundaries. Paths and roads there were none, except one short carriage-sweep leading directly from the house to the highway. Off to the west of the house sloped a half-dozen acres of meadow land, the rich velvety turf of which had known no plough for half a century. Sheep and cows had pastured it, and sometimes it had been mown. I mowed it and manured it too, and prided myself on the finest lawn to be seen in the county. At the foot of the slope came the feature which had chiefly induced me to buy the place. It was a broad placid stream fifty to one hundred feet wide, moving quietly down to a small neglected mill-pond that partially abutted my property. Across this stream I owned a narrow strip of land only an acre or two in extent, but enough to enable me to control the treatment of both shores of the stream. A rustic bridge joined these acres. The water was shallow, not more than, for the most part, two or three feet deep, and the grassy slope extended to the very edge. It was a brimming sheet of water, sometimes overflowing its banks several feet up the steep lawnside. Here was my chance, I believed, to grow aquatic plants in perfection. I proceeded at once to study the natural conditions of the spot, and tried to work on the same lines as nature had employed in this small territory ever since the dam had been built. Where the force of the stream had already managed to scoop out a small bay, I dug it still farther inland. In other words, I analyzed the forces in action

GREEN-LEAVED BAMBOO.
(ARUNDO DONAX.)

and aided and abetted their inclinations. If grasses and twigs had caught on a small projection of the shore and a little vegetation had sprung up and soil thus collected, I lengthened and broadened the projection and planted it with clumps of grasses, such as flag, bamboo, pampas grass, and the hardy *Eulalia Japonica*. Back of these, on more solid ground, I planted a willow and an alder, with some irises, and tender cannas and caladiums or elephant ears. I was careful, moreover, to be conservative even in this natural treatment of my shores. There was no frequent repetition of the promontory and bay idea. At only a few points was any change made in the original line of the shore. Such changes as I did make, however,

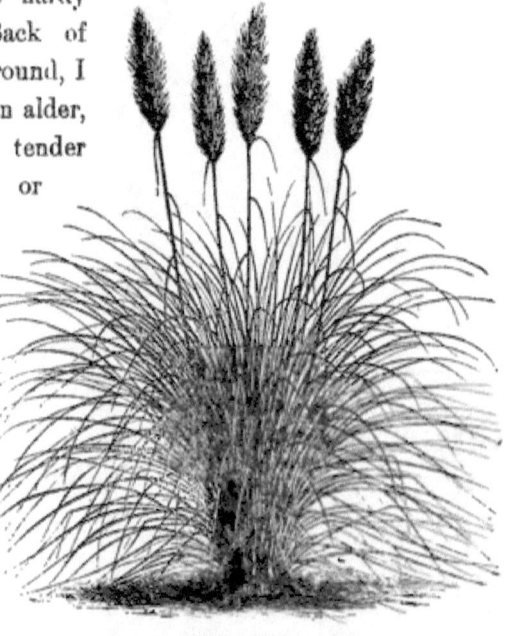

PAMPAS GRASS.
(GYNERIUM ARGENTEUM.)

were forcible and marked and carefully adjusted in the exact direction and angle that the stream would be likely to take when it worked its fantastic way before a rapid current or overflow. Grasses and shrubs suited to low grounds, of the kinds I have named, were scattered in small groups about the points running back, sometimes quite a distance, up the bank. In the midst of these groups grew some higher shrubs or small trees like the birch, for the sake of emphasizing the effect and giving variety of sky-line. I do not wish to be needlessly technical, but if you could see the two great Lombardy poplars, forty feet high, bordering and making a frame, as it were, for my place, you would understand what I mean by emphasis. Great towers of green, these poplars seem to be mounting guard over my small domain, and their long shadows at sundown reach far across the stream and the grass of the meadow beyond. I am not going to apologize for my poplars. They were and are grand, and I am proud of them. Tree-experts may warn me that they are liable to borers and bark-lice, and that they lose their leaves early in the season, and in many ways invite the use of the axe. It may be so. I have enjoyed them, however, for a number of years and they are entirely healthy yet, although surely a score of years in age. It will be a long time, therefore, before an axe under my direction will touch them. Even the tendency to lose their leaves early in the season would not induce me to use the axe, for their lofty spire-like forms dominate everything and establish that variety of sky-line so much to be desired by the lawn-planter. Let the limbs be bare and the trunk scarred and seamed with borers, the noble outline is there, and shrubs and small trees can be made to screen the lower and generally uglier portions. It should be remembered also, that an occasional pruning, as the years go on, tends greatly to renew and perpetuate the poplar's health and vigor.

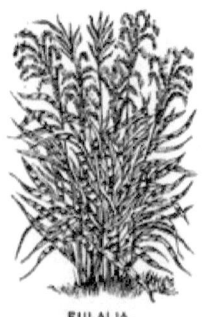

EULALIA.
(JAPONICA ZEBRINA.)

But, the reader will say, where is the lily-pond? You have told us about your lawn with its stream and old mill-pond, but where are your lilies? Well, I answer, do not be in a hurry. I assure you if I had not selected and arranged my lawn and water properties as I did, the lilies I might have set out would have been of much less account than they are. Remember the lilies on my former place. In

BORDER OF THE FOUNTAIN, UNION SQUARE. NEW YORK.—LOTUSES AND WATER-LILIES.

truth, without some of the characteristics of my present lawn the proper setting for the clustering water-lily gems would have been absent. And think what a setting they had now—great poplars, drooping willows, alders, waving grasses, purple irises, purple marsh-mallows growing on promontories of a brimming river backed by a sloping bank of rich greensward. In the coves, chiefly, of my stream and pond were set my lily-jewels. The bottom of the water was deepened and a foot of soil, not in spots but along the entire front, was replaced by the richest mixture I could make of mould and manure. Pond-lilies are great feeders, and I intended to give them the best chance I could to look their prettiest. For the *Nelumbiums* or lotuses considerable clay is needed. Fortunately, my soil had naturally plenty of clay. I used, moreover, other kinds of water-plants besides lilies, and some of them, as well as certain lilies, were tender, coming as they do originally from the tropics.

The tender ones I bought anew every year, at a moderate expense, from one of the few growers in America. I may have expended during some years one hundred and even one hundred and fifty dollars, but it was a small sum compared with the amount necessary to keep up a greenhouse fitted with suitable tanks. Water-lilies and aquatic plants winter badly in cellars. They are easily excited to grow by a little excess of light and heat, and as easily checked and injured by an excess of cold. Except a few kinds, such as the wonderful blue and purple water-lilies of Zanzibar, which I bought yearly, I have therefore managed to content myself with a number of perfectly hardy aquatics, including some of the best water-lilies and lotuses. Doubtless the biggest, grandest, and most effective of these was the lotus *Nelumbium speciosum*. This plant is the greatest feeder of all, and will thrive prodigiously in the richest, rankest mud that can be concocted. It will, in fact, crowd out most other plants, and should be thinned every year so as to appear in clusters and not in monotonous masses extending from shore to shore. This *Nelum-*

bium is widely known in India and Japan as the lotus, and is there considered sacred and is freely copied in their decorative designs. It is also probably the lotus of ancient Egypt.

Picture for yourself a pumpkin-leaf erected three or four feet high on a stem, and great buds that look, for all the world, like gigantic tea-rose buds, and you will have a

AN ARRANGEMENT OF LOTUSES AND LILY-PADS.

fair idea of the general appearance of the lotus. Of course, the leaves of the lotus are more finely veined and smoother and more shining of texture, and the flowers grander and richer in tint than the tea-rose bud; but, for all that, the pumpkin-leaf and tea-rose bud comparison is a suggestive one. The botanical name of the lotus, *Nelumbium*, signifying a rose or spray of a watering-pot, is very descriptive of the curious seed-pod. There is a fine *Nelumbium*, native to

America, a yellow lotus with excellent foliage, which is found in one or two places in New Jersey, but which chiefly abounds in Florida and other Southern and Western States. The leaves of this species are quite as noteworthy as those of the familiar *Nelumbium speciosum*. These are often two feet in diameter.

A GROUP OF JAPANESE LOTUSES.
(NELUMBIUM SPECIOSUM.)

The lotus leaves and flowers are decorative and striking in effect, but the true water-lilies, the *Nymphæas*, are, after all, I am inclined to say, the best ornamental water-plants. Following out my Lombardy poplar idea of emphasis, I used many lotuses in front of my brook and pond promontories. But in all my experiments with aquatic plants I never chanced on any pond-effects quite equal to that of my coves of *Nymphæas* in midsummer. Fancy a quiet, mirror-like surface of water, studded with clustering masses of lily-pads, enfolding half-open flowers, nestling yet buoyant. Every one is familiar with scenes in woodland nooks resembling this in kind. The remarkable difference on my place was that my trees and shrubs, grasses and flowers, came to the water's edge and were mirrored there, and that in front and about them floated and were reflected lily-pads of excellent size and coloring. The flowers also of these great tropical lilies were especially large and richly hued, some species being pure white, others red, and still others purple and deep blue. I have had these water-lilies and other water-plants growing on my place now for several years, but I confess that, even at the present time, familiar as they are to me, when I look at one of these blue lilies on an early summer morning I am impressed with the scene as an absolute revelation of beauty, a landscape feature positively unique.

I am not going, on this occasion, to give an account of all the aquatic plants I grow. I have the tender *Pontederia crassipes*, a floating plant with curious orchid-like purple flowers, water-poppies, pitcher-plants, cat-tails, and a score of other species and varieties that I shall not enumerate. All these kinds of water-plants doubtless add greatly to the attractions of decorative waters, but, after all, it is the lotuses and lilies, or lilies and lotuses, not giving the precedence to either, that every one ought to want. Having once had them, any decorative piece of water without them will seem almost uninteresting, no matter what other water-plants are employed.

Let me say here, before I forget, that spaces of clear surface among water-plants, with undisturbed reflections, are particularly necessary to secure the best effects. The whole surface of the pond should be no more covered up with water-lilies than fine rocks should be completely masked with climbing vines.

To explain to the reader which are the tender and which are the hardy kinds would be a lengthy task, and I must refer him to the nearest nurseryman who grows aquatics. Better not grow many tender plants, would be my advice to the ordinary amateur lawn-planter.

The success of this treatment of my stream certainly affords me great pleasure, and I need hardly say I am

AN ARRANGEMENT OF WATER-LILIES AND PAPYRUS.

proud of it. It has, however, done more than that. One or two of my neighbors are, I see, already following my example, with promising results. In the village, also, near by, there is a fountain, and in the basin I have persuaded the authorities to arrange some boxes of lilies and lotuses renewed every year with purchased plants, and in place of a great iron Neptune, painted white and surrounded by white iron cherubs spouting little jets of water, a graceful spray effect has been introduced. Water-lilies and lotuses lend themselves charmingly to the decoration of fountain basins, especially if they are used in moderation and do not cover up more than a fair half of the entire surface of the water.

Before closing this account of my experience in growing water-plants, I must refer to the introduction of water-lilies and lotuses in the parks of New York. Some four years since, a year or two after I became Superintendent of Parks, my mind was turned, as well as that of my assistants, to the subject of growing lilies in the Central and city parks. We knew they had been grown to a limited extent in Fairmount Park, Philadelphia, and conceived the idea of using them largely in New York.

At first we bought a considerable number, say five hundred dollars' worth, from Mr. Sturtevant, of Bordentown, N. J., the father of water-lily culture in America. For the last two years, however, we have bought little and propagated much, so that at present we have an abundance. We have tanks constructed in the green-houses, where, by means of high bottom-heat, we can grow the most tender aquatic plants. Our most ambitious, if not our earliest attempt, was the construction of a lily-pond. In Central Park we have nothing like the stream and pond effect on my own place, and we found that it would be necessary to treat our lakes in a larger and more expensive way. As a first essay we dug out a pond close by, and forming as it were part of, what is termed Conservatory Lake, just north of the gate at 72d Street and Fifth Avenue. The general shape of this pond was oval, with winding, irregular shores, bounded by a high bank on the east side and a great willow drooping over the north end. Rocks were disposed in the immediate banks, so as to suggest a natural formation rather than an artificial pond. The bottom, scarcely three feet deep, was cemented tight as a cup, and the water flowed gently in at one end and out at the other, and so through a basin into the sewer. Eighteen inches of soil was made rich with manure and deposited over the bottom. This soil was renewed more or less every year. Masses of flowering shrubs and small trees, such as the hydrangea, *Spiræa opulifolia*, and purple beech and birch formed a background of foliage on the steep hillside sloping up to Fifth Avenue. The lotuses *(N. speciosum)* in this pond were disposed in a solid mass at the north end along the steepest banks. There the observer can look down and see them mirrored on the surface

THE CENTRE OF THE FOUNTAIN,
UNION SQUARE.

of the water in the most effective way. Masses of the large hardy white lily *(N. alba candidissima)*, and the beautiful little white one *(N. pygmæa)*, the size of a half dollar, the Cape Cod pink lily, and several other kinds grow permanently in the mud of the bottom. Tender ones, like

BETHESDA FOUNTAIN BASIN
CENTRAL PARK.

the blue and red varieties *(N. Devoniensis, N. Zanzibarensis azurea* and *rosea)*, are planted in boxes filled with rich compost and removed to the park greenhouses every year. The season to enjoy this pond at its best is about ten o'clock in the morning,—later than this the heat of the sun gradually closes many of the blossoms, and earlier than nine some of the kinds have not yet opened their flowers. A sight of this pond in August and early in September is worth a considerable journey to see; and hardly less effective are the lotuses and lily plantations in boxes to be seen in the great fountain-basin at the Terrace.

Yet probably more effective, and certainly more attractive, on account of location, is the Union Square fountain, with its beautiful spray of water and vigorous water-plants, and in addition its outside collar of red alternanthera sward, planted with islands of geraniums. By electric light in the evening, or in the early morning sunlight, the effect of these lily-pads and lotus-leaves bedewed with globules of water is magical. Half a dozen, in fact, about all the fountain-basins in down-town New York are treated in this manner, and at almost any time before midnight, scores of people are gathered about them enjoying the beauties of the lilies and lotuses—nor, as the years go on, does the interest in them seem to flag. Indeed, among all decorations for architectural structures where a pool of water can be introduced, I believe there is nothing that can excel the lily and lotus. So confident am I of this, that I believe the time is not far distant when no fountain-basin will be considered completely equipped without them. In Central Park we have already begun to plant the shores extensively with them. At present this applies especially to the Pool at 100th Street and Eighth Avenue. There is a good deal of labor required in the preparation of rich soil on the shores, but we hope, nevertheless, in a few years to have our lakes as well stocked with lilies and lotuses as our fountain-basins.

CHAPTER XIII.

LAWN-PLANTING FOR SMALL PLACES.

THE word home has a pleasant sound. Indeed, one of the best signs of the times is a growing regard for home adornment. Practical considerations of simple comfort and show have long received too exclusive attention; but as we settle down more and more into a mature nation, the pleasantness of home gains in importance. In other words, our homes are becoming more characteristic, because we are learning duly to esteem and study them. They picture more truly the mind of the occupant or owner, because the occupant or owner is becoming more truly their architect and creator.

Doubtless fashion attracts many to this work, and makes vague enthusiasm the impelling motive, rather than love of art. But such motives or impulses are not altogether deplorable. Societies for the encouragement of decorative art flourish and grow strong. Hard times develop latent talent that would have otherwise lain fallow; and all things conspire to favor the advancement of home art. Then how home-like and refined and beautiful this work is making our houses! We may be very superficial nowadays,—very much inclined to run about the world; but surely our fathers, with all their domestic virtues, never had such lovely homes. Pretty devices in furniture, hangings, and a hundred simple things are noticeable everywhere as the work of the ladies and gentlemen of the house. Native taste, genius, association, and instinctive imitation, all combine to develop the true home artist. Yet models we must have, and principles we must recognize, and this in spite of the fact that most excellent work is done without conscious application of principles. Query: Does not this unconscious application of principles partake of the nature of genius? Let it be what it may, however, ordinary mortals, in their artistic struggles, are greatly helped by a few practical rules. Confiding in this belief, we ask a similar interest in both principles and practice of a definite, though not generally accepted, species of home art. We assert, in other words, that home art should not confine itself within doors, but should exert its influence on the immediate neighborhood of the house. Some of the most delightful hours of home life are spent on the piazza or lawn. It is, moreover, a pleasant hospitality that offers attractions on the lawn to the passer-by. But the sovereign difficulty that stands in the way of good lawn-planting, and especially of good lawn-planting for small places, is a widespread ignorance of lawn-plants. Numerous streets and shops offer instructive lessons to the decorator of the house and its contents. Hundreds of homes present tasteful examples of artistic work of many kinds. The study of lawn-planting, however, seems strangely neglected. Yet why is it? Are there no profitable examples to be found in parks or private grounds? And if there are, why do not people study them?

There are doubtless many who visit or communicate with such places, but how is it generally done? If they visit, they do it hastily and learn little. If they communicate, it is to ask about some plant which has struck their fancy. Whether it suits any position on their grounds they do not consider, and perhaps do not care. In like manner parks are looked over. They are but seldom studied. Now, if we are to have good work, the workman, or at least the deviser of the work, must know his material. You see, we are assuming that the lawn-planter of small places is also the owner. Seldom, indeed, can the owner of any small place afford a gardener of taste and knowledge; and the charm, moreover, of this peculiar species of work is its unprofessional character. It must have originality, variety, and no hackneyed forms, if it is to be of the best type. We hesitate, therefore, to fix anything like arbitrary rules, for fear they may be misunderstood and adhered to slavishly. Yet there are practical considerations and desirable artistic results growing out of the nature of plants that necessitate the use of rules. We cannot, of course, properly treat of the habits of plants in a short chapter, nor of all the rules that govern their employment on small places. Nevertheless, it will be our endeavor to set forth intelligibly a few important suggestions concerning work of this kind. We may illustrate them also by applying them to ordinary grounds. Lawn-planting for small places, as we propose it for popular employment, is a simple harmonious arrangement for the exhibition of individual plants. No one need fear, either, that the application of this principle will mar the effect of properly constructed masses.

Broad mass effect cannot be obtained satisfactorily, and therefore individual beauties must be emphasized in the selection and disposition of plants.

One of the most important considerations in planting a lot in this case as well as in others, is the disposition of shrubbery and trees about the lawn in a way that will secure single, open spaces of turf. These groups of shrubbery or trees should be arranged on the more prominent curves of walks about entrance gates, or the outer boundaries of the place. The object in view will be partly to secure the above-mentioned open spaces of turf, but chiefly to vary the effects and produce sudden, unexpected beautiful features. We should also seek to convey the idea that the path leads through the midst of a natural and picturesque group. These devices and the creation of miniature vistas will tend to give the place an appearance of greater size than is actually the case. It need scarcely be said that the curves of all the walks should be easy and flowing. Our sense of the graceful requires it, and practical experience proves its correctness. A horse, when taking the wagon directly to a given point without special guidance, always follows these long, easy curves. Indeed, the inexperienced driver is often bothered by the short curves of a circular road.

SMALL HOME LAWN.

A comparatively general principle is always to employ rhododendrons, hardy azaleas, Japanese maples, and other choice dwarf evergreen and deciduous shrubs directly about the house or on the walks near by. About the outskirts of the lawn, the entrance gates, and junction of paths, may be massed the larger-growing shrubbery and trees, if your door-yard is large enough to have any. They will serve to frame in the landscape, or to shut out undesirable views. We refer, of course, to medium-sized places of an acre or less. Within the skirting plantations of such places, few, if any, trees of large size should be used. Indeed, two or three elms, oaks, or lindens will come in time to occupy large sections of what should be entirely open space. Trees in great number, moreover, tend to make the plot look small and monotonous and the turf moss-grown and sparse. A few second-class trees, here and there, if the place is large enough, relieve and enrich the lawn without interfering with the effect of larger shrubbery. Large trees may be allowed at intervals on the extreme corners and outer boundaries, should the place be say half an acre in extent, to frame in the picture and diversify the contours and sky-line of exterior shrub groups. Sanitary conditions likewise demand a similar arrangement.

The position of the house also requires study. If space and full effect are desired, and no local peculiarities bar, it should be placed on one side so as to mass in a single lawn as much land as possible. This will broaden and enlarge generally the effect of the place. All fences should be screened more or less with shrubbery or hedges, although the last, as generally used, are formal and therefore objectiouable. Furthermore, few, if any, architectural adornment, such as statues, vases, etc., should be allowed. They are pretentious, artificial, and not in keeping with a natural style of the best landscape gardening. In the highly artificial gardenesque or geometric style they have, of course, their place, but of this we do not speak, as it is ill fitted for small rural homes. Summer-houses, gates and arbors, rockwork and waterfalls (the last two in secluded nooks, if at all), must be employed in the places under consideration to give whatever variety is desired other than trees and grass.

Another special point to be studied is the preservation of pleasing views, or vistas, in neighboring grounds. They may be framed in with attractive groups, which may at the same time plant out disagreeable, ungraceful objects. Provide, at least, one open range or view throughout the greatest depth of the lot, but not exactly through the centre line. A line, for instance, from the middle of the end adjoining the public road to the extreme corner in the rear is more desirable than several short vistas. This device tends greatly to increase the sense of novelty and distance, and lessens any apparent stiffness.

If the division fence must be kept up between adjoining lots, and no common lawn used, this fence should be also adorned with deciduous and evergreen trees and shrubs. These may be planted, if desired, at intervals to retain attractive glimpses and vistas as above suggested.

In all groups which define boundaries of the place, special care should be taken to avoid uniform horizon lines. Vary them with a few spire-like trees and shrubs now and then—birches and cypresses, *Tamarix Indica* and *Hibiscus Syriacus*,—which should also mark informally the corners of the lot, and complete, as it were, the frame of the picture. What we mean by *informally* is an avoidance of regular intervals or geometric arrangement.

As a rule, also, never plant a large, dark evergreen in front of, and mixed with, a lot of brilliant, light-colored, deciduous trees, for thus planted it will dwarf and weaken the effect of the latter. On some lawns of good size, however, a few massive dark evergreens may be used with effect in the extreme and, if possible, northwest corner of the lot. They will protect and give character to the place, and heighten the effect of the deciduous trees. A striking contrast may be obtained by interspersing a few white birches among, and in front of, these evergreens. They will serve, in this case, to brighten the picture both winter and summer,—though usually I prefer not to mix evergreen and deciduous trees. This harmonious and contrasting disposition of color requires careful study, and even perhaps a natural gift. For instance, it is better to introduce gay, bright colors in well-judged proportions. A few bright flowers of deep red, blue, or yellow, will have a better effect dispersed here and there about the lawns than in one great mass. Introduce them, so that by means of their different natures there will be always during the season a few gay points in the picture.

The turf borders of walks must present a true curve, and both sides be on a level. Their height should not be more than two inches or less than one. Great depth of border utterly destroys the effect of a walk.

Lawns generally—for we will say this much of grading—should never be reduced to a perfect level. They should be raised in the centre, or the surface be given the appearance of a hollow. The side lawn should generally assume a more or less slight incline toward the division fence. The rear lawn, if there is any of considerable relative size, should be graded, if possible, in like manner with the front. Of course, special conditions will vary any such rules. Their simple object is to increase the variety, and thereby produce a more pleasing and natural effect. All this, moreover, gives the place a larger and more picturesque appearance. In offering these few principles of an art capable of

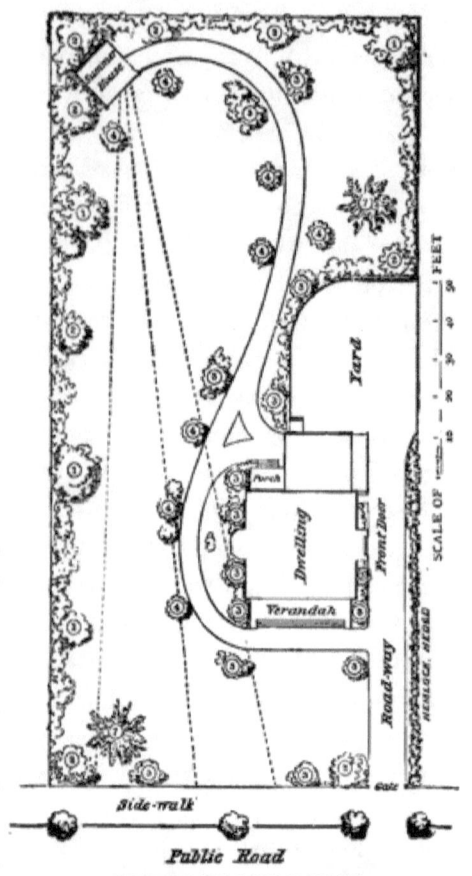

SUGGESTIONS FOR LAWN-PLANTING.

1, LARGE LAWN TREES; 2, TREES OF MODERATE GROWTHS; 3, DECIDUOUS SHRUBS OF MODERATE GROWTHS; 4, RARE AND DWARF DECIDUOUS AND EVERGREEN SHRUBS; 7, EVERGREEN TREES. LARGE SHRUBS EIGHT FEET APART,—SMALL SHRUBS FOUR FEET APART,—HEDGE PLANTS TWO FEET APART. RULES TO BE VARIED SOMEWHAT, ACCORDING TO THE NATURE OF THE PLANT USED.

producing so many diversified effects, I have endeavored to be sufficiently intelligible to secure their easy application. My language, however, may necessarily lack sometimes in clearness and picturesque force. I therefore present a design which fairly illustrates the simpler forms of lawn-planting as it should be exercised on small lots.

The first point that has been, and must always be, carefully studied is the location of the house in such manner as to keep as much of the lawn together as possible. Here the house is placed as it should be, near one side. If feasible, it should also be on the north or west of the lot, thereby securing the better protection for shrubs and flowers.

Immediately about the house may be gathered singly, or in groups, rare and choice deciduous and evergreen shrubbery, such as hydrangeas, hardy azaleas, Japanese maples, and the many beautiful dwarf conifers. These should be so arranged as to produce the most varied and favorable effect of color and form of which the plants are capable. It is usually necessary to thus retain only low-growing plants close to the house, for in this way only can the full architectural effect of the structure be secured. The exquisite and delicate attractions of choice plants demand also a position near the house where they can be easily seen. Any curve of the paths nearly adjoining a building may be thus ornamented, for the small size of the plants will leave all views and vistas as seen from the house unobstructed,— quite as important a point to be looked after as the proper exhibition of the architectural effect of the house. It will be therefore noticed that even the less immediate neighborhood of the house is left unplanted with large-sized shrubs or even second-class trees. The main feature of the place must evidently be the house, and therefore in devising prominent vistas and near or distant views we must take our stand at or not far from this point. Minor standpoints may of course be taken when some special effect is desired. Failure to contrive the landscape grouping from these established standpoints often weakens if it does not spoil lawn-planting, which is otherwise good and effective.

The curves of the walks or foot-paths are long and easy, reaching their destination in a natural and pleasing manner. All the junctions of paths and the main curves are planted with shrubbery in an irregular and informal manner. Furthermore, they are usually arranged with a view to suggesting the idea that the path is winding through single masses of flowers. It is not proposed in this plan to reserve any space for a vegetable garden, not only for want of room, but because it is notorious that vegetables thus grown are very expensive and troublesome. If exercise in gardening pursuits is desired, the same amount and a similar kind of work may be had in the culture of trees and shrubs as in that of vegetables with more generally satisfactory results. All necessary objects, not interesting in a picturesque way, such as drying-ground, entrance to the rear of buildings, tool-sheds, etc., should be shut out with deciduous shrubs. The front of these hedges or belts of shrubbery may be diversified by planting here and there occasional choice specimens.

The extreme end of the grounds may be also entered, if desired, by a path which should wind among shrubbery in somewhat obscure fashion, and come out suddenly on the lawn. The approach or entrance to the house is, in this case, somewhat formal and straight, for the sake of convenience, which must at times overrule considerations of beauty. It is well planted with shrubbery, however, to relieve all stiffness and vary the straight line. This system also introduces the pleasant element of surprise, as the full effect of the lawn is only presented after the place has been fairly entered. Flowing, graceful lines, with one exception, are retained everywhere, especially in the vistas that extend off to the full depth of the lot. On the most extended side, the vista takes a slanting direction across a croquet-ground, reached by a winding path and fronted by a summer-house in the extreme corner. This simple, inexpensive rustic structure—shown in the lawn-planting study—looks out toward the house over the croquet-ground, down the most attractive vista of the place. About it should climb vines, honeysuckles, etc., and some flowering shrubs. The entire feature is finely crowned and perfected by associating with it a slender, drooping, cut-leaved birch, with tender gray or light-green foliage and gleaming white bark. It will thus form one of the corner posts, or prominent points that define the outline of the picture, and, at the same time, constitute a most interesting and picturesque termination for a walk. One such feature is almost enough for a small place. Architecture should be confined, as a rule, to the house structure, and the lawn devoted to plants. Even rockwork, except in peculiar spots, has hardly a place on any small lawn, for reasons that should be obvious. Whatever portion of the summer-house appears from among the vines and surrounding foliage is intended to show a rustic, graceful, and solid structure. Simple rustic seats may, of course, be erected in suitable positions, but should not be made architecturally prominent. As a rule, however, chairs may be carried from the porch or veranda to any spot on so small a place. The planting on the walks directly fronting the summer-house should be made specially attractive by the employment of choice and dwarf trees and shrubs. The simple design of using a summer-house at all, has been to increase, within safe limits, the picturesque effect of the place, and to lend that portion of the scene a cosey, home-like aspect. Indeed, we have sought to give the entire place a similar natural appearance. Good lawn-planting should make it look, not as if it had been constructed in the ordinary sense of the term, but as if it had grown there, out of the special needs of the plants and of those expecting to enjoy them. Please note that we make most prominent the necessities of the plant. They must receive first attention, when the

A STUDY FOR LAWN-PLANTING.

best effects will follow in due course. Landscape architects are, perhaps, liable to fall into the habit of regarding plants as they would bricks or stones. An edifice of landscape architecture cannot be erected exactly as one chooses. Plants have their freaks and peculiarities in different positions, which even practical experience can scarcely foresee.

Beware of using on small places large-growing trees, and even on the outer boundary employ them sparsely. All such trees, like the Norway spruce or white pine, become in a few years, independent of their crowding mass, more or less unsightly for limited inclosures and necessarily close inspection. There should be an exact proportion between the size of a place and the eventual size—say in ten years—of all plants used for ornamenting it. For this reason, the rapid-growing, deciduous shrubs, with their wonderful variety of foliage and flowers and their moderate growth, are well adapted for small places. They not only attain moderate size, but can be duly restrained for many years by pruning. There are, also, many beautiful dwarf evergreen trees and shrubs well suited for lawn-planting on a small scale. Indeed, such plants may be kept, by pruning both root and branches intelligently, within a height of five feet for near a score of years.

It seems almost absurd to say that ornamental plants in their entire variety and special aptitudes for lawn-planting should be carefully studied by the lawn-planter. Nevertheless, many so-called experts seem to lose sight of the fact. With knowledge, however, and a cultivated taste, most delightful results can be obtained on a small lot by an outlay ranging from one hundred dollars to three hundred dollars, depending on the amount of choice plants used. Grading and fences are considerations governed by special conditions, and cannot, therefore, be taken into a general and typical estimate. This hardly seems an extravagant sum to devote to the exterior adornment of a home that has probably cost at least $4,000 for the building, and $2,000 more for a simple and tasteful furnishing. The general impression is widely spread abroad that the accomplishment of artistic effects in lawn-planting on small places, if possible at all, must be expensive and elaborate. Perhaps the idea comes from the fact that our parks and grand show places afford almost the only instances of artistic lawn-planting, and they, of course, are expensive. The lawn-planting efforts, moreover, of the jobbing gardener or owner of the place, are generally crude and based on no settled principles of art. It is this, perhaps, that gains credence for the belief that landscape gardening, as a picturesque art, is not only expensive, but does not suit small places. People may not state such ideas definitely to themselves; but they clearly demonstrate, by practice, a conscious or unconscious belief in their truth.

It has been, therefore, our desire to enunciate a few simple and important considerations of an art too much neglected, and to exemplify them practically from a plan intended for execution in a simple and inexpensive manner. There are necessarily many features and details, not here treated, that may be introduced on small places with much effect and without transgressing any fundamental rules of lawn-planting. We desire, however, to utter, before concluding, yet another warning against attempting too much when once we assume the artistic standpoint. Care for the proper exhibition and health of the plants themselves must be, after all, the prime consideration, in pursuance of which we cannot go far astray.

As I have already intimated, the rural adornment of the exterior of homes may rightfully demand and is receiving increased attention. It is improvement of taste in the same line, as that encouraged for the decoration of interiors, in that they both form important elements of home life. Unfortunately, many people have a way of regarding such work as requiring greater skill than is actually the case. It is really less difficult and expensive in proportion to the results obtained than most other forms of home art.

CHAPTER XIV.
CITY PARKS.

TO write of parks is to enter a field which is almost unlimited in extent. It has come now to the pass that every town and city of importance in Europe and America must have its park. It is the fashion. Whether the fashion is always well wrought out, is another thing. Unenlightened town authorities cannot always be depended on to employ competent talent, and to adopt a wise and comprehensive scheme of operations.

Yet, after all, parks are but larger door-yards or lawns, —or rather, in many cases, a series of them. The landscape-gardening lore applied to them is essentially the same as that employed in constructing the most modest home grounds. There is nothing really different in the general theory of the landscape gardening of parks from that of ordinary grounds. The apparent difference simply lies in the special application to some particular individual undertaking.

In actual practice, one park must, of course, be treated differently from other parks; but the lessons acquired by considering one piece of work of this kind, must always be helpful in carrying on other park-work.

In order, therefore, not to weary the reader with the enunciation of abstract principles, and detailing instructions that do not always really instruct, I am going to ask attention for a few moments to what I consider the best well advanced example of this kind of landscape gardening in America, namely, Central Park, New York City.

In considering Central Park, I beg leave to first introduce a few lines from the pen of Mr. Calvert Vaux, one of the originators of the essential artistic effect of the park.

"The principal defect of the ground originally appropriated to Central Park was that it offered very few comparatively level tracts of sufficient area to make a definite meadow-like impression on the eye. The ground is, for the most part, broken, undulating, picturesque, and rocky; and this is, confessedly, a desirable quality for a park site to possess, because it is a comparatively rare one. Most of the large parks—such as Hyde Park in London, the Bois de Boulogne in Paris, and the Phœnix Park in Dublin—are manifestly lacking in variety of natural surface; and every effort that art can make has to be resorted to for the purpose of relieving at intervals the general monotony of ground-line, which, in these parks, is the normal condition of things. Under such circumstances, it is evident that much can be done by planting trees of high and low growth, in such relation to each other that the sky-line will be agreeably diversified, while the level of the soil is but slightly varied. Nature works on so large a scale that it is rarely practicable to construct artificial eminences of sufficient magnitude to be really impressive. It has been done at the Parc du Chaumont, in Paris, quite effectively; but this is a rare example.

"It may be remarked, in this connection, that the sense of quiet repose ministered to by a large lawn surface is not satisfied by picturesque ground, however vigorously it may be planted; and, as the need for quiet repose in this work-a-day world is more constant than the need for vigorous stimulus, a lack of pastoral, meadow-like stretches of lawn in any large public park will always be felt by the habitual visitor to be a serious disadvantage."

Originally, a place for a large park was chosen along the East River, on the site of what was known as Jones Wood. This was not thought to be central enough, and, in consequence, Central Park was located within its present boundaries, with the exception that, for many years, its extent to the north only reached the neighborhood of 106th Street.

In 1857, the work of constructing Central Park was fairly undertaken, with Mr. Andrew H. Green the virtual head of the commission of eleven members appointed by the State, and not as a part of the Tweed charter of the city.

A topographical survey of the entire territory was first made, and then competitive plans, about thirty in number, were secured. The successful competitors were Messrs. Olmsted & Vaux. From that time until the present, the work of construction went steadily on, with some few exceptions, along the lines laid down in the original plans, nearly all being executed during the first twelve years.

Messrs. Olmsted & Vaux together, or either one alone, supervised this work, for the most part; and the confidence of the municipality having been won by Mr. Green, he was enabled for nearly thirteen consecutive years to successfully manage the finances and administration of this vast and complex civic enterprise. I feel, therefore, that it may be said with truth that Central Park could hardly have been built as it is to-day without the devoted interest, high administrative ability and artistic discernment displayed by the Hon. Andrew H. Green, at all stages of its development.

In order to secure some general idea of the treatment of Central Park, we will consider for a few moments its arrangement as it appears on the map. It is an awkward territory to treat, narrow and long, with about one hundred and fifty acres of Croton Reservoir occupying nearly the entire centre, from 85th to 97th Street. The clearly defined motive of the park is to secure a pleasant secluded country strolling ground directly in the heart of New York City. Perhaps the most difficult part of the park to design was the road system. It was, as all roads and walks are, a necessary feature, that would not in any case add to the beauty of the park. But opportunity for viewing the park must be secured, and so roads and walks were laid out on such lines as would exhibit the park best and mar it the least.

The main entrance, at Fifth Avenue and 59th Street, with its great after addition of the Plaza, was made at the corner of the park, extending in at an angle. This is always

THE MALL, CENTRAL PARK, NEW YORK CITY.

an effective way to enter a park. It makes the region seem larger and more varied in effect.

About half a mile along this drive, sixty feet wide, we come to the most important semi-artificial effect of Central Park, the Mall. It is a formal planted open-air cathedral of elms, showing long vistas of natural Gothic arches, with a wide walk in the centre and grass alleys on either side. The semi-artificial effect is relieved by irregular masses of trees planted all around the "cathedral of trees," thus shading off and merging the formal effect into the picturesque and natural one peculiar to the remainder of the park. The Mall is the most frequented part of the park. Beneath its noble arches people linger to enjoy the cool of morning or evening, or gather on bright afternoons in thousands to enjoy the music of a band occupying a stand near the north end. The Mall is about a quarter of a mile long, and at the extreme north end the cathedral of trees culminates in the Terrace, which is the most elaborate and manifestly architectural effect in the park.

A broad drive passes across the north end of the Mall, and along its entire width extends a broad high Nova Scotia sandstone balustrade, elaborately decorated with carved fruits, animals, and birds. Broad stone steps lead under this drive from the Mall itself; and from the north side of the drive two other sets of steps, bordered with carved balustrades illustrating the seasons, go down to a great Plaza, ornamented by the Bethesda Fountain. Beyond is the Lake, and still beyond, the woods of the Ramble that look illimitable. The view on an autumn day from the drive across the Plaza and fountain and across the Lake to the Ramble, where the woods are flushed with crimson and gold, is something to be treasured in the memory above all other scenes of the park.

To the east of the Mall, across the East Drive, is the Children's and Nurses' Lawn, extending from 72d Street, along Fifth Avenue to the gate at 67th Street. This place reminds one of an English lawn. It is a bit of five or six acres of fine turf, unbroken except by a few scattered shade trees of large size. Each tree is a fine specimen. There are horse-chestnuts and some excellent American beeches, oaks, tulip-trees, maples, elms, purple beeches, liquidambars, etc.

Under these trees and over the greensward play throughout the months of May and June, and occasionally later, hundreds of children both rich and poor. On a Saturday afternoon in May you will see scores of May-parties and hundreds of children covering every part of this lawn. The bright ribbons, the white dresses, and the greensward and trees, and above all, the happy faces, make a picture to gladden the heart of man. The attraction of the picture is increased when we consider that many of these children come from the great tenement-houses of the east side of town, and from some of the most crowded regions of the civilized world.

To the west of the Mall is another great lawn or meadow called the Green. Here base-ball is played on clear days, when the grass is dry, and under the shade of the bordering trees gather picnics. This meadow has no tree or shrub on its surface except on its extreme borders. It extends over to the West Drive, and is contrived, in connection with shrubbery and trees, as a western background, so as to give the idea of a larger area than really exists. There are only four open grass spaces or meadows of any size in Central Park; and as the main repose and highest enjoyment of the park reside chiefly in these spots, let the public beware of the intrusion of all glittering, discordant shows, military bodies, world's fairs, menageries, or race-courses. It is the poor who enjoy these places above all people—it is the children of the poor, and the mothers. We must not, therefore, spoil their heritage. The people should always treasure these open grass spaces of their parks. They are invaluable.

The Lower Meadow, near Seventh Avenue and 59th Street, is specially attractive. It has a great rock jutting out in it, and to the north at a higher level extends the seemingly large expanse of green. Round about run footpaths, bridle-paths, and drives, and at one corner of it is the children's play-ground, consisting of a great merry-go-round and the Kinderberg summer-house, one hundred feet in diameter.

On fine days in May and June this charming meadow is literally covered with playing children, thus fulfilling the most important functions of a park in a densely crowded city. Beyond these two meadows is the West Drive, sixty feet in width. In the neighborhood of 72d Street it passes on one side the Mineral Springs, backed by picturesque vine-covered rocks, and on the other by a lawn planted with fine shade trees—beeches, maples, elms, and, above all, several large specimens of Chinese magnolias (*Magnolia conspicua*).

THE ISLAND, NEAR BRIDGE, CENTRAL PARK, NEW YORK CITY.

Then the road strikes the Lake, looking on one side into a pool of rock-bordered water, with a spanning stone bridge at 77th Street; on the other side, over a broad view of lovely lake surface. This view is bordered with the sweeping branches of the wooded shores of the Ramble, and emphasized in the distance by a sandy beach and a point of foliage crowned by two great Lombardy poplars. There is a stone seat on the bridge close to 77th Street, where one can look over the shining surface of the Lake to the distant Lombardy poplars and possibly conclude that this is the most charming bit of landscape in the park.

At this point, however, the visitor is tempted away from the Drive into the Ramble, which must be considered as an episode needing special description. This quaint bit of wild-wood is chiefly made ground, and yet not in the least artificial-looking, for it is contrived quite simply out of the original simple and natural conditions, intricate as its paths and undulations may appear. It is identical in scale with what might readily be an ordinary country-place with the Belvidere as the mansion.

In front of the mansion is a fine central grass plat, and beyond wind paths up and down and across a stream, along the lake shore, or over great masses of rock down into a veritable gloomy cave. There are fine weeping beeches, azaleas, rhododendrons and plenty of perennial plants and shrubs blooming throughout the season. It is, in a word, a picturesque wild-wood nook, where one is hidden from and entirely forgets the city. An experiment like this might be hazardous, if the boundaries of the Ramble were not clearly defined by nature, because it does not

THE CAVE LANDING ON THE LAKE, CENTRAL PARK, NEW YORK CITY.

produce the ample, open-air lawn effect with reasonable shade, that should be the initial requirement in any city park.

Passing up the West Drive between two small hollow lawns ornamented with some fine specimens of evergreen, *Pinus excelsa* (Bhotan pine), and stone pines and hemlocks near 82d Street and Eighth Avenue, a loop drive leads up to a small plateau called The Concourse, where the eye wanders over miles of city houses, out to the Hudson in the distance. Here are many specimen evergreens of considerable excellence, creeping junipers, retinosporas, stone pines *(Pinus cembra)*, white pines in groves, silver firs of several excellent species and varieties, Oriental spruces, Atlas cedars, mugho pines, and some fine specimens of the evergreen thorn *(Cotoneaster* or *Cratægus pyracantha)*, with its shining small leaves and orange-red berries in autumn.

Beyond this portion of the park, towards the 85th Street transverse road, are two or three other small lawns on either side of the Drive. Throughout these lawns, since we left 72d Street, will be noticed along the West Drive as far as 110th Street quantities of evergreens. The West Drive was originally arranged for a winter as well as a summer resort, and is altogether the most attractive side of the park. Fashion has decreed, however, that the grand parade of carriages must go up and down the east side of the park.

Having reached the 85th Street transverse road, I will stop a moment and explain these peculiar features of the park. They are sunken roads extending from Fifth to Eighth Avenue, and there are four of them,—viz., at 65th,

NORTH MEADOW, CENTRAL PARK, NEW YORK CITY.

79th, 85th and 97th streets. Completely screened with trees and shrubs and seven-feet walls, spanned with frequent bridges, these driveways afford abundant convenience for traffic across the park.

On the 85th Street transverse road are situated the stables and workshops of the Department, completely hidden away. Here also is the entrance to the two great Croton reservoirs. They occupy one hundred and fifty-four acres of the heart of Central Park.

There is little of interest comparatively to be found in the park along the reservoirs. They block up and absorb almost the entire park for the distance they extend. When we reach, however, the north end of the park, clear of the reservoir, we come upon more charming meadow views.

The first is a glade of a few acres seen beneath the branches of noble pin-oaks, just before we reach the 97th Street transverse road. Here lawn-tennis is played, and the disposition of the trees is such that one can hardly believe it other than a genuine woodland nook. The scene is a thoroughly natural one, and far more park-like than anything in the Ramble.

Crossing over the 97th Street transverse road, and leaving with regret the grove of pin-oaks and the forest glade, we come to the great North Meadow of the park. It is a wonderful effect. Only nineteen acres, and apparently extending miles. The illustration gives a fair idea of it, but only as a picture can. The sheen of the grass, the varied tints of the foliage sweeping the turf to the left, the low-lying hillocks crowned with large forest trees, the great boulders entirely exposed or only half submerged, the meadow be-

OVERHANGING ROCK NEAR 110TH STREET AND SEVENTH AVENUE, CENTRAL PARK, NEW YORK CITY.

yond running back to seemingly unknown distances,—who will picture it truly? There is dignity, there is breadth, repose, restfulness, and yet a sense of isolation that is not absolute. It is genuine park scenery that the eye is tempted to linger on and the foot to walk on, and presents, if viewed as a single feature, one of the best examples we have of good park-work.

In May the bright costumes of numerous tennis players enliven its surface and attract many interested spectators. But to me it is more attractive when it lies in unbroken rest in the shimmering atmosphere of an autumn day with the red and gold of the maples and hickories framing and brightening its greensward.

Leaving the large suggestion of breadth and distance of the North Meadow, we pass up the West Drive to the Highlands of the park. As we cross the bridge spanning the stream which flows out of the pool of water near Eighth Avenue and 100th Street, called the Pool, we look in autumn on a splendid hillside of blood-red sumach, and turning the other way we see a rock-bordered stream winding along a forest-covered hillside. It is all charmingly wild and picturesque. When we reach the top of the great hill crowned with native trees we turn up a wide drive to the Circle a small open space of road, greensward, and dignified elms.

Turning back on our tracks and, after reaching the West Drive, passing down a steep winding way, we come to one of the finest single features of the park, a great overhanging rock. It is a picturesque object which is yet so natural-looking that it seems to have existed there always. On a

A GORGE IN CENTRAL PARK.

hot, dry day the gloom beneath it is literally "the shadow of a mighty rock in a thirsty land."

Near 110th Street we pass on the woody heights a great gorge filled with rhododendrons with a lily-pool at its base which produces a most natural and picturesque effect.

Opposite the entrance from Sixth Avenue we come to the Harlem Meer, a fine sheet of water of some twelve acres. Here there are sandy, pebbly shores and plenty of steep, rocky slopes coming down from the earthworks of old Fort Fish. Along the western shore of this lake at a somewhat higher level our drive now passes. We have come to the fashionable East Drive again, and opposite the entrance at Sixth Avenue and 110th Street most of the carriages turn.

The road winds at first picturesquely across a rock bridge over the stream that flows between the Pool and the Harlem Meer, and above this bridge appears a considerable waterfall. The walk along the stream above and south of the waterfall can be seen from the bridge to be picturesque and attractive with its wooded hillsides and on the east a grassy lawn sloping down to its eastern border. Having reached the top of the hill we come to the site of the old Mount Saint Vincent Convent, afterwards a restaurant, and finally burnt down and replaced by the present building. A little beyond this spot we come to the great North Meadow again and catch nearly as fine a view of its bright openness as we did from the West Drive. There is really little of interest now on the East Drive until we pass the reservoir and come to the east side of the Ramble.

The birches, evergreens, and vines on the rocky banks are fine at this point and there is a small deep dell to the east of the drive adjoining the 79th Street transverse road that is worth stopping to look at. Its sides are planted with beeches, oaks, elms, and maples, and at the bottom the grass seems to grow with peculiar richness and vigor.

As we come down the hill past the branch road leading out to 79th Street we look over to Fifth Avenue across a hollow or bowl extending from 79th to 72d Street. The sloping sides of this region, intended for a conservatory, enclosing as a central feature a small sheet of water with a lily-pond to the north, close by, make an attractive picture. These slopes are further adorned with fine specimens of firs, spruces, beeches, elms, and maples, and also with large groups of deciduous shrubs planted on the slope adjoining Fifth Avenue. There is a noteworthy mass of *Rosa rugosa* and among the shrubs are many Japanese snowballs, hydrangeas, *Rhodotypus kerrioides*, *Spiræa Thunbergii*, etc. The common shrubs are numerously represented by *Spiræa opulifolias*, red-twigged dogwoods, weigelias, standard honeysuckles, and philadelphuses.

The lily-pond is of irregular form, bordered with rocks and planted at intervals with lotuses, water-lilies, *Cyperus papyrus*, and the quaint and charming floating pontederia.

Thus we have made the round of the park and come to the Casino Restaurant, which is worth visiting in early or late May of all seasons, for the sake of the wonderful wistaria effect crowning the Pergola, a summer shelter overlooking the Mall at this point. The purple clusters of flowers lie in piles among the tossing tendrils and leaves until against the blue sky beyond the effect is that of a purple and green cloud resting on the arbor.

Before concluding this brief itinerary of the park, however, I must take the reader on horseback, as it were, to two or three bits of charming scenery on the bridle-paths, which can be seen nowhere else as well. The first is on a curve around the southwest side of the lower green near Seventh Avenue and 59th Street. There is a great rock here, and an ever widening meadow, with a distant view over another meadow and plenty of trees and shrubs round about. The sweet influences of spring at this point are not to be surpassed anywhere else in the park.

Another charmingly secluded spot may be found by passing up the bridle-path to the stone bridge at 77th Street and Eighth Avenue to a pool of water with a loop road leading to the water's brink and a great sheer rock on the opposite shore. The shrubs on the bank at this point are attractive, in both spring and autumn, including spireas, dogwoods, *Lonicera fragrantissima*, weigelias, privets, and masses of honeysuckles over the small rocks on the edge of the water, and *Ampelopsis tricuspidata* and Virginia creepers on the stone bridge and sheer rock. I would advise the reader to mount a horse and ride through the park, if only for the opportunity of sauntering down this loop bridle-path at 77th Street and Eighth Avenue.

There are, besides, choice bits of landscape along the bridle-paths between 81st Street and 86th Street and up by 97th Street among the pin-oaks. But in no other way can the great North Meadow be seen so well as on horseback from the bridle-path that runs round its entire extent. On the east side the bridle-path is completely embowered with trees, and from these you look out with peculiar enjoyment over the expanse of the North Meadow.

There are five and one half miles of bridle-paths, and nine miles of drives, and thirty miles of foot-paths in Central Park. Altogether, there are eight hundred and fifty acres in Central Park, including the one hundred and fifty acres of reservoir.

It might doubtless be interesting to speak of many other individual features of marked interest in Central Park. I do not, however, think it expedient in such a general description and illustration of general principles as this to be drawn into such emphasis of details. Indeed, the manifest superiority of the design as a whole is its general adequacy to the effect sought, which was simple park scenery in the midst of a city.

This seems a proper place to remark that another great attraction possessed by Central Park is the essential unity of its design. Here is a park laid out on paper according to definite artistic conceptions and then executed substantially as conceived in the beginning.

Before closing my remarks on Central Park I desire to direct especial attention to the popular-amusement feature insisted upon in its arrangement. The chief and most important office of Central Park is not to furnish agreeable driving territory for the *beau monde*, the millionaires, and the lovers of horseflesh. It is not a scheme to please and attract the fashionable, but it is a playground for the young people, a pleasant open-air breathing space for the mothers and fathers who desire to go into the country and cannot get there.

As a part of this scheme for the pleasure and well-being of the multitude there is music on the Mall twice a week, goat-carriages, donkeys, merry-go-rounds, summer-houses, grounds for croquet, lawn-tennis, base-ball, foot-ball, and lacrosse, and, above all, grounds everywhere for picnics in spring and early summer. Last year there were picnic permits issued to over seventy-five thousand children, whose wants were ministered to by park employés without charge.

In order to secure the greatest amount of pleasure from these games, the turf requires special and solicitous attention. It must be mown frequently, and manured yearly; and above all it must not be used when soft from rain, and liable to be torn up by the feet of visitors.

Before closing this chapter on city parks, I must say a few words about small city squares or greens. They are generally not large enough to consist of more than a few square yards or half a dozen acres. Usually they come on some irregularly shaped space situated at the junction of two or more streets. Properly they should be termed "Greens," like the Bowling Green, at the foot of Broadway, New York City. The green effect of the grass should be made the chief and most important feature of their treatment.

Some fence of a simple and inconspicuous character should surround the plot, and this fence should be masked and ornamented with shrubs and trees, but the interior should be simple open greensward, with a few bright bits of bedding, and trees enough for shade along the paths. The semi-artificial lines and masses of formal bedding are out of place in the strictly rural scenery of Central Park, but in the city parks they look well amid the architectural lines of the surrounding buildings.

Every small city park should have a widening of the pathway towards the centre, and if possible an open plaza where the children may play and the visitor linger. Architectural adornments may properly be employed in small parks, so long as they do not seriously interfere with the open grass effect. There may be even busts or statues, but especially suitable are drinking fountains, and fountain basins, with great sprays of water.

The fountain basins may be effectively ornamented with lotuses, water-lilies, and other decorative water-plants. All such adornment of small city squares or greens tends to appropriately enliven and enrich the general appearance of a crowded city, where the effect of everything is artificial, and more or less formal or tedious.

I should warn those who propose to plant these small city squares, that the surrounding conditions are not primarily favorable for the growth of plants. The air is apt to be hot, dry, and dust-laden, if not actually impure. Consequently the soil should be thoroughly enriched, and the most vigorous and hardy trees and shrubs employed. Evergreens seldom do well in large, crowded cities. It is better to plant certain hardy, deciduous trees and shrubs, such as the privet, weigelia, snowball, *Spiræa opulifolia*, American thorn *(Cratægus Crus-galli)*, philadelphus, American elm, honey-locust, American linden, Norway and sugar maples, and the Oriental plane trees.

The care of these small city squares is often difficult on account of the crowds that congregate or pass through, and on account of the heat and dust, but it can be done by continual watering, cleaning, and cultivating. Canal Street Park, New York, is situated in perhaps the most difficult position in the city of which it is possible to conceive. The surrounding houses are tenements, produce stores, and the like, and the incessant traffic consists largely of trucks and carts, laden with coal, refuse, vegetables, and the roughest material. Dirt is ubiquitous, and the heat at times is great. And yet the grass is always green here, and the shrubs, trees, and bedding plants, always thriving. The park is only 195 feet long by 69 feet wide, but it occupies the entire attention of one gardener, and two police officers, either one of whom is on guard at night and during the day.

It is a pleasure to see the mothers with their children gather here on the settees throughout the long sultry summer nights, and realize that this unspeakable boon can be secured at such comparatively low cost. Every city should seek to adorn these small greens, to increase their number, and to enlarge their boundaries.

CHAPTER XV.

RAILWAY, CHURCHYARD, AND CEMETERY LAWN-PLANTING.

A RAILWAY LAWN.

N encouraging sign of the times is the interest which has been manifested of late by our railroad officials in the appearance of the stations on their lines. Many of these buildings and surroundings, which were formerly eyesores, have been so beautified by the judicious expenditure of some thought and a little money, that they now lend an added charm to the landscape; and were they to be removed, they would be missed with regret.

I had occasion lately to visit one of these recently improved stations. The natural surface of the ground rose rapidly in the rear of the building, and along the edge of the great rock mass, cut through just here by the railroad, gurgled a small, tumbling rill across the road, under a board or two. Except just about the station, where everything had been thoroughly cleared away, bits of rock abounded, and these had been utilized in a picturesque manner. Immediately around the station ran a carriage road, with a convenient oval circuit for turning. On one end of this circuit, near the station, was a weeping beech, and the other extremity was occupied by a group of flowering shrubs, that, although too freshly planted to blossom that year, already impressed the eye as an attractive mass of bright green foliage. Here and there, near the house, were planted pleasant shade-trees, such as the linden, oak, and maple. It should be remembered that by thus planting large shade-trees, the architectural effect of the building was greatly enhanced, because the side toward the railroad, which is the true front, was uninterfered with. Passing mention is made of this, because objection might otherwise be fairly raised to shutting in the building with trees. The entire work had been completed rapidly, but with evident thoroughness. Rich, well-tilled soil had been secured, and the paths were solid and properly constructed. All the edges of the walks were bordered by cut sods, and the remaining ground was sown with grass seed that, by the good luck that sometimes accompanies good management, had come up evenly. A single path wound through the small domain, carried hither and thither so as to obtain the best views of the river near by, as well as the utmost variety of surface. It was surprising how large the place seemed, as one rambled over this undulating path. The matter-of-fact visitor was even betrayed into the expression that it was as good in its way as anything in Central Park.

There was little bedding stuff that required to be constantly renewed; only a few bits of color in the way of scarlet geraniums and the like, planted as a salient point in some shrub group. Almost everything was simple and permanent in character. Hardy flowering shrubs were freely used, because some one of them bloomed during every month of spring and summer. There were small-sized trees, like the purple beech, stuartia, and magnolia. A few groups and single specimens of evergreens stood in a section near the rockiest part of the grounds and somewhat by themselves. These consisted almost entirely of dwarf, slow-growing kinds, such as the mugho pine, stone pine, creeping juniper, and some of the beautiful retinosporas. Peering out from the rocks and background of woods and shrubbery that surrounded the spot, were white-barked weeping birches, golden oaks, and other trees of equally individual character. A rhododendron or two bloomed also among the nearest rocks, as well as several hardy azaleas. Along the little run of water were set out various herbaceous plants that flower freely and brightly in the green turf nearly all summer, and come up again next year without being renewed. Over the rocks grew climbing vines, Virginia creepers, moneywort, and periwinkles, as well as sedums, and many other varieties of herbaceous plants fitted for such spots. A little of everything that properly pertained to a lawn was here, for variety had been one of the main objects sought, in order that the tedium of the waiting passenger might be alleviated as much as possible.

I cannot properly explain how charmingly the combinations were contrived to thus produce, by a complete variety, the most continued pleasure and surprise. Uninitiated as they were, the railroad men at once recognized the attractions of this variety, even in its crude and freshly planted state, and grimly, after the way of such men, expressed approval.

I asked the station-master how all this had been done, and how it was to be kept in order. He said that a close survey of the ground and existing plants was made last fall. During the winter, maps and planting lists were worked up; and in the spring, a lawn-planting foreman came on the ground, with half a dozen men, and with the help of the map, and one or two visits of the landscape architect, they accomplished the result.

As to keeping it in order, the work is easily done, he said, by men who are sent from the company's office, at stated times, to mow grass, and to weed and prune. All the station-master is asked to do is to watch that everything is kept in apple-pie shape, and if weeds and grass show signs of getting ahead, to telegraph for help.

THE CHURCHYARD.

Churchyards and cemeteries were once essentially identical. All this, however, is rapidly changing. For sanitary and other good reasons, the cemetery is now separated from the church; but, unfortunately, with the growth of modern cemeteries is associated curtailment of churchyards. This is greatly to be deplored. Would it not be wiser to even moderate, if necessary the ornamentation of the interior, and secure trees and grass and flowers? A few may be impressed with holy awe by sculptured nave and glowing window, but the whole world that passes by is benefited by trees and flowers. My object, therefore, is to see if I cannot help to increase the love and knowledge of lawn-planting, as applied to the grounds of buildings for worship. In the belief that it is a reasonable and beautiful object, I will endeavor to point out how certain trees not only harmonize with such surroundings, but also how they possess special and practical value in the positions they occupy. The accompanying illustration shows what can be effected in a country churchyard.

A CHURCH LAWN.

Such trees as stand near the church are rightly dignified and statuesque. For the same reason, they generally stand singly or in small groups of three. The larger ones, like the American elm in the centre, or the ginkgo *(Salisburia adiantifolia)* to the right, have a more or less erect character. On the other hand, the yellow-wood (*Virgilia lutea*), to the left of the last, has a broad head and curving outline of trunk and branches, suggestive of the high finish of the turner's art. Harmony and variety are specially sought in the design of this plot. Remarkable specimens of weeping sophora stand in one or two spots, and seem essentially adapted to the surroundings of a church.

Noteworthy and valuable weeping trees are the elms on either side of the gate. They have been planted later than many other trees visible in the picture, and are of the campestris species, Camperdown variety. Evidently British from their name, they bear little resemblance to our American elms. Slow of growth and compact of form, at no time are they lofty and spreading. They belong evidently to the rounded type of foliage contour. The rich, dark green leaves droop and fold over each other in a regular manner, in many cases quite systematic. You will notice in the picture, however, that these particular specimens have taken a fancy to lean toward each other in a manner that even trees will sometimes assume. Pruning secures for this tree a perfect form, until it attains considerable age. In short, it may be ranked well up on our short roll of merit of really good weeping trees. The weeping sophora, of which there are two, is possibly more elegant in appearance, with drooping garlands of neat, acacia-like foliage. It is not, however, as hardy, either in summer or winter, as the Camperdown elm. I need hardly rehearse the excellence of the weeping sophora, having already treated of it elsewhere. Furthermore, I want to call your attention again to the broad, round-headed yellow-wood (*Virgilia lutea*, or, according to best authorities, *Cladrastis tinctoria*). It is the most cheerful tree on the grounds, and, moreover, though rare, an American plant from the banks of the Tennessee. The foliage is not dense, and does not clothe the interior branching of the tree, which, in a way, lays open to view a peculiar development of trunk and limbs. About their rounded contour is stretched tightly wrinkled swathings of smooth, light-colored bark. Small and graceful, the leaves are light green, more or less like those of an acacia or sophora, and the flowers white and in form drooping, like those of the wistaria. The pyramidal oak, too, forms one of the best trees for a church lawn. Its upright lines are bold and picturesque, as relieved against the more horizontal ones of the church. The tree is, moreover, massive and, for an oak, very rapid in growing.

In seeking to gather about the church trees that accord with the place, the lawn-planter, by employing the *Virgilia lutea*, has been most successful. The color shades off effectively, through the varying hues of ginkgo, weeping elm, pyramidal oak, and stately American elm, to the deepest, noblest tone of all produced by the grand Nordmann's fir, near the right-hand corner of the church. Here a dark, noble mass, with rich, silvery tints, rears itself into a symmetrical, perfect feature, which impresses the eye much as the ear is affected by some deep, solemn strain from the old organ within the church. This fir, indeed, serves, with its companion evergreens, to give the place its special character. By good luck, hills and trees to the north and west have so protected this spot that evergreens of somewhat tender nature stand the winter well. Thus, we have the

Irish yew, rich and dark and erect as a sentinel, as well as its parent *Taxus baccata*, also dark, if not altogether statuesque. Other evergreens bear, of course, their due relation to this harmony of color and form. Graceful, grotesque, weeping spruces, golden and fern-like Japanese cypresses or retinosporas, columnar weeping silver firs, and fountain-like weeping hemlocks, alike contribute each its separate mark on the broad effect of the whole. It is a symphony of trees as impressive in many ways as the swelling chords of the church organ. Nor does the velvet turf, extending in broad, unbroken spaces, fail to perfect the general appearance of the scene. Statuesque dwarf evergreens, as well as more lofty trees, occupy the space immediately about the church walk, or fence, leaving wide openings between. The fence, carrying out the same idea, is low, with but two rails, and as inconspicuous as possible. Care is taken also not to overload the lawn with choice, low-growing, sombre evergreens, as represented by most of the yews, spruces, and firs. Just as the effect of the graver elms, oaks, and maples is lightened by the tints of the yellow-wood and ginkgo, so the evergreens pass here and there into bright golden forms, and again into low deciduous trees, which are not, in any sense, shrubs. Thus the glowing leaves of certain Japanese maples are used as single specimens, and especially the low-grafted form of the Kilmarnock weeping willow. This tree is very symmetrical and even graceful, if properly pruned; but, as usually known in its high-grafted form, its stem early decays. In the sketch accompanying the church illustration is shown the low-grafted form, which is comparatively free from bark-cracking on account of the protection the branches afford the stem. The effect of the employment of this weeping plant in the churchyard is specially happy, for it hardly represents a real shrub, which is, in this case, scarcely admitted, and yet it breaks, with its irregular, graceful lines, any possible monotony among the statuesque dwarf evergreens. Of course, the ivy on the wall and the crimson autumnal tints of the Japan creeper (*Ampelopsis tricuspidata*) are here in all their glory. Altogether, there is an organic completeness in the selection of the various plants that proves the lawn-planter to have had a genuine sympathy for his work, as well as abundant practical knowledge.

THE CEMETERY.

The excessive and tasteless use of stonework in our cemeteries has been unnaturally fostered by love of display and by the fact that cut stone is more permanent and needs less care than shrubs and flowers, which are not only difficult to select to-day, but liable to perish to-morrow. Hence grew up the vulgar fashion of using stone inordinately, nominally in honor of the dead, but often merely for the sake of fashionable display.

Plants, however, have long been employed, entirely independent of what the fashion might be, and in their use, therefore, lies the really heart-felt offering to the memory of the departed. More than twenty years ago, one or two cemeteries, notably Spring Grove, Cincinnati; and Laurel Hill, Philadelphia, attempted a reform which aimed at doing away with fenced and hedged burial plots. Hartford laid out a cemetery on a similar plan, and a portion of Woodlawn Cemetery, New York, has a park-like character, unblemished by fences or even tombstones. Cincinnati has certainly been the pioneer in this movement, and to Mr. Strauch, superintendent of Spring Grove Cemetery, of that city, belongs the credit of most persistently and systematically following out what may really be called a new principle.

In Woodlawn Cemetery, New York, may be seen a fair example of what is generally considered a good park-like cemetery. Shrubs and trees are planted about in irregular fashion upon a lawn. The lots are clustered here and there in groups, and their boundaries are designated by small stones or stakes hidden in the grass, the graves themselves being made in an inconspicuous manner. With the exception of creeping vines, not a tree, shrub, or flower is planted unless by permission of the authorities. Flowers are allowed on the graves, but no plants bearing flowers may be set out except under these restrictions. Everything is under the control of a central authority, which is supposed to know exactly how to produce the finest landscape effect possible under the circumstances. That such effects are actually accomplished may be fairly questioned by competent judges; but that is not the fault of the system.

Many people, however, possess cemetery lots where stones exist, and they must make the best of things as they are. They may not wish to destroy existing evergreen hedges entirely, in which case they can leave a plant in each corner and on either side of the gate, otherwise they will find it advisable to follow the plan here presented as regards its general system. This system consists chiefly in open stretches of perfect greensward throughout the entire lot, except on the extreme edges and at the head and foot of the graves. No formal hedge is necessary, but a border of foliage, to break and modify the stiffness of the necessarily stiff-looking fence. This work can only be accomplished properly by dwarf evergreens, the forms of which are

A BURIAL PLOT.

statuesque and dignified, as comports with the spirit of the place. I refer to such plants as the Swiss stone pine, the conical and Gregory spruces, and the many agreeable dwarf varieties of retinosporas. These plants have the supreme advantage of the most lovely variety and contrast of color, when properly arranged, and have at the same time the ability to retain their dwarf forms for a score of years with a minimum of pruning. Variety of color is too little considered in most landscape gardening of a permanent character, and the unfitting mature size of many plants in confined positions is equally disregarded.

This lot, it will be seen, has a weeping beech on the border of the lot, and three or four slow-growing plants—roses and variegated-leaved Japanese maples—by the grave itself. This is designed to secure a peculiar grace for this special spot, which may be enhanced by allowing a vine or two, ivy or Japan creeper, to twine about the base of gravestone or monument. All plants used in the centre of the lot should be pruned and managed with the greatest care, or they will become, in spite of their dwarfness, too luxuriant in growth for the place they occupy. Above all things, the vines should not be allowed to cover all the surface of the stones and monuments. Any seeming neglect and disorder must detract greatly from the proper dignity of the spot.

CHAPTER XVI.

NOOKERIES ON THE HOME GROUNDS.

OW shall we treat our garden or lawn nookeries? to coin a phrase which means, I take it, an aggregation or congeries of nooks and corners combined into a single isolated picture. On general principles nooks of the garden attain a value not only because in them, as Lord Bacon quaintly puts it, "when the wind blows sharp you may walk as in a gallery," but because these nooks afford the attraction of a surprise, that may be in the truest sense, when properly taken advantage of, a pleasurable surprise. In a word, there must be a succession of nooks, surprises in numbers, all within the limits of one small spot, to make your true nookery, for a bare corner is in no sense a nookery. Memory must surely recall to all of us such spots down in the orchard or behind the barn, and in the edge of the woods at the back of the house. The old apple tree with the grape-vine trailing over it, down by the drinking-

hole for cattle in the corner of the orchard, was a delightful nookery in its way, with its rich turf and charming wild flowers, or weeds as some would call them. Abounding, too, in nookeries of the pleasantest sort was the old flower garden, with its box-lined borders and larkspurs, and hollyhocks, where, for instance, in a far corner, we come suddenly on an old arbor festooned with grape-vine, honeysuckle, and trumpet creeper. I think, though, according to my remembrance, the best nookery was to be found down on the edge of the grove, with its pool of water on one side and its bays of shrubby growth and aisles of tree trunks on the other. The rushes and lilies of those remote, still waters, and the wild flowers and climbing vines, Virginia creepers and bitter-sweets in the recesses of the woods, even now linger with me as types of what genuine nookeries should be.

After recalling the constituent parts of such scenes, it ought not to be hard to adorn, and, if necessary, create these pleasant nookeries in our gardens. It is not a question of extensive or even exquisite culture, but only a few well-directed efforts from year to year and the place takes care of itself. Every one surely can find a secluded nook in the garden or lawn, and there are many things we can do of the easiest nature that will tend greatly to perfect these delightful surprises. Wild flowers can be fostered and even planted in such a way as to preclude all idea whatever of the presence of the hand of man. Hardy shrubs, too, may be used in the most effective manner for this purpose, by planting them singly or in colonies in a thoroughly wild-wood manner. But, I believe, nothing better than the intelligent employment of climbers and creepers will create such pleasant, artistic surprises in these nooks, and illustrate the proper way to treat them. With them alone we can do wonders. Take that old stump before you and wreathe it with festoons of the long, crimson flowers of the trumpet creeper—*Tecoma radicans*. Nothing in its way can be finer except the employment of *Tecoma grandiflora*, with its great orange-colored flowers. So vigorous and stout are these climbers that they soon grow into a tossing, wild mass of leaves and trumpet-shaped flowers, to the entire obliteration from view of the old trunk over which they grow. Do not confuse, however, these trumpet flowers with those of the scarlet trumpet-vine or honeysuckle—*Lonicera sempervirens*—with the bright, glossy, green leaves that often last nearly all winter. Every one thinks of honeysuckle flowers as sweet-scented and yellow, white or red; but how many stop to examine the rich, glossy shades of honeysuckle leaves, so admirably adapted for carpeting bare spots or draping heaps of stone and stumps and tree trunks? There are many varieties of honeysuckles which are, every one of them, worthy of employment.

In some of these sheltered nooks we might even use the unequalled English ivy, particularly if we use it as a carpet; but we certainly can have the so-called Japan ivy, *Ampelopsis Veitchii*, or *tricuspidata*, in this country the most perfect of hardy creepers for clinging by rootlets to stone or wooden surfaces. Few plant effects can surpass in summer the glossy color and artistic forms of the leaves and tendrils of the Japan ivy, or the crimson and gold of its autumn tints. But we must not forget the other varieties of *Ampe-*

lopsis in contemplating the charms of the Japan ivy, for few things are more effective in our tangled wild-wood corners than great masses of the common Virginia creepers—*A. quinquefolia*. How its piled-up leaves festoon the tree trunks with overlying masses of shining green in summer and of scarlet and blood-red in autumn every one familiar with fall effects must remember. Of an entirely different, but none the less very effective, nature is the Virginia silk—*Periploca Græca*,—with long, pointed, shining leaves, small flowers, and brownish-red stems, reaching out with almost unrivalled speed of growth away up the stem of the tree. For the adornment of the upper part of the trees and rock masses we must not forget the rich clusters of foliage and charming garlands of flowers of the purple and white wistarias. Wistarias, allowed to reach out, flower and leaf most abundantly in their upper parts, and are, therefore, specially adapted for garlanding a tree or roof far up in the air without reference to covering its lower part. Then there is the neat-leaved akebia; the bold and picturesque, large, light-colored leaved Dutchman's pipe; the autumn-crimsoned purple-berried bitter-sweet, all lovely climbers for our purpose. But of all charming climbers, I verily believe the clematis must bear the palm. The variety of color and form of its flowers seems endless, extending as it does, from the noble, dark-purple *Clematis Jackmani* to the delicate, small, white and yellow flowers of *C. flammula* and *C. apiifolia*. And they are equally fine in the nookery, whether carpeting bare spaces of ground or garlanding and draping rocks and trees.

Before leaving a subject thus closely allied to the very

heart of nature I would note again, with increased emphasis, that one of the peculiarities of the proper treatment of these pleasant corners, whether in garden or woodland, is that it may be said, almost, that the more you plant and the less you cultivate and cut with the sickle, scythe, and pruning knife, the more surely you attain the end desired. Conventional methods are all out of place in the true garden or lawn nookery. Grasses, mosses, tree trunks, fantastic, "lovely climbers and wild flowers, weeds even, and manie a plant that the fastidious woulde cast forthe," tall, purple thistles and asters, and great docks and sorrels, all make up a picture in such nooks, that, irradiated, perchance, by the level beams of the setting sun, surpasses "beyond compare" any number of cart-loads of scentless bedding plants, mechanically arranged and ribbon-bordered.

CHAPTER XVII.

MY FRIEND THE ANDROMEDA.

DO not know why it is, but the appearance of a tree frequently presents itself to my mind in a semi-personal, or I might almost say human, way. This is fanciful, no doubt, but only another instance of the facility with which the mind clothes simple objects of the senses with its own less simple drapery of the imagination. Association of ideas may, perhaps, account for it. When a tree is graceful, slender, or drooping, we think immediately of womanly metaphors, like the poet's epithet of "Lady of the Woods," as applied to the birch; and I fail to see any objection to such an innocent misconception. It not only pleases without doing harm to any one, but it does more. Such an attitude of mind tends to develop a more sympathetic consideration and study of plants under varying conditions. Horses, dogs, and even some comparatively worthless human beings, gain and have gained, during all time, much of this sympathetic

consideration. May we not, in its humble sphere of life, plead a similar claim for the tree? Every member of the lawn affords us a more profound and lasting impression, viewed from this seemingly fanciful standpoint of so-called personal sympathy, than if we keep ourselves resolutely realistic in our feelings. I assure you, gentle reader, results will prove that the encouragement of these scientifically inaccurate vagaries of the imagination is neither bad for the tree nor the man, nor even for science. My thoughts are disporting themselves somewhat after this manner to-day, while my attention rests musingly on a lovely specimen of an *Andromeda arborea*, known also as *Oxydendrum arboreum*, or sorrel tree. The October sun and air enrich and strengthen its tints and outline, and, in more than one way, its beauty arouses the most palpable feelings of pleasure.

To most observers, indeed, it may be only a bright-leaved tree; but to me as I look at it, come still fairer images and associations. I remember many a morning before this one when I have looked with pleasure on this tree. Last summer, in July, and August even, I used to enjoy its white-tasselled flowers, bending and delicately graceful as those of any hot-house plant. I insisted then on pointing it out to my friends with, perhaps, what they felt to be the mere pride of ownership; and was wont to declare that here was a tree that not only bore lovely flowers, when scarcely another tree was so adorned, but that also proved good in color and attractive in form throughout the season. One of the few plants that neither paled its shining green nor lost its firmness of leaf texture from May to October.

On these occasions I was apt, on very slight provocation, to grow warm in praise of my andromeda. It was everything that was lovely. The leaves were always shining and gracefully curving. Bark and twigs were refined and attractive in texture, coloring, and picturesque contour. In every way this plant was full of beauty as pleasing as that of its August flowers. Several sober, matter-of-fact friends have, I know, smiled from time to time at my enthusiasm on the subject of this andromeda. But what matters that? It is only their loss that they are unable to see with my eyes; and, in one sense, my gain. The charms of a flower are, to the possessor, rather increased than otherwise by the sense that few people have the wit to appreciate them; but it is a little selfish, I know, to feel thus, although entirely human, and I am trying to make my peace with conscience by enlarging on the topic to-day.

Truly, this brisk October morning, as I am dwelling on the lovely crimson color of my favorite, bright with sunlight and dew, and adorned with pendant seed vessels, I am disposed to doubt whether my enthusiasm, in all its fulness, has not been after all somewhat crude and unappreciative. Notwithstanding its evident excellence, it occurs to me now that this plant has beauty that is still greater than commonly appears, because it is so seldom suitably employed. It is not, like your oak or beech, sufficient unto itself in its isolated grandeur; but it is a tree that needs association to develop its highest possibilities of attraction. Like some rich beauty, whose loveliness is stimulated and brought out by the charms of other forms and faces, to pale again when left alone or neglected; or like the gifted and witty mind that needs the sympathy of kindred spirits to put it on its mettle, the andromeda silently craves to be artistically disposed and grouped with other plants.

I comprehend this morning, seemingly for the first time, that my andromeda, my dear andromeda, is ungainly. A crooked, slender stem, though, in a certain way, fine and picturesque, supports its graceful mass of foliage in a decidedly unsatisfactory way. Surely this plant was not made to stand alone. On the contrary, I am inclined to think it decidedly affects society. Next spring, therefore, I am going to keep it in the conspicuous position it now occupies, but, at the same time, make it happy by surrounding it with friends and relatives. A mass of rhododendrons shall cluster in its rear, for they show a fine relation to the andromeda in both appearance and nature; and they are, moreover, rich and noble plants. These rhododendrons, in the outline of their grouping, will present deep bays and promontories of foliage, with points and flanks and bare places, masked with choice low-growing shrubs, like mahonias and evergreen thorns, the bush form of Chinese wistarias, and the golden and variegated weigelia. My andromeda shall not appear exactly on one of the points of these rhododendrons, to which its leaves bear too close a relation for intimate grouping; but it shall be isolated and, at the same time, surrounded and connected with the mainland of foliage by the mahonias and evergreen thorns. The weak parts of the base of my plant will be thus masked, as so many plants apt to develop naked bases need to be masked, and its more excellent qualities brought out in finest relief by its association.

Several years hence, perhaps, I may be looking at my andromeda, in its new position, as I am looking at it now, and, I am sure, in that case, it will comport itself with greater dignity and grace than it has ever done aforetime. Its crimson tints will seem richer when relieved against the shining green of the mahonias and rhododendrons; and its naturally taller form will rise with more striking and harmonious effect from amid the broad-spreading masses of adjacent greenery. And why should I not give fitting companions to my fair andromeda? It is to me of greater value than my pictures, and yet I re-hang and re-group my pictures with the greatest care. Certainly, sympathy of this sort is not wasted on plants, which should be treated as sensitive children that need to be deeply influenced in the best way by sympathetic personal comprehension and care.

INDEX.

A

Abies amabilis, 140
  Cephalonica, 84
  Cilicica, 83
  compacta, 84, 140
  concolor, 84
  Douglasii, 84
  lasiocarpa, 84
  nobilis, 83
  Parsonsii 84, 140
  pectinata pendula, 30
  pichta, 83
Acalypha, 223, 232
Acer Colchicum rubrum, 55, 57
  dasycarpum, 55
  Japonicum, 58
    aureum, 58
  lætum, 55, 57
  Lorbergii, 57
  macrophyllum, 55
  Pennsylvanicum, 150
  platanoides Schwerdlerii, 56
  polymorphum, 28, 57, 122, 130
  pseudo-platanus, 55
    Leopoldii, 56
    lutescens, 56
  rubrum, 55, 122
Achillea, 213
  fillipendulina, 175
  millefolium roseum, 176
  Ptarmica, fl. pl., 176
  tomentosa, 170
Aconite, winter, 169
Aconitum autumnale, 191, 214
Adonis, spring, 160
  vernalis, 160
Æsculus parviflora, 101

Ajuga reptans alba and rubra, 161
Akebia, 113
  quinata, 28, 104
Alder, black, 131
  cut-leaved imperial, 37
  Japanese, 37
Alders, 28
  American, 37
  European, 37
Almond, white, double flowering, 51
Alnus firma, 37
  imperialis laciniata, 37
Alternanthera, 209, 223, 225, 227
  amœna, 228
  aurea, 228
    nana, 228
  paronychioides, 228
  versicolor, 228
Althea, 99, 262
Alyssum saxatile, 160
Amarantus, 225
  salicifolius, 232
Amorpha, 100
Ampelopsis, 131
  tricuspidata, 28, 104, 131, 290
  Veitchii, 131
Andromeda arborea, 28, 126, 313
  Mariana, 101
Anemone, 212
  Caroliniana, 159
  hepatica, 165
  Japonica, 191
  nemorosa, 159
  patens, var. Nuttalliana, 159
  pulsatilla, 160
  sylvestris, 160

INDEX.

Anthemis tinctoria, 176
Anthericum liliago, 176
  liliastrum, 176
Aquilegia, 213
  Canadensis, 159
  cœrulea, 170
  chrysantha, 170
  vulgaris, 171
Arabis alpina, 161
Aralia Japonica, 28, 107
  spinosa, 28
Arbor vitæ, American, 82
  Asiatic, 82
  Chinese golden, 146
Arbutus, trailing, 212
Architecture on small lawns, employment of, 267
Arenaria verna, 160,
Aristolochia sipho, 104
Armeria maritima, 171
Arundo, 193
  donax, 242
    variegata, 210
Asclepias, 176, 214
  tuberosa, 176
Asperula odorata, 171
Asphodels, 177
Asphodelus luteus, 177
Aster amellus, var. Bessarabicus, 178
  longifolius, var. formosus, 191
  Novæ-Angliæ, 191,
  ptarmicoides, 178
  Shortii, 191
Asters, 178, 191
Astilbe Japonica, 163, 213
Aubrietia Leichtlinii, 161
Aubrietias, 161
Aucubæfolia, 43
Autumn, 191
Azalea, American, 49
  amœna, 30, 48
  Ghent, 29, 49
  hardy, 68, 69, 264
  mollis, 49

B

Bachelor's button, 174
Bamboo, 242

Bamboo, white, 210
Banana, 223, 234
Baptisia, australis, 178
Barrenwort, 162
Bedding, around Arsenal, Central Park, 224
  color of, Union Square, 218
  elliptical arrangement of, 225
  existing prejudice against, 217
  grass type of, 227
  methods of preparing plans for, 225
  narrow border of a circular fountain basin, etc., 222
  planting of, 236
  pruning or pinching of, 227
  shrub background, 222
    form of, 230
  solid background, 220
  spring, 236
  summer, 236
  time of planting, 236
  tree type of, 235
Beech, American, 111, 112
  European, 111
  purple, 58, 59, 252
  weeping, 28, 111, 152
Bell-flower, large, 189
Berberis, 30,
  aquifolium, 30
  Japonicum, 30
  Thunbergii, 131
Berberry, purple, 130
Betula Dahurica, 38
Biota elegantissima aurea, 146
Birch, black, 37
  canoe, 37
  cut-leaved, 37
  purple, 252
  purple-leaved, 37
  white, 58, 120, 262
  yellow, 37
Bitter-sweet, 132
Blazing-star, 186, 213
Bleeding-heart, plumy, 172
Blood-root, 212
Bluet's, 158
Bois de Boulogne, 272
Bowman's root, 182

INDEX. 319

Broom, Scotch, 29
Bugle, white- and red-leaved, 161
Bulbocodium vernum, 164
Butter and eggs, or single orange phœnix, 166
Butterfly weed, 176
Buttonwood, American, 92

C

Caladium, 243
Callicarpa purpurea, 131
Callirrhoë involucrata, 178
Calycanthus floridus, 72
    lævigatus, 72
Campanula Carpatica, 178
    grandiflora, 189
    rotundifolia, 171
Campanulas, 178
Candy-tuft, 213
    corris-leaved perennial, 172
Canna, 206, 219, 223, 224, 232, 243
    Ehmanni, 233
    Indica, 233
Cardinal flower, 193, 213
Cassia Marylandica, 179
Castor-oil plant, 224, 235
Catalpa, 62, 107
    Bungeii, 107
    dwarf, 107
    golden, 94
Cat-tail, 249
Cedar, Atlas, 29, 282
    of Lebanon, 143
    red, 29
Cedrus Atlantica, 29
Celastrus scandens, 132
Cemetery, Japan-creeper for, 306
    maples, Japanese, for, 306
    park-like arrangement of, 304
    plants for, 304
    roses for, 306
    spruce, conical, for, 305
        Gregory for, 305
    Swiss stone pine for, 305
    Woodlawn, New York, 304
Centaurea candidissima, 230
Cerastium Biebersteinii, 161
    tomentosum, 162

Cercis Japonica, 108
Chamomile, yellow, 176
Cherries, double flowering, 42
Cherry, Japan weeping, 43
    white, double flowering, 43
Chionanthus Virginica, 62, 94, 107
Chionodoxa Luciliæ, 169
Chrysanthemum, 191, 214
    lacustre, 191
    maximum, 191
Chrysanthemums, Chinese and Japanese, 198
Churchyard, cypress, Japanese, for, 302
    elm, American, for, 299
        Camperdown weeping, for, 300
    fir, Nordmann's, for, 301
    ginkgo, for, 299
    hemlock, weeping, for, 302
    ivy or creeper, Japan, for, 303
    maple, Japanese, for, 302
    oak, pyramidal, for, 301
    silver-fir, weeping, for, 302
    sophora, weeping, for, 300
    spruce, weeping, for, 302
    Taxus baccata, for, 302
    willow, Kilmarnock weeping, for, 302
    yellow-wood, for, 300
    yew, Irish, for, 302
Cladrastris tinctoria, 120
Clematis, 28, 76, 205
    apiifolia, 104
    Davidiana, 179
    flammula, 104
    integrifolia, 179
    Jackmanii, 77
    lanuginosa, 77
    patens, 77
    recta, 179
    Virginiana, 104
    white, sweet-scented, 104
Clethra alnifolia, 29, 100
Coffee-tree, Kentucky, 28, 94, 120
Colchicum autumnale, 199
Coleus, 206, 219, 223, 231, 232
    golden bedder, 232
    Kirkpatrick, 232
    Verschaffeltii, 232
Columbine, Canada, 159

Columbine, golden, 170
  hardy, 213
  Rocky Mountain, 170
Columbines, 179
Colutea, 100
Compass-plant, 196
Cone-flower, large, 195
Coreopsis, 213
  lanceolata, 191
Cornus florida, 40, 126
  sanguinea, 150
  alba, 29
Corydalis nobilis, 163
Cotoneaster, buxifolia, 30
  pyracantha, 30, 108
Cranberry-tree, 29
Cratægus, 30
  coccinea, 28
  crus-galli, 28, 293
  oxyacantha, 47, 48
  pyracantha, 30, 108
Creeper, Virginia, 131, 290
Crocus, 167, 204
  autumn, 199
  Susianus, 168
  versicolor, 168
Crucianella stylosa, 170
Cucumber-tree, 64
  yellow, 64
Currant, Indian, 13
Cydonia Japonica, 39
Cyperus papyrus, 289
Cypress, Chinese, 102
Cypress, obtuse-leaved, Japanese, 151
  Southern, 102
  vine, 205

D

Daffodils, 165, 166, 167
Dahlias, single and double, 199
Daisies, Michælmas, 191
Daisy, Giant, 195
  turfing, 212
Daphne Cneorum, 113
  Genkwa, 29, 41
Daphne Japanese, 41
  Mezereum, 41

Delphinium formosum, 180
  grandiflorum, 180
  elatum, 180, 204
Delphiniums, 179
Deutzia crenata, 72
  fl. pl., 72
  Fortunei, 72
  gracilis, 48, 72
  scabra, 72
  fl. pl., 72
Dianthus barbatus, 172
  deltoides, 171
  plumarius, 172
Dicentra eximia, 172
  spectabilis, 164, 172
Dictamnus fraxinella, 180
Dielytra spectabilis, 164
Diervilla, or weigelia, 74
Digitalis purpurea, 181
Dogwood, 100, 290
  red-stemmed, 29, 130, 150, 289
  white flowering, 40, 126
Dracocephalum Ruyschianum, 181
Dragon's head, hyssop-leaved, 181
Drainage, 4
Dropwort, 190
Dutchman's Pipe, 28, 104

E

Echeveria metallica, 228
  secunda glauca, 228
Echeverias, 209, 219, 228
Elæagnus hortensis, 29, 113, 128
  longipes, 29, 113
Elephant ear, 235, 243
Elm, American, 152, 293
  cork-barked, 152
  weeping, 152
Emphasis, parts for, 218
  sky line, construction of, 244
Epimedium, 162
  macranthum, 163
Eranthis hyemalis, 169
Erianthus Ravennæ, 210
Erica herbacea carnea, 157
Eryngium alpinum, 181
Eulalia Japonica, 243

INDEX.

Eulalia Japonica, variegata, 210
   zebrina, 210
Euonymus alatus, 29
   European, 131
   latifolius, 130
Euphorbia corollata, 181
Exochorda grandiflora, 73

F

Fagus ferruginea, 112
   sylvatica pendula, 110
Fences on small places, treatment of, 260
Festuca glauca, 210
Fever few, or golden feather, 228
Fir, Cephalonian, 84
   compact silver, 84
   dwarf silver, 140
   Grecian silver, 83
   Hudson Bay, 84
   lovely silver, 140
   noble silver, 83, 140
   Nordmann's silver, 83, 140
   Parson's silver, 140
   Siberian silver, 83
   silver, 140
   silver, weeping, 30
Flax, perennial, 173
Forget-me-not, creeping, 212
Forsythia Fortunii, 39
   suspensa, 29, 39
   viridissima, 29, 38
Fothergilla, alnifolia, 29
Fountain-basins, water-lilies suited to, 250
Foxglove, common, 181
   purple, 213
Fraxinus concavæfolia, 94
Fringe, white, 94
Funkia ovata, 182
   subcordata, 182

G

Gaillardia grandiflora, 182
Galanthus Elwesii, 169
   nivalis, 169
Garden, arrangement of, 202

Gas-plant, 180
Gay-feather, Kansas, 186
Genista scoparia, 29
   tinctoria, 29
Gentiana acaulis, 162, 213
   Andrewsii, 192
Gentian, 213
   closed, 192
   stemless, 162, 213
Geranium, 217, 219, 223, 225, 232
   blood-red, 182
   General Grant, 230
   horseshoe, 230
   sanguineum, 182
   silver-leaved, 230
      Mountain of Snow, 231
Gillenia trifoliata, 182
Ginkgo, Japan, 120, 152
   tree, 29
Globe, European, 175
Glory of the snow, 169
   of the spruces, 80
Glyptostrobus sinensis, 102
Gnaphalium, 209
Golden bell, 38
   weeping, 39
Golden-rod, 196, 214
Golden tuft, 160
Grading, semi-artificial, 20
   the lawn, 6, 7
   wholly artificial, 18
Grandmother's garden, 201
Grape-vine, 205
Grass seed, difficulty in securing pure, 3, 10
   for lawns, varieties of, 11, 12
   planting for lawns, 3, 11
Groundsel, 195
Grounds, sloping, 18, 20
Gynerium argenteum, 210
Gypsophila paniculata, 183

H

Harebell, 171, 178, 213
   Carpathian, 178
Hawthorn, Paul's red double-flowering 48
   European, or English, 47

Hazel, purple, 60
Heart, bleeding, 164
Heath, winter, 157
Helenium Hoopesii, 183
Helianthus Maximiliana, 192
　orgyalis, 192
Helleborus niger, 197
　altifolius, 198
Hemerocallis Thunbergii, 192
Hemlock, 80, 282
　weeping, 29
Hepatica triloba, 165, 212
Herbaceous plants, arrangement of, 200
Hercules' club, 28
Hibiscus Californicus, 193
　Moscheutos, 192
　Syriacus, 99, 262
Hollyhock, 183, 204
Honey-locust, 28, 293
Honeysuckle, 28
　Belgian striped monthly, 76
　bush, 72
　Canadian, 76
　evergreen, 113
　Hall's evergreen, 76
　Tartarian bush, 72
Hornbeam, American, 28
Horse-chestnut, 61, 101
　dwarf flowering, 101
　red-flowering, 61
Hoopesii, 183
House on small place, position of, 260, 264
Houstonia cœrulea, 158
Hyacinths, 168
Hyacinthus orientalis, 168
Hydrangea, 264
　Japan climbing, 77
　paniculata grandiflora, 99
Hypericum, 99

I

Iberis, 213
　corræfolia, 172
Ilex verticillata, 131
Indigo, blue false, 178
Iris, Chalcedonian, 169
　crested dwarf, 164

Iris, cristata, 164
　Florentine, 173
　German, 184
　Germanica, 184
　golden-netted, 169
　Iberica, 169
　Japan, 214
　Kæmpferi, 184
　pumila, 164
　reticulata, 169
　Siberian, 173
　Siberica, var. hæmatophylla, 173
　verna, 164
Itea Virginica, 29
Ivy, Japanese, 28

J

Jasmine, yellow, 34, 38
Jasminum nudiflorum, 29, 34, 38
Jonquil, fragrant or campernelle, 166
Judas-tree, Japan, 108
Juniper, bluish-tinted, 146
　common Canadian, 82
　creeping, 30, 282
　Irish, 82
　savin, 30
　Swedish, 82
　weeping, 82
Juniperus Canadensis, 82
　oblonga pendula, 82
　prostrata, 29
　Sabina, 30
　squamata, 29
　tamariscifolia, 30
　venusta, 82
　Virginiana glauca, 29, 82

K

Kalmia latifolia, 30, 70
Kerria Japonica, 29, 74
Kniphofia alceoides, 210
Kœlreuteria, 59

L

Laburnum, common, 63
　Scotch, 63

Landscape gardening, geometric style of, 261
Larch, 29
　Japan, 38
　weeping, 29, 38, 152
Larix Europæa glauca, 38
　leptolepsis, 38
Larkspur, 179, 204
　beautiful, 180
　large-flowered, 180
　tall, 180
Lathyrus latifolius, 193
Laurel, broad-leaved, 30
Lavender, sea, 174
Lawn after sowing grass-seed, maintenance of, 13, 14
　arrangement of Washington Irving's, 205
　exhibition of individual plants on, 250
　plantations, arrangement of, 6
　planting at small places, 258
　railway, creeping juniper for, 297
　　moneywort for, 297
　　mugho pine for, 297
　　periwinkle for, 297
　　plans for, 297
　　plants suited for, 297
　　retinospora for, 297
　　rhododendron for, 297
　　stone pine for, 297
　　treatment of, 296
　　Virginia creeper for, 297
　thorough preparation of, 238
Lawns, cultivation of, 5
　grading of surface of, 263
　small, approach to house on, 265
　　cost of plants for, 269
　　location of trees on, 264
　　treatment of, 265
　　vegetable garden on, 265
　　vistas on, 261
Ledebourii, 72
Leek, cobweb house, 197
　common house, 197
Liatris, 186, 213
　pycnostachya, 186
　spicata, 186
Lilac, 50
　Chinese, 51

Lilac, common, 51
　Persian, 51
Lilies, water, nymphæas, 248
Lilium auratum, 185
　Batemanniæ, 185
　Canadense, 185
　pardalinum, 185
　pomponium, 169
　Pyrenaicum, 186
　speciosum, 185
　superbum, 185
　tigrinum, 185
　　splendens, 185
Lily, blue plantain, 183
　day, 183, 192, 213
　hardy white, 253
　leopard, 185
Lily-pond, cost of plants for, 246
　importance of open spaces of, 246
　in Central Park, construction of, 251
　instructions for making, 242
　natural effect of, 249
　right way to make a, 241
　wrong way to make a, 239
Lily, Saint Bernard's, 176
　small white, 253
　tiger, 185
　Turk's cap, 185
　Cape Cod water, 253
　water, in the pool, Central Park, 253
　　in Union Square, appearance of, 252
　white plantain, 183
　yellow turban, 186
　Zanzibar water, 253
Linden, American, 293
　golden-barked, 110, 150
　red-twigged, 150
Linum perenne, 173
Liquid ambar styraciflua, 95, 124
Liriodendron tulipifera, 63
Live forever, 195, 212
Liver leaf, 165, 212
Lobelia cardinalis, 193
Lonicera Canadensis, 76
　flexuosa, 72
　fragrantissima, 29, 72, 290
　Halleana, 76
　sempervirens, 104

Lonicera, sineusis, 104
  Tartarica, 72
  xylosteum, 72
Loosestrife, purple, 186
Lotus, 246, 252
  best soil for, 246
  leaves, appearance of, 247
  yellow, 248
Lychnis Chalcedonica, 186
  scarlet, 186
Lycium barbarum, 29, 75, 99
Lythrum Salicaria, 186
  viscaria splendens, 187

M

Magnolia acuminata, 64
  Asiatic, hardiness of, 46
  broad-leaved, 65, 96
  Chinese, 44, 46
  conspicua, 44
  cordata, 64
  dark purple Japanese, 46
  glauca, 65, 67
    longifolia, 65
  gracilis, 46
  Halleana, 46
  hypoleuca, 66, 67
  Kobus, 66
  Lennei, 44, 46
  macrophylla, 46, 65, 95
  Norbetiana, 44
  parviflora, 66, 67
  purpurea, 46
  slender, 46
  Soulangeana, 44
  stellata, 44, 46
  swamp, 65
  sweet-scented, 65
  Thompsoniana, 65
  tripetala, 66
  umbrella, 66
  Watsonii, 66
  white swamp, 65
Mahonia, 30, 113, 131, 146
  aquifolium, 30
Mallow, crimson, 178
  garden, 194

Mallow, marsh rose, 192
Maltese cross, 186
Malus aucubæfolia, 43
  coronaria odorata, 43
  Halleana, 43
  spectabilis, 43
Malva Alcea, 194
  moschata alba, 194
Manures for the lawn, 8
Maple, ash-leaved, 55
  broad-leaved, 55
  English field, 55
  Japanese, 28, 55, 57, 122, 130, 264
  Norway, 55, 61, 119, 293
    Schwerdler's purple-leaved, 56
  scarlet, 55
  silver, 55
  striped, 55, 150
  sugar, 55, 122, 293
  swamp, 122
  sycamore, 55
    Leopold's, 56
    silver-leaved, 56
Meadow-rue, 174
Meadow-saffron, 199
Meadow-sweet, 190
Menispermum Canadense, 104
Milfoils, 175
Milkweed (Asclepias), 214
Mock orange, 71
Monarda didyma, 187
Moneywort, 212
Monk's-hood, 179
  autumn, 191, 214
Morning-glory, 205
Mountain everlasting, 212
Mouse ear, 161
Munstead giant, 171
Musa ensete, 234, 235
Myrica cerifera, 29

N

Narcissus, 165
  bicolor, 166
  incomparabilis, 166
  maximus, 166
  odorus, 166

INDEX. 325

Narcissus, poeticus, 166
  pseudo-narcissus, 166
Nasturtium, 228, 229
Nelumbium or lotus, 246
  speciosum, 246, 252
Noble fumitory, 163
Nookeries on the home grounds, 307
  akebia for, 310
  ampelopsis quinquefolia for, 310
  ampelopsis tricuspidata, or Veitchii, for, 309
  arrangement of, 308
  clematis apiifolia for, 310
  flammula for, 310
  Dutchman's pipe for, 310
  Japan ivy for, 309
  lonicera sempervirens for, 309
  Periploca Græca for, 310
  Tecoma grandiflora for, 309
    radicans, 309
  trumpet-creeper for, 309
  trumpet-vine or honeysuckle for, 309
  Virginia creeper for, 310
  Virginia silk, 310
  wistaria, 310
Nymphæa alba candidissima, 253
  Devoniensis, 253
  pygmæa, 253
  Zanzibarensis azurea, 253
    rosea, 253

O

Oak, chestnut, 96
  English, 97, 123
  golden, 97, 123
  over cup, 152
  pin, 96, 112
  pyramidal, 29, 97, 112, 120, 123, 152, 301
  red, 96
  scarlet, 96
  Turkey, 123
  weeping, 97
  white, 96
  willow, 96
  willow-leaved, 112
Œnothera Missouriensis, 187
Oleaster, garden, 128

Opuntia Rafinesquii, 187
Orris-root, 173
Oxydendrum arboreum, 126, 313

P

Pæonia officinalis, 173
  tenuifolia, fl. pl., 173
Pampas grass, 210, 243
Pansies, 236
Pansy, bird's foot, 158
Papaver bracteatum, 188
  nudicaule, var. croceum, 188
  orientale, 188
Parc du Chaumont, 273
Park, Central, acres in, number of, 291
  beginning of, date of, 273
  bridle path of, arrangement of, 290
  competitive plans for, 273
  forest glade of, 284
  gorge with rhododendrons, 288
  green, 72d St. and 5th Ave., arrangement of, 277
  Harlem Meer, neighborhood of, 288
  highlands of, 28
  lawn, children's and nurses', arrangement of, 277
  lower meadow, arrangement of, 277
  mall, arrangement of, 276
  miles of paths and roads in, 291
  north meadow of, 284, 290
  pin-oaks of, 284, 290
  play-grounds of, 291
  pond near 72d St., 289
  ramble, arrangement of, 280
  roads, transverse, of, 284
  rock, overhanging, in, 286
  selection of site of, 272, 273
  terrace, 276
  the lake, arrangement of, 280
Hyde, lack of variety in, 272
Phœnix (Dublin), 272
small, architectural adornments on, 293
  Canal St., New York, care and size of, 294
  city squares resembling, 292
  fences for, 292
  fountain basins for, 293
  plants for, 293

Pasque flower, European, 160
Pea, everlasting, 193
Peach, double flowering, 43
Pear, Western prickly, 187
Pennsylvania catchfly, 163
Pentstemon, 213
  barbatus, var. Torreyi, 189
  cobæa, 189
Peonies, herbaceous, 173, 204
Pepper-bush, sweet, 100
Pergola, wistarias on, 289
Periwinkle, 212
Persimmon, American, 108
  Japanese, 108
Petalostemon decumbens, 189
Pheasant's eye, 166
Philadelphus, 71, 289, 293
  coronarius, 72
  dwarf golden, 72
  grandiflorus, 72
  laxus, 72
  speciosus, 72
Phlox amœna, 159
  annual, 174
  Carolina, 174
  dwarf, 159, 160
  garden, 194, 204, 213
  maculata, 194
  nivalis, 159
  paniculata, 194
  starry, 174
  stellaria, 174
  subulata, 159
  white, 159
Picea alba, 80
  excelsa elata, 29
    Gregoriana, 80
    inverta, 29
  Orientalis, 141
  polita, 81, 142
  pungens, 85, 142
Pine, Austrian, 144
  Bhotan, 82, 144, 145, 282
  dwarf Scotch, 82, 144
  dwarf white, 144
  golden Japanese, 145
  Japan parasol, 30, 145
  mugho, 30, 83, 144

Pine, stone, 282
  sun-ray, 145
  Swiss stone, 144
Pink, cushion, 172
  fire, 174
  garden, 172, 203, 213
  maiden's, 171, 172
  moss, 159
  wild, 163
Pinus cembra, 30, 144, 282
  excelsa, 82, 144, 145, 282
  Massoniana variegata, 145
  mughus, 144
    compacta, 144
    uncinata, 144
  strobus compacta, 143
Pitcher-plant, 249
Plane-tree, Oriental, 92, 293
Platycodon grandiflorum, 189
Plumbago Larpentæ, 195
Plum, double flowering, 43
Poet's narcissus, 166
Point of view on small places, importance of, 263
Poker, red-hot, 193
Pond-lilies, habit of, 246
Pontederia crassipes, 249
Poplar, 98,
  aspen, 38
  balsam, 98
  Lombardy, 29, 244, 248
    health of, 244
  tulip, 122
Poppies, hardy herbaceous, 188
Poppy, great scarlet, 188
  Iceland, 188
  water, 249
Populus tremuloides, 38
Portulaca vine, 204
Primrose, English, 163
  evening, 187, 194
Primula vulgaris, 163
Prinos verticillata, 29
Privet, 113, 290, 293
  Californian, 210, 214
Pruning vines on rocks, 26
Prunus cerasus, fl. pl., 42
Pseudotsuga Douglasii, 84

INDEX. 327

Pyrethrum, 209, 223, 225, 228
  aureum, 228
  uliginosum, 195
Pyrus Japonica, 39

Q

Quercus concordia, 123
  Daimio, 112
  palustris, 96,
  phellos, 96, 112
  robur pedunculata Concordia, 97
    var. pedunculata, 97
Quince, Japan, 39
  large-flowered, 40

R

Ranunculus speciosus, fl. pl., 174
Raspberry, purple-flowering, 188
Red-hot poker, 210
Retinospora obtusa, 30
Retinosporas, 146, 282
  golden, 146
Rhododendron, 30, 68, 69, 113, 146, 206
  Catawbiense, 35
  Dauricum, 35
Rhodora Canadensis, 40
Rhodotypus kerrioides, 29
Rhus cotinus, 68
  glabra laciniata, 29, 129
  Osbecki, 124, 129, 130
Ribbon-grass, variegated, 210
Rock-cress, 212
  Alpine, 161
Rocks on sloping ground, arrangement of, 26
Rock tunica, 175
Rockwork, planting vines in, 28
  right way to make, 15, 29
  semi-artificial, example of, 22
  tree- and shrub-planting in, 28
  wholly artificial, illustrations of, 18
  wrong way to make, 30
Rosa rugosa, 80, 289
Rose, Baltimore Belle,
  Baronne Prevost, 78
  Christmas, 197, 214
  climbing, 78

Rose, damask, 203
  General Jacqueminot, 78
  hardy, 78
  Japan Ramanas, 81
  Mme. Plantier, 78
  Queen of the Prairies, 78, 190
Rubus odoratus, 188
Rudbeckia maxima, 195

S

Sage, meadow, 189
Salisburia adiantifolia, 29, 299
Salix caprea, 37
  laurifolia, 98, 109
  pentandra, 98, 109
  regalis, 37
  rosemarinifolia, 29
Salvia pratensis, 189
  splendens, 233
Sambucus nigra aurea, 29
Sandwort, 212
  spring, 160
Sanguinaria Canadensis, 212
Saxifraga cordifolia, 158
  heart-leaved, 158
Scabiosa Caucasica, 189
Sciadopitys verticillata, 30, 145
Sea pink, 171
Sedum, 195, 212
  acre, 195
  Fabaria, 195
  Sieboldii, 195
  spectabile, 195
Sempervivum, 197
  arachnoideum, 197
  calcareum, 197
Senecio Japonica, 195, 196
Senna, American, 179
  bladder, 100
Shrubs, small dwarf, 264
Silene Pennsylvanica, 163
  Virginica, 174
Silphium laciniatum, 196
Sky-line for trees and shrubs, 260, 262
  variety of, 260
Small places, arrangement of walks and roads on, 259, 266

Small places, borders on walks of, treatment of, 262
   boundary lines on, treatment of, 261
   foliage on, evergreen and deciduous, 262
   grouping of trees and shrubs on, 260
   house on, position of, 260, 264
Sneezewort, 176
Snowball, 75, 131, 293
   Japanese, 75, 289
Snowberry, 131
Snowdrop, 169, 204
Solanum, 224, 235
Solidago, 196, 214
   Canadensis, 197
   rigida, 197
   Shortii, 197
Sophora, weeping, 152
Sorrel tree, 99, 126
   autumn appearance of, 314
   bark of, 314
   bush form of, 315
   flowers of, 314
   rhododendrons in connection with, 315
Speedwell, 190
   gentian-leaved, 190
Spiræa, 290
   Billardii, 102
   bullata, 109
   callosa, 29
   callosa alba, 29, 102
   crispifolia, 109
   Douglasii, 102
   Fortunei, 71
   Japonica, 163
   lobata, 190
   opulifolia, 252, 289, 293
   aurea, 71
   pentandra, 109
   prunifolia, 71, 109, 129
   Reevesiana, 29, 71
   salicifolia, 102
   Thunbergii, 129, 289
   tomentosa, 102
   trilobata, 71
   ulmaria, 190
   venusta, 190

Spruce, Alcock's, 142
   Colorado, 142
   Gregory's, 142
   Gregory's dwarf, 80, 142
   Norway, 142, 144
   Norway weeping, 29
   Oriental, 142
   tiger-tail, 81
   weeping, 142
   white, 80
Spurge, flowering, 181
Staggerbush, 101
Starworts, 191
   Russian, 178
Statice latifolia, 174
Statues on small place, use of, 261
Stipa pennata, 210
Stokesia cyanea, 197
Stone-crop, common, 195
Stuartia pentagynia, 99
Sumac, 129
   Chinese, 124, 130
   cut-leaved, 129
Summer-house, location of, 266
Sunflower, 192, 214
   graceful, 192
Surprise, element of, 266
Symphoricarpus racemosus, 29, 131
   vulgaris, 29, 131
Syringa, 50
   Chinese, 51
   Persian, 51
   vulgaris, 51
Swallow-wort, 176
Sweet gum, 95
   pea, 204
   -scented shrub, 72
   -william, 204

T

Tamarix Africana, 29, 74
   Gallica, 74
   Indica, 29, 74, 99, 262
Taxodium, 102
Taxus baccata, 85
   baccata elegantissima, 85
Tecoma grandiflora, 105
   radicans, 28, 105

Thalictrum speciosum, 174
Thorn, American, 293
  box, 99
  cock-spur, 28
  evergreen, 108, 126, 148, **282**
Thrift, 171
Tilia dasystyla, 110
  sulphurea, 110
Tradescantia Virginica, 175
Tritoma or Kniphofia, 193
  Uvaria grandiflora, 210
Trollius Europæus, 175
Trumpet creeper, 28, 105
Tulip, 236
  Artus, 237
  Duc Van Tholl, 237
  La Belle Alliance, 237
  tree, 63, 95
Tunica saxifraga, 175
Turf, importance of open spaces of, 273
Turtle head, 214

U

Ulmus parvifolia, 109

V

Vegetable garden on small lawns, 265
Vernonia Noveboracensis, 197
Veronica amethystina, 190
  gentianoides, 190
  longifolia, 190
  subsessilis, 190
Viburnum, 74,
  lantana, 131
  opulus, 29, 75
  plicatum, 75
Vinca rosea, 233
Viola cornuta, 175
  pedata, var. bicolor, 158

Violet, 158
  bird's foot, 158
  horned, 175
Virginia creeper, 26, 28
  silk, 28, 113
Virgin's bower, upright, 179

W

Wahlenbergia grandiflora, 189
Walnut, black, 92
Weed, New York iron, 197
Weigelia Lavallei, 103
  rosea, 74
Weigelia, 74, 102, 290, 293, **315**
  dwarf variegated, 103
White fringe, 62, 107
Willow, 98
  drooping, 245
  goat, 37
  golden, 130, 150
  laurel-leaved, 98, 109, **126**
  rosemary-leaved, 29
  royal, 37
  weeping, 128
Wind-flower, Japan, 213
  snowdrop, 160
Wistaria, 28, 77, 205
  Sinensis, 77
Woodruff, 171

Y

Yarrow, downy, 170
  Egyptian, 175
Yellow-wood, 120
Yew, golden, 85
  Irish, 85, 150
  silver-tinted, 85
Yucca filimentosa, 29, 190
  recurva, 29

www.ingramcontent.com/pod-product-compliance
Lightning Source LLC
Chambersburg PA
CBHW020246240426
43672CB00006B/653